The Making of the Hawthorne Subject

The Making of the
Hawthorne Subject

Alison Easton

▼ UNIVERSITY OF MISSOURI PRESS
Columbia and London

Copyright © 1996 by
The Curators of the University of Missouri
University of Missouri Press, Columbia, Missouri 65201
Printed and bound in the United States of America
All rights reserved

5 4 3 2 1 0   99 98 97 96 95

Library of Congress Cataloging-in-Publication Data

Easton, Alison, 1943–
    The making of the Hawthorne subject / Alison Easton.
        p. cm.
    Includes bibliographical references (p.   ) and index.
    ISBN 0-8262-1040-6 (cloth : alk. paper)
    1. Hawthorne, Nathaniel, 1804–1864—Criticism and interpretation. 2. Sub-
jectivity in literature. I. Title.
    PS1892.S9E27 1996
    813'.3—dc20   95-36101
                                                                        CIP

∞ This paper meets the requirements of the
American National Standard for Permanence of Paper
for Printed Library Materials, Z39.48, 1984.

Designer: Kristie Lee
Typesetter: BOOKCOMP
Printer and Binder: Thomson-Shore, Inc.
Typeface: Minion

For my Edinburgh people—

father, mother, sister, brother, cousins, friends,

and teachers on two sides of George Square

Contents

Preface

▼ H A W T H O R N E ' S   P R O J E C T concerns subjectivity. It is an attempt to understand and come to terms with the clash of what he eventually named "desire"—all that is unrecognized and unrepresented within the social order—with what he called "circumstance"—those external, largely social conditions within which the subject must live and that she or he is constructed by and yet also partly constructs. This division between subjective and objective is no simple one. Instead, the individual is the site on which many conflicting, often socially derived views struggle for primacy, and both consciousness and the unconscious are given particular shape by the demands of the social formation.

Hawthorne found himself with two theories of the human subject that were his cultural inheritance: Scottish Common Sense psychology and the Romantic ideas of the individual. Neither proved adequate for him, but both affected the way he conceived the dilemma. Over the first twenty-five years of his career he explored, experimented, imagined, and negotiated his way toward a better model, one that would take account of multiple needs, desires, ideologies, and conflicting subject positions—all the contradictions that are the consequence of becoming a subject and existing in social relations. He had to invent a new vocabulary or adapt given ones to deal with what he thought he saw. With *The Scarlet Letter* he reached at last his fullest conceptualization and fictional realization of these issues.

It is the several stages of this intellectual and artistic enterprise that I have attempted to chart here. The third crucial term for Hawthorne's argument is "sympathy," not as it is usually understood within a Romantic framework, but as it was remarkably redefined by Adam Smith in his *Theory of Moral Sentiments*. It is the operation of this imaginative sympathy that comes to focus, though not resolve, many of the issues that Hawthorne found himself confronting.

This approach implies a development in Hawthorne's work, something that critics, with one outstanding exception, have ignored. Explicitly or implicitly, they simply deny that development occurred, and his writings, though discussed in many contemporary and historical contexts, are rarely placed in the full context of his other works written at the same time. Indeed, not even a complete chronology of these works exists—an extraordinary critical situation. As a result, what has been largely missed is the sense of a complex, evolving project and the revealing intertextual play of meaning that emerges when we look at the whole. With a clearer chronology, it is possible to see how Hawthorne's work forms a dialectical development, twenty-five years of accumulated experimentation, ongoing debate, and often consciously constructive change culminating in *The Scarlet Letter.*

In considering this development, it is vitally important to consider the full range of Hawthorne's writings during this period. The first twenty-five years of his work challenges us with a striking and bewildering diversity, ranging from his earliest tales and first novel, *Fanshawe,* through nearly a hundred more tales and sketches to *The Scarlet Letter,* not forgetting all the notebooks, letters, children's books, reviews, and edited compilations. Commentators hitherto have almost always solved the problem of this diversity by being highly selective in what they discuss, turning a blind or embarrassed eye to what fails to fit their preoccupations. None have attempted to make sense of the whole. With the insights afforded by a more detailed chronology, this confusing picture of widely differing material, forms, and positions resolves itself, familiar texts are given a significant context, and neglected pieces find their place in an overall pattern. Through the terms evolved from his cultural inheritance, "desire," "circumstance," and "sympathy," Hawthorne turns out to be thinking about some of the most important issues of our current critical debates on subjectivity.

▼

I have many people to thank, starting with Andrew Hook, who first introduced me to nineteenth-century American literature. I am grateful to Quentin Anderson, Arnold Goldman, and Marcus Cunliffe for their insights and support while I was working on a doctoral dissertation on Hawthorne many years ago, and to friends at Sussex,

Aberdeen, and Lancaster (particularly John Labbé) for their help at that time. In writing this present study my greatest debts are to Geoff Ward and Alan Friedman, without whom this study might never have seen the light of day. Thanks are also due to Keith Hanley, who in the closing stages of preparation wonderfully marshaled all kinds of assistance; to Simon Parker, who helped with the final library work; and to Anne Stewart, who produced the final version of the manuscript so quickly. Many thanks too to the Humanities Research Policy Committee of Lancaster University for financial assistance in preparing the manuscript. Tony Pinkney, Richard Dutton, Marion Wynne-Davis, Michael Wheeler, and Raman Selden all offered help, advice, and much-needed encouragement. (I might now bear in mind Benjamin's strictures on "fat books!") I am deeply grateful to the University of Texas at Austin, which made me a Visiting Scholar for six months in 1984, and for the help of many friends at Austin, notably Liz Butler and Alan Friedman, who gave me a home there. The University of Missouri Press has been a delight to work with—I cannot imagine kinder and more helpful editors. I would also like to thank the Press's anonymous readers of my manuscript—their reports were much appreciated. For love and support over many years that I could always rely on, I thank very many friends, and in particular the Osborn, Phillips, Easton, and Cosslett-Myers families—not forgetting Hester. My debt to the many commentators of Hawthorne and New England has, I trust, been acknowledged in my commentary; other exciting studies, which I can only note, appeared after work had been completed on this one—long may they continue.

Note on Editions

▼ I HAVE USED where possible *The Centenary Edition of the Works of Nathaniel Hawthorne,* edited by William Charvat et al. (Columbus: Ohio State University Press, 1962–), twenty volumes to date, and all page references, unless otherwise indicated, refer to this edition. Page references prefixed AMUEK indicate Hawthorne's contributions to the *American Magazine of Useful and Entertaining Knowledge* in *Hawthorne as Editor,* edited by Arlin Turner (1941; Port Washington, N.Y.: Kennikat, 1972). Page references prefixed LN indicate *Hawthorne's Lost Notebook, 1835–1841,* transcript and preface by Barbara S. Mouffe (University Park: Pennsylvania State University Press, 1978). Page references prefixed TS indicate The Library of America edition of *Tales and Sketches* (New York: Viking Press, 1982), which has been used for the four Biographical Sketches, "Thomas Green Fessenden," and "Jonathan Cilley."

The Making of the Hawthorne Subject

"I Am a Good Deal Changed

Since Those Times"

Introduction

▼ THE FIRST FULL-LENGTH critical examination of Hawthorne's work initiated a critical tradition that has persisted with outstandingly few exceptions: "[H]is mind proper—his mind in so far as it was a repository of opinions and articles of faith—had no development that it is of especial importance to look into."[1] True, Henry James does then go on to make a distinction between intellectual and artistic development; nonetheless he still asserts that Hawthorne's writing shows no sign of any significant evolution of ideas and forms. This view has been and continues to be the underlying assumption of nearly all critical analyses of Hawthorne's work.

True, there is no immediately evident line of development in the first half of Hawthorne's career. Some of the tales that at first seem closest to *The Scarlet Letter* were in fact written in the first years of his career, twenty years before his first "major" novel. Many of the one hundred or so short stories and sketches composed in the years between his first novel *Fanshawe* and *The Scarlet Letter* may seem tangential or remote from the latter's formal and thematic complexities, and indeed may seem an artistic embarrassment to those who wish to argue for the radicalism or technical sophistication of *The Scarlet Letter*. Instead of texts being discussed as "early" or "later" works, the critical tendency has been to judge them in terms of "good" or "inferior," "major" or "lesser," "significant" or merely "conventional," without really examining the second term in these binaries. It does not seem sufficient explanation simply to say that Hawthorne was an ironist who loved paradox and subversion, but who wrote to suit the market when he was in financial straits or was desperate for an audience. There has been very little attempt to discuss the total range of his work, or to try to make sense of the great variety of his work at this period and bring together all his pieces of writing within a larger, evolving pattern (if such a pattern exists). Though few critics are as forthright as G. D. Josipovici, his view only makes clearer what is implicit in the standard approach: "And yet, when all is said and done, there is much about Hawthorne that is unsatisfactory. . . . There remains *The Scarlet Letter* and a handful of stories. And there remains the question: why are they so good and the rest so bad?"[2]

As a result, until recently virtually no attention has been paid to the date when Hawthorne wrote any particular piece. Instead, the most characteristic strategy is to select certain works from the mass of texts irrespective of when these were composed, and to fit these together in an entirely achronological examination of a theme, technique, or materials. There have been only a tiny number of exceptions to this approach among the vast array of studies on Hawthorne. Where lip service is paid to the date at which Hawthorne wrote a work, the date may well be inaccurate.[3]

All this is particularly important during the first half of Hawthorne's writing life, the period of his career when he composed only short works. After the completion of *The Scarlet Letter* in 1850 he concentrated, with the exception of one short tale, exclusively on writing novels. There are certain critical studies that deal with many of these tales, but they do not do so in a chronological or developmental way, finding instead "a strange lack of direction" in this mass of texts.[4] Some studies obliterate any sense of development by choosing a very early date by which Hawthorne is assumed to have achieved complete artistic control; or, conversely, they diminish or distort our perception of these early works by arguing that Hawthorne's writing took a long time to crystallize, or that it is only Hawthorne's later works that show most clearly the assumed central concerns and forces of his writings.[5] Other critics may take a broadly developmental view, but find an "apparent dwindling rather than growth."⁶ Others tend to cut a broad swathe through the tales rather than to make fine discriminations within the total range of tales, so that it has been typical to take the entire period from 1825 to 1849 as constituting the first phase of Hawthorne's work. This smooths over some very awkward disjunctions and differences within the period, though some studies have at least briefly acknowledged the problems of Hawthorne's "plural and experimental beginnings."⁷ There have also been local, partial studies of certain phases within this long period that have not explored how these phases relate to the rest of his story-writing career.⁸

There have been only two comprehensive developmental studies: Alfred Weber's *Die Entwicklung der Rahmenerzählungen Nathaniel Hawthornes: "The Story Teller" und andere frühe Werke* (1973) and Nina Baym's *The Shape of Hawthorne's Career* (1976). Weber makes a speculative reconstruction of the aborted *Story Teller* collection (composed in the early 1830s) along with all of Hawthorne's preceding works. Baym looks at the entire corpus of Hawthorne's work from 1825 to his death in 1864 in order to establish the notion that his "literary career *was* a development, in the sense of a series of consecutive changes."⁹

My interest in the first half of that career, the shorter fiction and the achievement of *The Scarlet Letter,* has drawn me into an attempt to date all the tales as precisely as possible—a tricky but not impossible task, and one that the Centenary Edition did not undertake. What my study offers is a working hypothesis based on all presently available evidence about dates of composition.

The situation is particularly confused because Hawthorne tended at first to write tales for specially planned collections. These were then rejected by publishers and split up, and some of these pieces were published separately while others were retained for the next planned volume. In consequence, the date of publication may be very different from the date of composition. Nor is there much external evidence. Some letters and the history of certain annuals and journals provide information, and much of this material has been assembled by Elizabeth Lathrop Chandler, Nelson F. Adkins, and Seymour L. Gross in their studies of Hawthorne's early works and projects. Library borrowings of source material can also be a useful mechanism for dating: Hawthorne worked slowly and deliberately, so there is a likely (though not definite) chronological tie between these borrowings and the actual composition of a tale.[10] For two reasons I have used internal evidence from the tales themselves as little as possible. Apparently autobiographical references to his writing found in some works may simply be fictive invention. In addition, an undated work's thematic or formal resemblances to other datable pieces cannot be taken as a definite indication of a similar date of composition. So the evidence is quite complex, and I have relegated much of it to the notes to spare all but the keenest Hawthorne scholar.

From my dating exercise has emerged a sense of there being a number of distinct and coherent stages to Hawthorne's career as a short-story writer, each with a separate character, only some of which have been discussed before. His career is not a matter of a simple, continuous, unitary evolution over twenty-five years. Instead, the tales and sketches appear to cluster in different groups that form a sequence. Each of these phases has a sufficient number of datable tales to form its core, surrounded by other similar tales that, though their date is less certain, were probably written around the same time.[11]

I have avoided speculating about Hawthorne's intentions or purpose except where these had been stated and available for investigation and interrogation. "Development" can often be seen in terms of some supposed goal toward which the works proceed or from which they fall away, but here there is no single organizing principle that unites all of these six phases of his work, no template from which all the tales are produced. Instead there is a continuous dialectic, twenty-five years of accumulative experimentation, ongoing debate, and often consciously constructive change. As a result *The Scarlet Letter* seems neither a sudden flowering nor a wholly new direction, but the outcome of continuous work.

The extent to which his art alters is thus properly revealed. Hawthorne himself seems to have been aware of this: "I am a good deal changed since those times," he remarked to his publisher James T.

Fields in April 1854 about *Mosses from an Old Manse* (17:201), and he describes *The Snow-Image* collection (1851), which contained some of his earliest work as well as the last of his short pieces, as "indices of intellectual condition at far separated epochs" (11:6).

Approaching Hawthorne's early work in this way, it is at last possible to make better sense of the bewildering diversity of material, form, and attitude found on reading the whole of his output during these years. Criticism has until now averted a disapproving or baffled eye from too much of this, dismissing or neglecting or shelving it pending future enquiries. It is indeed difficult to imagine how Hawthorne came to write in such widely differing modes and with apparently such varying attitudes, but we need to wrestle with this critical conundrum, and if we do, there is so much to be discovered.

The reason I have set myself the huge and unprecedented task of considering everything that Hawthorne wrote during this time is that there seems to be an internal rationale within each phase that becomes more clearly discernible if we take on board everything and avoid privileging some tales over others (tempting though that undoubtedly is). Each work is a piece of a scattered mosaic, and each is necessary to its reconstruction. Within this significant, multifaceted pattern, "minor" or neglected works are given a place. In such a context, puzzling tales can be freshly interpreted, and even when a tale continues to be read within customary critical parameters, it is now possible to see the part it plays within the overall structure of the author's developing work.

I need at this point to explain what this study will not foreground in its investigations. I have not concerned myself here with a view of Hawthorne's development that is primarily biographical. Exciting psychobiographical material has been published recently that will add further complexities and questions to the positions I trace here from his published writings. The social and cultural determinations that these biographical and other studies investigate increasingly help us to understand Hawthorne's historical situation in terms of class and gender. If I do not pursue this here, it is not because I think it unimportant but simply because my project made its own demands and resulted in quite long enough a book as it is! I have chosen to focus here on the intertextual, the play of meanings between individual works, the echoes that persist and motifs that change and contrast. These very extensive developmental patterns of image and idea demand detailed exposition if we are to understand the extent to which meaning within these tales is in part continuously created by them. Other excellent commentators are already in the process of investigating more closely the cultural contexts in which this play of meaning operates.[12]

▼

Lying at the center of this continuous dialectic is a concern to define the human subject. It is no accident that Hawthorne was directly involved in this issue. He was writing at a historical juncture that we can now recognize as a period of complex economic, class, and national changes, and he shared with members of the emergent middle class great anxieties about self-definition. This crisis of self-hood was produced in part at least by twin pressures: the competitive individualism, ideologies of self-sufficiency and paradoxical servitudes of the expanding marketplace; and the domestic repressions, idealizations, and covert stresses of the new and privatized bourgeois family life. As Joel Pfister has argued, Hawthorne's "persistent thematic focus on subjectivity and personal life can be read as a literary expression of historically specific and ideological concerns."[13] Hawthorne is not alone, of course, in responding to these changes, but what is particularly interesting is that, entangled though he was in its complexities, Hawthorne nonetheless confronts these issues of subjectivity consciously and deliberately. True, he universalized the dilemmas of his class, but his diagnosis remains an important one.

In proceeding in this project, Hawthorne initially had recourse to two theories of the human subject that were his cultural inheritance, namely Scottish Common Sense psychology and Romantic notions of the individual. Neither of these proved adequate for him. The first point to note is that in opposition to Romantic views of self, Hawthorne's individual cannot hope to be the sole creator of her or his being and world. There seems in Hawthorne's work to be no clear sign of an autonomous, substantial, fully consistent "self" preexisting the individual's entry into social relations; at best there is only an embryonic self full of desires. Certainly, as in both Common Sense and Romantic psychologies, the locus of reality does indeed remain the individual consciousness perceiving and responding to the exterior world, but in Hawthorne's work this consciousness can only very rarely attempt to originate its own meaning. Instead, subjectivity becomes the far more common site on which many conflicting, mainly socially derived views struggle for primacy.[14]

To Hawthorne's characters the phenomenal world may at times seem "out there," that is, external and antithetical though at times desirable. However, this structural sense of alienation from social formations is ultimately shown to be a misapprehension about the nature of relations between individuals and the social organism. What we encounter in these texts is therefore not such a simple division between the subjective and objective. That Romantic opposition of self and other, while never quite discarded since it provides a vocabulary to express a continuing conflict between individual desire and external circumstance, is nonetheless largely superseded by a conception of a subjectivity that is far more fully (though not wholly) constructed socially. A key recognition for Hawthorne's work is that we exist not only in relation to, but also because of and through other people, institutions, and the social meanings that they are shown to reproduce and to some extent produce. The Romantic failure to find that autonomous "self" led to this conclusion. Because a residual belief in independent being lingers on, Hawthorne's works do not wholly embrace an essentially social explanation of psychic processes; nonetheless this concept is much modified, at times in not entirely consistent ways. There seems to be an understanding both that consciousness and the unconscious are to a great extent given a particular shape by the demands of the social network, and that by refusing positions within society, the individual would merely inhabit a void.

So these works argue that acceptance of oneself as a human subject must in part involve learning to recognize oneself in a series of subject positions in the social order. This is a continuing process.

To a large extent ideology and social discourse (the discourses, for example, of Duty, Morality, Law, the Family, or Church) construct the human subject in specific relations to social relations, although we need to see the degree to which Hawthorne accepts this at the various stages of his work and the extent to which he is aware how his own thinking must itself be shaped by the discourses of his culture. Ideology does bring a certain fixity to those subject positions (particularly for women, who are much less well represented, if at all, in the social order than men), but it also appears to make social relations intelligible and may give some kind of coherence to the person both in the face of contradictions within society and despite the way that the individual must occupy sometimes conflicting positions.[15]

The second point to note is that Hawthorne is also making important adaptations to received Common Sense formulations of the human subject. Although these formed an important part of his university education and he continued to study them during the early years of his career as a writer, he does not simply reproduce this philosophy or confine himself within its borders. Superficially, Common Sense conceptions of the self might seem in certain ways similar to the Romantic, in that the philosophers argued for a "continuous personal identity ontologically prior to thinking," and believed that there were innate ideas that made perception an act of interpretation.[16] But Common Sense thinkers regarded these ideas as God-given and therefore fixed. Social identity and the nature of moral authority were similarly regarded as fixed because the mind, when in their view working properly, was not an active creator of meaning but rather a divinely programmed machine that worked according to these rational laws of reason (a position opposite to Romantic conceptions). A person's identity could then only be achieved through participation in the community that was sanctioned by Reason and God. "Reality" was public, shared social intercourse; the individual was shaped by her or his engagement with physical and social reality. A commonly felt need for social order in that post-Revolutionary era made this philosophy politically conservative and suspicious of the imagination as a threat to society.

This rationalist conception of the human subject was as a result both blind to contradictions and divisions in the person within social existence, and quite unable to give an adequate account of the workings of the unconscious—both very important elements in Hawthorne's thinking.

It quickly becomes clear that a social model of the human subject that revises and moves beyond those Common Sense limitations will encounter considerable problems. Entering the social order brings self-awareness, and this activity of consciousness brings subjectivity into being as the individual participates in the discourses of society. But subjectivity means both being subjected to the social order and becoming aware of aspects of oneself as a result of this subjection. It is this self-consciousness that brings a sense of division—something very characteristic of Hawthorne's characters.

The human subject is not unified in Hawthorne's writings, even at the times when it believes itself to be whole. True, there is a conscious self that can participate in the social order because it has taken up a given and therefore publicly recognized position: "The subject in ideology has a consistency which rests on an imaginary identification of self: this is simultaneously a recognition (since it provides subjectivity, enables the subject to act), and a misrecognition (a recognition which involves a representation in relation to forms which include the work of ideology)."[17] But there is also the self that is represented only partially or not at all, and that challenges the socially identified self in various ways and indeed intrudes itself into consciousness, where it is then experienced as contradiction. This is a part not constituted by society; it is what society has had to repress as the price of sociality. It has no place given to it in the social order; it is therefore hard to represent, and it was not recognized by Common Sense philosophers.

So, although one could simply accept that the individual must necessarily be both subject and object and that there is a normal and inevitable alienation that comes with social living, for Hawthorne's characters these conditions of existence mean instead a state of inner conflict, an intolerable sense of a fragmented self and an awareness that each person embodies society's own contradictions. So these characters seek new subject positions to resolve this incompatibility or contradiction, hoping to find an integrated self-image, seeking it in society because the solution to their problems cannot be outside culture, given the way in which the human subject is constructed.

We must, however, recognize that this search for a harmonized self partly reflects an ideology of the unified self that is Hawthorne's cultural inheritance and therefore a shared hope or illusion. Society holds up a mirror and offers the seductive possibility that the self might be whole, might be a totality. What we see with his characters, and arguably in the general thrust of the writing itself (because it does not seem to relinquish that hope either, even while demonstrating how hard it is to have a clear notion of what that self might be), are the struggles and squirmings of persons who believe in such a concept of wholeness—a fictive sense of unitary selfhood bolstering up the ego. The struggle brings a complex mix of resistance and accommodation: on the one hand resistance to the fixity, restriction, and sense of alienation involved in being a subject within this particular society; and on the other hand accommodation to that society's structures because there is nowhere else in which a person can have being in a way that is meaningful to her or him. As a result there is an odd melange of radicalism and conservatism in these works. Typically they face both ways, on a threshold between the two selves, the represented and the unrepresented, and over the years Hawthorne must either invent a new vocabulary or adapt a given one to describe what he sees.

Chapter 2

"Fantastic Dreams and Madmen's Reveries"

Seven Tales and *Fanshawe*

1825–1828

Here I am . . . in the old dingy and dusky chamber, where I wasted many good years of my youth, shaping day-dreams and night-dreams into idle stories—scarcely half of which ever saw the light; except it were their own blaze upon the hearth. I wish now that I had not burned them; for perhaps there might have been one among them fit—or capable of being made fit—to lead the new collection of tales. However, my youth comes back to me here; and I find myself, sad to say, pretty much the same sort of fellow as of old—(16:126)

▼ IT IS OCTOBER 1845 and Hawthorne, nearing the end of his short-story writing career, is writing to one of his editors, E. A. Duyckinck, with a strong sense of continuities as he contemplates the scene of his first literary efforts. This is a characteristic letter, self-dramatizing, self-denigrating, self-concealing, yet it suggests certain matters that are important in his first surviving works. It makes us ask what he meant by "day-dreams" and "night-dreams," and what is the connection between these two terms; what were the difficulties encountered in giving such material "shape" (a term that we shall see he also uses in an 1829 letter to his publisher Samuel Goodrich); and why he tried to destroy so much. Hawthorne never wholly rejected or accepted this work. His sister-in-law reported that he had "said some of these *[Seven Tales]* were perhaps the most powerful he had written, but felt they were *morbid*. . . . He was not sure that he had burnt all that deserved that fate."[1]

But these works were not necessarily an abortive beginning. They give insight into what first engaged his imagination and the literary form it took, and they also partly determine the direction his work subsequently took. Hawthorne came to reject the unmodified introversion that characterizes these works and that can be traced to the use of the Gothic unleashing an unsocialized self and subverting normality and authority. The lack of ethical or psychological resolution in these works derives from an oversimplified notion of two starkly opposed psychical and social realms and from Gothic forms that can express but not explicate that opposition. These were the problems that Hawthorne was to reassess in the next phase of his work.

▼

First we must briefly reconstruct those literary beginnings, for few indeed of his first compositions escaped burning. When a Salem publisher took too long to decide whether to publish his work, Hawthorne withdrew and destroyed his first projected collection, *Seven Tales of My Native Land*. If the narrator's account in "Alice Doane's Appeal" is based on autobiographical material (and there are grounds for believing this since there are other clear parallels in that tale with Hawthorne's own life), then we can say that two of these tales "chanced to be in kinder custody at the time, and thus by no conspicuous merits of their own, escaped destruction" (ii:269). These two were probably "Alice Doane" (an early version of "Alice Doane's Appeal") and "The Hollow of the Three Hills."[2] His first novel, *Fanshawe*, published at Hawthorne's own expense (as was typical at that time), received mostly favorable reviews, but it did not sell, and after asking his sister and best friend to burn their copies, he kept its authorship a total secret for the rest of his life (3:308–12).

It is possible to trace the history of the composition of these works. It appears that those two apparently very different kinds of writing overlap chronologically, though it is not certain which Hawthorne began first—the stories or the novel. Accounts conflict, but the likeliest interpretation of the evidence is that he wrote *Seven Tales* while still at college. He returned to Salem after his graduation (September 1825). There, according to his college friend Horatio Bridge, the tales were "prepared for the press" (thus implying that they were composed elsewhere). *Fanshawe* was also probably started at college: Hawthorne wrote to his sister that he had "made good progress on my novel"—unnamed, but the implication of Elizabeth Hawthorne's account is that this was *Fanshawe.* The novel was then taken up again during the wait for *Seven Tales* to be published (the collection was withdrawn in autumn 1826) and was made ready for publication in October 1828.[3] It is this interrelationship between *Fanshawe* and *Seven Tales* that will be investigated here.

▼

In writing about *Seven Tales* Hawthorne focuses on the Gothic, and in this element lies the key to understanding the central focus of both these tales and *Fanshawe.* In a letter to Goodrich in 1829, commenting apparently on "Alice Doane," he says:

> You will see that one of the stories is founded upon the superstitions of this part of the country. I do not know that such an attempt has hitherto been made; but, as I have thrown away much time in listening to such traditions, I could not help trying to put them into some shape. The tale is certainly rather wild and grotesque, but the outlines of many not less so might be picked up hereabouts. (15:199)

Although Hawthorne felt he was breaking new ground, his choice of subject is not entirely surprising. Judith Wilt points out a similar childhood "obsession with romantic and supernatural adventure tales from both oral and written sources" in the early literary imaginations of Scott, Charlotte Brontë, and Dickens, and the Gothic novels that Hawthorne so admired in his adolescence and that provided models for some of his earliest works were, as David Punter shows, a middle-class appropriation of the terrors of such folk stories. Such terrors had a fascination for two reasons. As Wilt has suggested, they expressed the ambiguities and anxieties of a rapidly changing society whose dominant rationalist, realist ideology had difficulty in accommodating many hidden fears, alienation, fragmentation, and a disconnection with its past[4]—fears to which the new United States must have been as susceptible as industrializing Europe. Secondly, the Gothic also deals with transitions at a more individual level in the young person, aware of the social order but not yet part of it, surrounded by people and powers that can hardly be understood, let alone controlled.[5]

Gothic is a way of imagining the unimaginable, the classic mode of gaining access to areas not readily available within the realist confines of the social novel.[6] Its use here unleashes barely comprehended unconscious impulses, anarchic feelings unaccountable by contemporary rationalism, feelings that blot out the social world, distort normal perception, destroy authority, question the nature of identity, and make value judgments very difficult (indeed sections of the community are shown to be corrupted by it). The core of "Alice Doane's Appeal"—apparently what remains of the original "Alice Doane"—is a disturbing nightmare, a concatenation of extraordinary horrific effects. It draws on primal psychological material narrated in the confessional first person: the central image is of children (Leonard and his sister) weeping over their father's corpse, and this image merges into the adult picture of isolated and guilty Leonard standing in tears over his murdered brother, his other self. The terror is derived from the inadmissible, antisocial, taboo part of the person.

It is, however, noteworthy that this is the single unadulterated use of the Gothic in Hawthorne's work, possibly because it expressed only entrapment within an individual mind and a desire to destroy that part of oneself. There is no catharsis. Although the murder seems at first to liberate the hero from this terror, the actual effect is to intensify the tale's introversion and imprisonment within the mirror walls of the self. Fear of this introversion is reinforced by images of possible incestuous attraction and fearsome doubling:

"[t]here was a resemblance from which I shrank with sickness, and loathing, and horror, as if my own features had come and stared upon me in a solitary place, or had met me in struggling through a crowd" (II:271). The doppelgänger is a kind of mirror, and to meet yourself thus is a horrifying business. Leonard is killing an unconscious, or latent, or suppressed part of himself (hence the dreamlike quality of the action).

Mirrors will prove to be a potent image at various stages of Hawthorne's development. Here the mirror-like double expresses an encounter within the self that is conceived as split between a socially benign, conformist exterior and an apparently demonic inner being. The parts of the psyche that are not normally represented in the culture are here fully, indeed literally, embodied—Leonard looks in a kind of mirror and sees something other than what he thought himself to be. The mirror that could reassure one of the self's presence now shows that the self is divided into two. This self-division is itself the product of an ideologically induced desire to see the social life in rational and morally optimistic terms: as a result, the encounter with the part it loathes, fears, or tries to ignore is profoundly disturbing. In the tale these now rampant fears obliterate even the whole community's usual self-image as well, so that eventually it appears only in the form of "spectres" of the damned—a projection of the individual's own terror at himself.7

Because this experience has no acceptable place in the social symbolic order, Leonard's consciousness is doomed to remain unexpressed there, and because of the way that the self has been constructed into two strongly opposed parts, there cannot be grounding of the subjective fantasy in an ordinary external social reality, nor can dreaming bring about reunification. The situation is resolved instead only through violent destruction of the mirror: "the similarity of their dispositions made them like joint possessors of an individual nature, which could not become wholly the property of one, unless by the extinction of the other" (II:272). The psychic roots of the self are abandoned in favor of the ideological ideal of a unique, unified self.

"The Hollow of the Three Hills" is not as profoundly introverted a tale, but is nonetheless similarly caught up in exploring the act of introspection. Again the Gothic supernatural is the medium through which "fantastic dreams and madmen's reveries" are "realized among the actual circumstances of life" (9:199). The artist is here represented by the witch who is able to summon up the scenes of the tales, but has no other power to change—her smile is merely "lamplight" (9:200) illuminating the events. These scenes are entirely located in the mind of the protagonist. Although the phrase "the actual circumstances of life" appears to privilege the exterior world, that world is not directly present in the tale that focuses on the lady's consciousness; the world "beyond" this exists only in her imagination and is viewed from a position of exclusion from the cultural order. The basic situation is one of isolation and disconnection. This is paralleled in the situation of the chained inmates of the madhouse "whose own burning thoughts had become their exclusive world" (9:203). Thus at the very outset of his career we can see Hawthorne constructing one of his recurrent motifs, the prison or "sepulchre" (9:200) of the heart. As we can see from its roots here, this image is predicated on a particular conception of a psychic world—a conception that comes into being because the full range of the self is not represented in the social order.

To make the protagonist a woman (normally expected to embody all that the culture held dear) is to destabilize even further certain settled ideas about the social world. The male desire for salvation may have been embodied in the sexually pure Alice Doane, but as a merely conventional image of moral value it is easily threatened and never fully restored. Here that threat is fully realized in the "fallen" woman as protagonist and in the ancient witch.

In the world of both "Alice Doane" and "The Hollow of the Three Hills" there is no ethical or psychic resolution, no social accommodation or Romantic transcendence.[8] The reader is not presented with moral meaning confidently affirmed; there is little or no sense of an outside observer reporting events or of explicit authorial intervention. Instead, in "The Hollow of the Three Hills" the readers' experience and responses are carefully kept parallel to the protagonist's in a way that further intensifies the tale's focus on her consciousness, and at one point her experience is made identical to that of the readers' when her visions are described as "the dim pages of a book, which we strive to read by an imperfect and gradually brightening light" (9:201). Because the conclusion is voiced by a gloating witch, the reader cannot easily derive a conventional moral satisfaction from the adulteress's punishment. It is true that the tale's morality is implicitly bound up with seeing the woman as the violator of domestic values, but by locating the tale's judgment in the lady's repenting inner self, which has internalized social judgments, there is no escape from this subjectivity. She dies in agony unable to absolve herself, and the entrapment within the mind is unrelieved. The split self, now embodied in one divided identity rather than in two people as in "Alice Doane," cannot here be resolved by destroying one half.

In comparison with "The Hollow of the Three Hills," the original "Alice Doane" appears to have been even less structured toward a moral conclusion; the tale largely subverts institutional value systems. When an unconscious, unforeseen impulse thus opposes the artist's conscious morality, reentry into the everyday world is blocked. The author appears not to be wholly in control of his material in that he cannot impose structure on the tale's experiences (an effect possibly exaggerated in the rewritten "Alice Doane's Appeal"). It is only the more consciously socialized narrator of the story's later 1830s frame who has learnt to desire (if not achieve) "that better wisdom, which draws the moral while it tells the tale" (11:267). This art that creates such a moral vacuum is disturbing: Leonard had wanted to kill the vision that his "diseased" imagination and "morbid feelings" had conjured up (11:270), and his creator appears to nurse similar feelings.

There are further suggestions in the tale that the imagination here works in disturbing ways. The hoarfrost covering the scene is presented as a symbol of the transforming and defamiliarizing power of art. The wizard's powers too are ambiguous (it is not clear whether he or Leonard is responsible for events), but these powers will make more sense if they are seen as an image of the power of the creative writer who invents a plot but whose characters then seem to have some disturbing and amoral will of their own. One of Hawthorne's early notebook entries in the 1830s expresses something of this: "A person to be writing a tale, and to find that it shapes itself against his intentions; that the characters act otherwise than he thought; that unforeseen events occur; and a catastrophe which he strives in vain to avert. It might shadow forth his own fate—he having made himself one of the personages" (LN [19]).[9]

The imagination's creations are seen in both these works as images of demonic possession rather than merely dreams, and it is in such terms that it is described in "The Devil in Manuscript." This tale from the early 1830s, given the parallels between some of its material and extra-literary accounts of the fate of Hawthorne's early writing, is apparently a retrospective, fictionalized, and mockingly self-dramatizing account of the composition of *Seven Tales:* "I have a horror of what was created in my own brain, and shudder at the manuscripts in which I gave that dark idea a sort of material existence'" (II:171). The young writer-narrator links defeat by the devil within his stories with the artistic failure of the tales themselves. The "devil" here represents the inability of the work to free itself from the compulsions and limitations of its creator's or its character's psychic life with the result that it remains trapped within this. Furthermore this kind of composition is presented as bringing a peculiar sort of subjective isolation: "I am surrounding myself with shadows, which bewilder me. . . . They have drawn me aside from the beaten path of the world, and led me into a strange sort of solitude—a solitude in the midst of men—where nobody wishes for what I do, nor thinks nor feels as I do" (II:172).

Hawthorne's own response to these early tales was divided. Although latterly he rejected "Alice Doane's Appeal" even for inclusion in his final collection, *The Snow Image* (II:390–91, and 6), he had been interested enough in the original *Seven Tales* version of the tale to salvage the work in the early 1830s and recast it as "Alice Doane's Appeal." This reworking has a quasi-autobiographical frame containing extraneous details of the narrator's own history as a writer. Since these details have no immediate reference to the tale in hand, their presence in the frame may suggest the importance of the original story to Hawthorne in defining the subsequent direction of his literary career. The narrator remembers his pen "now sluggish and perhaps feeble, because I have not much to hope and fear, was driven by stronger external motives, and a more passionate impulse within, than I am fated to feel again" (II:269).

The contemporary cultural context of *Seven Tales* may be the source of these conflicting attitudes. Scottish Common Sense philosophy, the reigning intellectual view of the day and staple academic fare at Hawthorne's college, linked dreaming with madness. Indulgence in the imagination was regarded as dangerous because it would cut one off from what Common Sense philosophy regarded as the real world. Imagination was seen as a threat to society, and as a result, as Terence Martin shows, "the world of the imagination thus became in a special way a region of terror." As Martin further suggests, this was a philosophy for a post-Revolutionary society that was seeking stability both socially and intellectually.[10] Practical-minded, this society rejected undue speculation (thus avoiding both Hume's skepticism and Berkeley's idealism) and sought freedom from the very past that Hawthorne's work appears to have wanted to explore. This society defined the real in terms of a God-created physical world and believed in universal innate feelings. Only children, it was thought, failed to live fully in this world of actuality (a view possibly confirmed by the primal content of "Alice Doane").

These Common Sense ideas created a widespread hostility to fiction. Martin here cites Levi Frisbie to exemplify the current notion of ideal fiction:

"Our moral and intellectual condition may be still further improved," he [Frisbie] says, by the "diffusion of correct tastes, sentiment, and opinions" of literary men and scholars. "The literature which we want is effective, practical, useful literature, the literature of the intellect and the heart. The men, whom we particularly need, are those, who may guide and form publick opinion and sentiment in matters of taste, in morals, in politicks, and in religion."[11]

The author of "Alice Doane" and "The Hollow of the Three Hills" was likely to feel uncomfortable about his creations in the face of such an ideology; indeed his first novel reflects the conflict set up by these attitudes. His early writing reflects what David S. Reynolds sees as a "bifurcation" between the conventional and the subversive literary currents in American culture by this date. Whether intentionally or not, this earliest work has become what Rosemary Jackson calls a "literature of subversion," which gives voice to what is invisible or silenced in the culture and which is an expression of censored or at least unsatisfied desire.[12]

▼

Fanshawe's "smiling gothic" clearly contrasts with the hellfired Gothic of "Alice Doane" and "The Hollow of the Three Hills,"[13] yet of more significance is what all three works have in common: the compulsive quality of dreams. In the case of *Fanshawe* this is narcissistic daydreaming. But whereas the two short stories do not clearly relate to the ordinary world of quotidian experience and customary expectations to which any literary work that hoped for a public at that time must speak in a recognizable voice, *Fanshawe* in its surface narrative attempts an investigation of the relationship between these dreaming and waking worlds.

The enterprise of tracing this relationship is made easier because here the dream is not the terrifying desires of nightmare but is more like a daydream and an expression of desire where the daydreamer is transfixed by his introversion, staring as if in a mirror at the imagined self. The novel's hero is a scholar whose natural habitat, the library, would have been dismissed by Common Sense philosophy as artificial and false—this philosophy generally regarded the drawing room and the "forum" as "reality," that is to say the spheres of familial and political interaction.[14] By paralleling Fanshawe's career with his fellow student Walcott's, the novel conceives of life as a choice between two very different worlds: the solitary inner world, and marriage and a socially active life. Like the tales, the division is conceived in stark terms. The conflict between the attractions and demands of each is made artificially simple (though undeniably more dramatic) by embodying one of the mutually exclusive modes of existence in each man, rather than by exploring these possibilities within a single person.

On the level of plot, the novel's ending might appear to endorse Common Sense values—Walcott gets the girl and Fanshawe dies. This conclusion would certainly be more satisfying to popular taste and was possibly deliberately designed that way while the fate of *Seven Tales* still hung in the balance (3:305–6, 308). On the surface it normalizes the demonic nightmares of those other early tales. Nonetheless the novel does not conform more than superficially to conventional tastes and attitudes. At bottom the novel indulges Fanshawe at the expense of the rest of his world, and Common Sense is shown not to have all the answers. Indeed, the novel's oddities, frustrations, and incoherences turn out to make more sense if we do not try to approach the novel as a validation of commonly agreed notions about reality and the social life.

Several elements indicate a lack of commitment to a Common Sense view of things, indeed a lack of interest in the social order. The introversion of Fanshawe's world of learning is not unattractive: "like one who was a ruler in a world of his own" (3:346). His detachment dooms him to an early death, but is the source of an apparently superior moral power. In contrast, all the other characters, involved with their families, work, and sense of duty, are shown to be strangely vulnerable.

The novel's evaluation of character and event (the area in the novel where one would expect the greatest engagement with significant issues to do with being a subject within the social order) suggests an authorial lack of interest in these matters. This assessment is never other than bland and abstracted from the narration, there is no real questioning of values, and the creation of character is done by reference to certain fixed values, held to be prime virtues by social beings but here unrelated to the main body of action. Potentially important material is left unexamined or unintegrated into the narrative or thematic argument: for example, Butler's depravity, whether innate or acquired; his aunt's gratuitously evil misdirections; the new emotional depths found at his mother's death.

Fanshawe himself is the most problematic. He is inconsistently and inadequately motivated, and the novel's emphasis on adventurous action makes it more difficult to describe a character not often impressive in appearance, conversation, or action, and distanced by an inability to be happy with "the common occupation of the world" (3:443). His unchosen love for Ellen is introduced in one paragraph of reported thought and two of indirect summary (3:350–51); his vacillation is not presented as inner conflict; the implications of self-destruction in his search for independence, knowledge, and fame go unexamined; and his apparently inevitable fate disposes of any real turmoil.

Yet Fanshawe's disturbing act of renunciation is the central focus of the novel, and the other characters are peripheral to this. He is the novel's main interest, but for all his fascination, the novel is unable or unwilling to elucidate its hero. The novel itself demonstrates an awareness of the problem, for it attempts to explain this away by reference to Fanshawe's own character: "That he was conscious of such hopes, there is little reason to suppose; the most powerful minds are not always the best acquainted with their own feelings" (3:443).

Perhaps the narrator is right. Fanshawe is caught in the realm of the infantile Imaginary, that pre-oedipal union of child with mother where the world seems made for oneself and one's self for the world; he refuses to enter the social order. Loss and a sense of difference are therefore literally unthinkable because he avoids the frustration of living as a social subject. In consequence he has not developed a subjectivity because he has never moved from the mirror of introspection that supports the Imaginary.

We can best account for all these elements by looking at the nature of the satisfaction the novel offers. In spite of its potential to investigate the problematic relationship between inner life and social existence (something made pressing by *Seven Tales*), it makes no demands of its audience, which remains passively enjoying a self-contained daydream that, with the exception of Butler's mother's death, is never well grounded in the objective world. Indeed, as long as Fanshawe is insulated from the rest, the dream of scholarship and the dream of being loved can both be indulged without having to connect them or relate them to the pressures of actuality. This, then, is a fiction just as introverted as *Seven Tales*. Fantasy is frequently the uncritical fulfillment of unsatisfied wishes or the correction of an unsatisfying social reality, the effortless fantasy of escape for those who are powerless or paralyzed. Gothic's exploration of desire latches onto something of this in its reflection of the injustices and inequalities of people's lives and their sense that their fates are unchosen.[15] Fanshawe's combination of power and passivity testifies simultaneously to fantasy's freedom and the actual, underlying choicelessness that had provoked such compensatory fantasizing. Butler on the other hand shows the perils of any attempt to act out these desires. He is Fanshawe's alter ego, an actively resisting hero whose actions can be seen by society only in terms of subversion, evil, and guilt—a Gothic hero more in the mold of *Seven Tales*. There was therefore no need for a sophisticated plot, motivation, resolution, range of characters, moral or psychological purpose. Here the ego safely triumphs as it can when the daydreamer is hero. This is the omnipotence of thought that Freud associated with narcissism or the very small child.[16] Fanshawe's timeless world is indeed dreamlike: his scholarly life is an "eternity of improvement . . . without a termination" (3:350), and his moment of possessing Ellen "contained no mixture of hope, it had no reference to the future—it was the perfect bliss of a moment—an insulated point of happiness" (3:452). Even the novel's creator seems to stand with a foot in each of two worlds, the actual and the imaginary, without having to blend them into one—the novel contains unassimilated scenes and incidents from Hawthorne's own Bowdoin days.

Only woman—the sexual other—could disturb this daydreaming of a self safely insulated from the social order that it refuses to enter. Ellen constitutes a threat when she proposes marriage, but her power is shorn by her illness and Fanshawe is able to turn her down—unlike the retiring scholar of *The Scarlet Letter* who involves himself disastrously with a woman. Anything that would disturb the illusion of a safely gratifying world must be marginalized, such as Butler's gratuitously evil aunt who challenges the safely idealized stereotype of woman. Here the novel's deterministic structure, unlike that of the two surviving stories from *Seven Tales,* reflects a pleasure in such lack of choice. Death is a devoutly wished for consummation rather than a tragedy—an expression of the death wish, that longing for Nirvana with all tensions gone.[17] Posthumous fame is better than the oblivion reserved for socialized Walcott.

This view of *Fanshawe* is confirmed in an authorially self-conscious way by later works that depict literary composition by very youthful writers almost exclusively in terms of this daydream fiction of safely unimpeded desire. "Monsieur du Miroir," a decade later than *Fanshawe,* recalls how the narrator-writer, in the classic image of narcissistic fantasy, had gazed in the mirror to inspire "bewitching dreams of a woman's love" (10:169), and "A Select Party" (1844) describes the portals of the literary castle in the air as thronged with "beings of crude imagination, such as glide before a young man's eye, and pretend to be actual inhabitants of the earth; the wise and witty, with whom he would hereafter hold intercourse; the generous and heroic friends, whose devotion would be requited with his own; the beautiful dream-woman" (10:63).

"The Vision of the Fountain," written not long after *Fanshawe* in the early 1830s, is wholly devoted to examining the processes of the youthful imagination in these terms. The narrator describes how, as a boy, he created a fictional story from the glimpse of a girl seen as he gazed Narcissus-like in a pool (this setting even recalls slightly one place in *Fanshawe* [3:438–39]). Like *Fanshawe,* fiction is generated from the introverted gaze. This daydreaming introversion is clearly more benign than that of "Alice Doane" and "The Hollow of the Three Hills," nonetheless it has the similar effect of cutting the dreamer off from what would be regarded as the "real" world, making him confused about what is real and what imagined, and leading to withdrawal into "an inner world" (9:216). The subsequent evaporation of the fantasy, however, reflects the later attitudes of Hawthorne's 1830s work.

"Graves and Goblins," also written in the early 1830s, further parallels this reading of *Fanshawe.* Its protagonist, a ghost, is like Fanshawe in several ways: he thinks it was good to die young, he is now unhappily in love. What is interesting for the present argument is that this ghost version of Fanshawe is the inspiration for the creative writer: "I steal into his sleep, and play my part among the figures of his dreams. I glide through the moonlight of his waking fancy, and whisper conceptions, which, with a strange thrill of fear, he writes down as his own" (II:297). The phrase "waking fancy" suggests daydreaming rather than the dreams of the deep unconscious. It is, however, a view of fiction applicable only to *Fanshawe* among Hawthorne's works, and it is important to note that it disappears from his thinking on art thereafter, except as something evoked only to be critically rejected.[18] No wonder he latterly suppressed the novel.

▼

It is clear that the apprentice Hawthorne wrestled with his material. The links that these surviving works establish between literary creativity and dreaming or demonic power (or both) suggest a sense on the author's part that he has created something outside the boundaries of his contemporary social order and hence unacceptable. The works were too radical for a society that, although revolutionary in its public institutions, liked to think of itself as emotionally conservative. Though it is true that *Fanshawe* was in part a typical popular American novel of the period, we have seen that in Hawthorne's hands the fantasizing tendency was intensified until it seemed a genre not susceptible to serious moral development. It is typical of the kind of Gothic described by Robert D. Hume, a world essentially individual and subjective rather than social and exterior in its concerns, and one whose limits are never transcended.[19]

However, in certain ways "The Hollow of the Three Hills" proves an exception. Unlike either *Fanshawe* or "Alice Doane," this tale was latterly regarded by Hawthorne as worth reprinting. It went into *Twice-told Tales* in 1837, his first collection that, as its Preface indicates, was designed to establish a public for his work. This tale was not for burning. While "Alice Doane" and *Fanshawe* are in most important ways unique in the corpus of Hawthorne's work, "The Hollow of the Three Hills" turns out to foreshadow certain concerns and strategies in his later writing, and is evidence that he did not completely change course in reaction to this first phase of his career, as Baym and Weber have both suggested.[20]

Instead of the simple *Fanshawe* dichotomy between the isolated and the socially integrated, and the "Alice Doane" black foray into the wild territory of the unconscious, "The Hollow of the Three Hills" did take as its subject one alienated soul's attempt to reconnect with her social identity. True, she fails, and the tale is, as we have noted, deeply introverted. But the tale's main narrative thrust is toward making that external world real to the woman. Both the use of physical scene (instead of interior monologue or confessional dialogue) and the stress on the senses contributes to this. The lady's ability to visualize that world is dependent on her growing willingness to acknowledge fully her connection with it.

Thus the action of the tale, though in essence a mental event, has its source in what is conceived of as an external world. Indeed what we are shown of the lady's subjectivity is almost entirely constituted by the social world, the self ideologically defined by personal roles (daughter, wife, mother)—unlike her celebrated successor Hester Prynne. It is because the lady's subject position as a woman is so fixed that her psychic life is pushed into in the uncivilized, wild area of existence.

Some of the tale's "shape"—its clarity of narrative outline and its lack of emotional or moral muddle in contrast to *Fanshawe* and what remains of "Alice Doane"—derives from this use of a generally accepted feminine stereotype. Hawthorne made it an easier but more superficial subject for himself both morally and psychologically by adopting such an image of woman, since the female subject is fixed here by social signs but is not represented by that order. The relationship of the adulterous woman to that family world, though distressing, is thus clearly and simply presented. These "fantastic dreams" can be more easily "realized among the actual circumstances of life" than those of the other protagonists of this phase or the phase to come. The work Hawthorne went on to do in his next phase, *Provincial Tales,* gained from the expressive means found in "The Hollow of the Three Hills," but took on subjects with far less simple

conceptions of the nature of the human subject. The entrapping
nature of introversion in all these first pieces posed a challenge that
the *Provincial Tales* attempted to take up, and the social meanings
that had faded and even disappeared in those early works were to
become operative again in these subsequent works.

Chapter 3

"Am I Here, or There?"

The *Provincial Tales* Period

1828–1831

▼ IN 1863, NEARLY FORTY YEARS after writing *Seven Tales,* Hawthorne had apparently forgotten about "Alice Doane" and "The Hollow of the Three Hills." In a letter reviewing his career for Samuel Cleveland, he wrote: "The first tales that I wrote (having kept them in manuscript, for lack of a publisher, till I was able to see some of their demerits) I burnt. Of those that finally came before the public, I believe that 'The Gentle Boy' and 'Roger Malvin's Burial' were the earliest written" (18:521). These named stories formed part of his next projected collection, *Provincial Tales,* and it is in this group of tales that Hawthorne establishes, far more clearly and centrally than in *Seven Tales,* the central concerns of his work for the next twenty or so years. His new use of historical material helped to clarify his sense of the dual dimension of identity, in particular its origins, and to recognize fully how subjectivity is structured in particular societies. While some of the most substantial tales of this period need to be examined in detail, other apparently very different sketches and stories also composed at this time can be shown to be closely related to his exploration of subjectivity and adequacy of social discourses to express it.

Both tales mentioned to Cleveland contain the same primal image first found in "Alice Doane," of the child weeping at the feet of his dead father—Ilbrahim in the forest crying at his father's grave, and Reuben weeping at the site of Roger Malvin's bones—but the *Provincial Tales* are no mere continuation of *Seven Tales.* They do not occupy the same dream territory as Hawthorne's earliest work. They explicitly reject the romantic daydreaming of *Fanshawe*, and they attempt to contextualize the nightmare of "Alice Doane" so that its source and relationship to the social order can be investigated: "The tangled and gloomy forest, through which the personages of my tale were wandering, differed widely from the dreamer's Land of Fantasie" (10:352). Not content to rest with a simple bifurcation into the conventional and the subversive, Hawthorne seeks explanations for the introversion bedeviling his earliest work and continuing here: Reuben unable to love except where he sees a reflection of himself in his son; Brown apparently projecting his self-hatred onto his fellow villagers; Robin Molineux rejecting his kinsman; the Wives of the Dead trying to reach beyond the solitude of grief to sisterhood; and the antinomianism of the Quaker Catharine obeying her inner voice.

The sense of dream within a waking world pervades each tale: the characters feel they straddle two worlds; daydreaming Robin cries out, "Am I here, or there?" (11:223). Like a "sleep-walker" ("Roger Malvin" [10:355]), characters are shown dreaming in a waking world, or not knowing whether or not they dreamed their experiences. Thoughts, we are told in "My Kinsman, Major Molineux," become "visible and audible in a dream" (11:23), and the later procession is "as if a dream had broken forth from some feverish brain" (11:228). These tales show that dreams are not simply the passive reflection of a chaotic unconscious, but rather the individual's attempt to transform the raw materials of both waking life and latent wishes into something intelligible.

▼

In one respect *Provincial Tales* does resemble *Seven Tales:* it was never published as a collection. The scattered tales appeared anonymously in various magazines at different times in subsequent years, and to reconstruct the collection many different pieces of evidence have to be pieced together. The best we can hope for is a working hypothesis, based on all the existing evidence, much of it extratextual.

The tales are first mentioned in Hawthorne's letter in December 1829 to the Boston editor Samuel Goodrich, who had read *Fanshawe* and written asking to see some of Hawthorne's work:

> These which I send have been completed (except prefixing the titles) a considerable time. There are two or three others, not at present in a condition to be sent. If I ever finish them, I suppose they will be about upon a par with the rest. . . . none of the pieces are shorter than the one first sent you ["Roger Malvin's Burial"]. If I write any of the length you mention, I will send them to you; but I think I shall close my literary labours with what I have already begun. (15:199–200)

From Goodrich's reply (9:489) acknowledging receipt of the tales in January 1830, we know that *Provincial Tales* definitely included "Roger Malvin's Burial," "The Gentle Boy," "My Kinsman, Major Molineux," and "Alice Doane" (the original version, since "Alice Doane's Appeal" makes reference to what is probably Charles W. Upham's book on Salem witchcraft published in 1831).[1]

It is virtually certain that "The Wives of the Dead," which was published with "Roger Malvin," "The Gentle Boy," and "Major Molineux" in the *Token* of 1832 (and therefore was ready for publication in mid-1831), was part of the collection. The tale is too short to be among those originally sent to Goodrich, whose request for shorter pieces was evidently met a few months later by two works specially written for the *Token,* one of them similar in length to "The Wives of the Dead."[2] "The Wives of the Dead" was therefore probably written after December 1829, but its historical setting of the Louisberg siege is mentioned in the biographical sketch, "Sir William Pepperell" (published in the 1833 *Token* but in all likelihood written at the same time as three other markedly similar biographical sketches published earlier in late 1830 and early 1831). The common source for both "The Wives of the Dead" and "Sir William Pepperell" was William Douglass's *British Settlements in North-America,* borrowed by Hawthorne from Salem Library in February 1828 and January 1830.[3]

The "two or three others" not yet completed that the original letter mentions were probably "The Wives of the Dead," "The Gray

Champion," and "Young Goodman Brown." The latter two have appropriate subject matter. "The Gray Champion" can be given a likely date from Hawthorne's library borrowings of its source material, Thomas Hutchinson's *History of Massachusetts* in December 1826–January 1827 and again in April 1829, and by a visit to the grave of the regicide judges in 1828. "Young Goodman Brown" has less evidence for its date, but two of its sources were borrowed from the library—Hutchinson in 1826–1827 and 1829, and Cotton Mather's *Magnalia* in April 1828. There are, however, no records of borrowing his key source, Mather's *Wonders of the Invisible World.* The tale may have been completed after Upham's lectures in 1831 at the Salem Lyceum on the 1692 witch-hunts (lectures so celebrated that "Young Goodman Brown," unlike all the other *Provincial Tales,* did not need to start with a summary of the story's historical background). A likely explanation for why "The Gray Champion" and "Young Goodman Brown" were not published until 1835 is that they were retained by Hawthorne for inclusion in his next projected collection, *The Story Teller.*[4]

Provincial Tales dominates his work at this period. There are eight other slight pieces: the four historical Biographical Sketches, three of which were published in the *Salem Gazette* between November 1830 and January 1831 along with two stories, "The Battle Omen" and "The Old Woman's Tale." "The Battle Omen" has links with *Provincial Tales* but fails to develop into a fully realized narrative. "The Old Woman's Tale," while also having some similar material to "Alice Doane" (the telling of superstitions and the crowd of dead townspeople, although without any demonism), seems, unlike all the other tales of this phase, to mock the Gothic with its teasingly inconclusive ending, and presages the tone of work in Hawthorne's next phase. "Sights from the Steeple" and probably "The Haunted Quack" belong to this period chronologically, but they were apparently written to meet Goodrich's requirements for the *Token* market and in content are clearly the first sign of the kind of work Hawthorne was to produce in the next phase of his career (see chapter 4).[5]

Although Hawthorne did include "Alice Doane" in *Provincial Tales* and we can have only a partial sense of what he had written previously in *Seven Tales, Provincial Tales* nonetheless constitutes distinctive work that is attempting something different.

▼

In *Provincial Tales*, five of the six stories draw attention to their historical base with introductory paragraphs of purportedly factual context. More than merely "background," in each case the introduction constitutes the particular historical moment in which a certain social order constructs a character's subjectivity. Through the inclusion of precise dates, the outlining of the political and ideological contexts, and citation of textual authorities and the historians and annals used as sources, the tales thus advertise their subject as being partly about history both in the sense of charting the processes by which a society and its people are constructed, and of showing how that society fabricates a story of its origins. This material is used in a manner that is distinctive in certain aspects from other later historical tales and sketches.[6]

This is Hawthorne's first use of such material, but there is a close relationship between the early Gothic novel and the "historical novel" that emerges around the same time in both European and American literature. As Punter remarks, "Gothic itself seems to have been a mode of history, a way of perceiving an obscure past and interpreting it," a past that was seen as barbaric and terror-filled.[7] So, while Hawthorne's use of Gothic had hitherto been more caught up in the personal past of particular individuals, the move toward a more sharply defined historical context for his characters seems part of that general literary development in examining a culture. This historicizing of the division within the human subject is vital since, as he goes on to show, subjectivity is given a distinctive shape by the nature of a particular society (Puritan, Revolutionary, capitalist).

This shift toward creating an ostensibly accurate picture of a historical actuality drawn from his extensive study at this time of American history does not, however, create a realistic, objective world as counterweight to the fantasy and introversion of his earlier work. Much more usefully, history provides here the socially constructed external stage on which the human subject acts out its psychic turmoil, a turmoil that does not simply emerge from within the individual but rather is the product of that society—the frustration and confusion that results when the social order fails to acknowledge and meet individual desire. Moreover, a historical tale can examine the very images through which peoples in the past have expressed their inner compulsions (for example, as Michael J. Colacurcio has observed, witchcraft in seventeenth-century New England provided "a vocabulary for the publicly ignored contradictions" of that culture).[8]

In contrast to Hawthorne's contemporaries' enthusiasm for merely sentimental and patriotic historical tales, the historical material here contextualizes the nightmare of his earlier work, making possible a richer analysis of his growing sense of the processes by which subjectivity is constructed and of the way that this creates a split within the person between a self that is recognized in the social order and a self that is not represented in given roles and discourses. For these *Provincial Tales* characters, their subjective lives are created and positioned through the processes by which the individual is allowed to enter the social order.

Seventeenth-century New England history was particularly useful in investigating such disjunctions. Its base in theology and debate provided Hawthorne with sharply defined material and dialectical structures that he could explore with some degree of detachment. A further consequence of using such material was to enhance his sense of human beings as creatures of a specific time and place (whether the seventeenth or nineteenth century) and thus subject to historically changing influences. History was not merely a decorative backcloth for supposedly timeless, "universal" problems of human existence. As Lawrence Buell has demonstrated, Hawthorne worked within the Arminian-Unitarian tradition of Puritan historiography, whose critical, rationalist, and liberal appraisal, emphasizing a process of evolution, led to historical and ethical relativism and was opposed to the orthodox Congregationalist absolutist view of New England past.[9]

The major exception, at this point in Hawthorne's career, to this sense of cultural relativity and evolution is the tale's treatment of women who are depicted and judged by nineteenth-century values as if these values were absolute. While it is likely that women were subjected to more rigidly defined roles than men, this seems to be accepted without analysis or irony, whereas male characters are forced to question similar social conditions. In this, the *Provincial Tales* stories come close to the conservatism of the Biographical Sketches (to be discussed presently), where Ann Hutchinson is condemned for mistaking "the strong division-lines of Nature" for "arbitrary distinctions" (*TS* 18). It is, however, those very arbitrary distinctions that the *Provincial Tales* stories highlight when dealing with male characters. Robin's response to the remark that a man may have "several voices"—" 'Perhaps a man may; but Heaven forbid that a woman should!' " (II:226)—is a view shared by Hawthorne's other works at this period where the few female characters are either portrayed as domestic angels (Dorcas's pure white tablecloth in the middle of the wilderness) or are condemned for their dereliction of this publicly established role. The tales have been frequently analyzed as if the fate of the male protagonists was generally applicable, so it is necessary to point out the separate destinies of men and women within these works. "My Kinsman, Major Molineux" suggests that Robin's fate impinges on political as well as personal freedom, yet from women's point of view it is a matter of one patriarchy being overthrown by another. Only "The Wives of the Dead" treats women other than as mere conventional ciphers, but even here their identity is merged with their husbands: the source of the women's self-division is the men's deaths, because the men had provided the women with an imaginary wholeness and had reflected an image that actually fixes them in society.[10]

It is the four Biographical Sketches that both clarify the particular fictional ways in which Hawthorne will handle this historical material and trace the source of that problematic relation (already discernible in his work) between radical and conformist elements. These sketches are contemporary with *Provincial Tales* and linked in content (usually only in a minor way) with some of them:

"Mrs. Hutchinson" with "The Gentle Boy," "Sir William Pepperell" with "Roger Malvin" and "The Wives of the Dead," "Dr. Bullivant" with "The Gray Champion." The relationship of the sketches to *Provincial Tales* may seem at first problematic, given great differences in attitude and method, but they have an important role in his work at this time, disclosing the tensions between individual subjectivity and forms of social and ideological determination, particularly at the level of representation.

Like a photographic negative of the tales, the sketches are dark where the tales are light, and light where they are dark. They foreground social analysis rather than dramatic scene and character. The rare dramatic scenes are presented as self-consciously constructed illustrations of some abstract analysis by a detached narrator who insists on a clear nineteenth-century perspective, with its values and hindsight. Character is knowingly presented as an index of social conditions and created entirely from exterior appearance and action, without exploration of consciousness: typically, "The portrait of the ancient Governor . . . will owe any interest it may possess, not to his internal self, but to certain peculiarities of his fortune" (*TS* 12). Although the central figures in each sketch are never mere products of unified social influences, nonetheless the sketches strongly emphasize their roots and destinies in a particular time and place and, though at a slight tangent to their world, they are carefully shown to reflect and represent it entirely.

Furthermore, while confusion, pessimism, and the supreme difficulty of any kind of interpretation are, as I shall presently argue, prime characteristics of *Provincial Tales,* here the sketches' ostensibly liberal voice turns out to be that of unquestioned, establishment values, the rational nineteenth-century majority's view. So, in spite of interest in somewhat ambivalent persons, this analytical voice makes for a smoothly conformist surface. There might be a flicker of irony in this adopted voice, but it disappears when, for example, we get a virulent attack on successful women writers taking over the opening of "Mrs. Hutchinson."

However, the sketches are important to Hawthorne's task of mediating between the interiority of his first writing and the demands

of external cultural conditions: they show him the limitations inherent in this way of relating subjectivity and the social order.
Both "Dr. Bullivant" and, more fully, "Sir William Phips" begin
by acknowledging the difficulty of fully realizing convincingly and
in fictional terms the individuality and living experience of people
from a past culture: "They seldom stand up in our Imaginations
like men" (*TS* 12). The writing of history was a matter of debate
in Hawthorne's time, particularly the historians' responsibility to
bring history "alive." As "Sir William Phips" sees it, the methods
of history are contrasted with those of literature, where the creative artist's imagination can release itself from the constraints of
history's sociological analysis (an analysis that, as the sketches have
demonstrated, is at once too abstract and ideologically conformist).
The imaginatively created world, it is argued, is nearer to truth than
the publicly accepted picture. It is a concept that is clearly at odds
with the far more limited and passive concept of the imagination
provided by Common Sense philosophy, which posited a faculty to
be cultivated that remains "subject to common standards of beauty
and morality," merely designed to "bridge the gap between sensation and idea, between external stimulus and internal perception of
beauty and goodness."[11]

The sketches' proposition that historical "fact" can be combined
with the creative imagination, combined with their failure to achieve
this, is an important discovery in relation to the *Provincial Tales*
stories, where rather than being ideally two complementary modes,
"history" (in the sense of the culture's received assessment of events)
is at odds with their imaginatively recreated processes of identity.
The reason for this conflict is made evident in the sketches. Their
conservatism derives from the kind of historical material clearly
constituted by social discourse and ideology, in contrast to the
creative imagination that constructs individual subjectivity on many
pages of *Provincial Tales*.

Of all the stories of *Provincial Tales*, "The Gray Champion" most
closely follows the sketches' notions about the relation between
"literature" and "history." It also, symptomatically, shows the least
concern for describing individual subjectivity—the conservatism of

those social discourses militates against this. This formula does not produce the desired result. The tale's method is to add some invented material to a base predominantly made up of generally agreed historical fact, and its purpose is to create a national myth that will reflect something of the "character of the people" (9:13). However, as "Roger Malvin's Burial" realizes, a patriotic story of ideologically acceptable heroes can only be constructed by "casting certain circumstances judiciously into the shade" (10:337), in effect by rejecting some of the factual evidence (in the case of "Roger Malvin" we touch on legendary heroics of Lovell's Fight where in fact frontiersmen had been scalp-hunting for bounty on the Sabbath).[12]

"History," then, may be the wrong kind of fiction, one that re-produces ideology rather than analyzing it. "The Gray Champion" largely ignores this uncomfortable realization. Although it makes reference to hypocrisy, massacres, and self-provoked martyrdom, such material is mentioned only briefly, without consistently developed irony or any other attempt to assimilate it into the total picture. Two discourses conflict without acknowledgment. At one moment the narrator is conventionally patriotic, at other times and more rarely the irony is so deadpan as to be virtually imperceptible. The complacency of this simple narrative is only temporarily disturbed. It is a conventional hortatory tale with its "moral" for its "scene" (9:13), authoritarian in literary form like its protagonist, and the undisturbed reader is aligned automatically with one side ("our ancestors," "our liberties" [9:9]). The tale, in avoiding the overt challenge or necessary confusion that a more complex handling invited, reveals that a coherent imaginative picture cannot be created out of conventional attitudes to its country's history.[13] Crucially, it contains no individual character's viewpoint (in this respect "The Gray Champion" is unlike the other *Provincial Tales* stories), and social structures are described in a way that aborts any deep questioning.

This pattern is confirmed by "The Battle-Omen," the tale closest to "The Gray Champion" in its focus on public concerns and absence of individual subjectivity. It describes, from a late-eighteenth-century rationalist point of view, a quiet yearning that events like those of "The Gray Champion" might actually be true, but the tale does not pursue its questions, ultimately opting for a "superstitious" ending not materially different from the lightweight, ahistorical "Old Woman's Tale," which purports to tell one of the traditional and wholly improbable legends of the Connecticut valley. It is only the other more subjectively written of the *Provincial Tales* stories that investigate in any depth the possibility that this tale's sense of "Providence" might be only an invention of the human mind.

So "The Gray Champion" and "The Battle-Omen" veer away from a more subjective perspective, not surprisingly since, as "Alice Doane" and "The Hollow of the Three Hills" had realized, it is a more disturbing perspective from which to view the world. The sketch "Mrs. Hutchinson" had noted, watching those around the woman teacher, that to turn from the common consciousness, from orthodoxy and shared assumptions, is to "feel like children who have been enticed far from home, and see the features of their guides change all at once, assuming a fiendish shape in some frightful solitude" (*TS* 21). These images are replicated exactly in the description of Goodman Brown's departure from the socially sanctioned path to heaven.

At this point it is useful to compare the tale "The Gentle Boy" with the sketch "Mrs. Hutchinson," for in the tale we can see that sketch form converted into fiction and the attempt made to combine an individual viewpoint with an ostensibly objective analysis of external circumstances. Its protagonist Catharine is partly modeled on the sketch's view of Ann Hutchinson, but here the situation is handled with greater ambivalence, despite Catharine being judged by the same nineteenth-century standards as Mrs. Hutchinson. The tale begins with a lengthy, quasi-sociological analysis of the Puritan colonists' dispute with the Quakers (it is even longer in the original published version of 1832), which is similar in enterprise to the Biographical Sketches. However, while it is observed that the Quaker actions "abstractly considered, well deserved the moderate chastisement of the rod" (9:69), the tale abandons such an "abstract" perspective for a dramatic treatment of the material with reasonably well-developed characters and action. This is important since emotional affect is part of the tale's argument as well as its method—how one responds to Ilbrahim is presented as a moral touchstone for characters and readers alike. Although the persecution, rescue, and death of an innocent child is a conventional nineteenth-century focus of sentiment, most of the characters in this tale are more complicated than the two-dimensional persons of the Biographical Sketches or the emblematic figures of "The Gray Champion": Ilbrahim's pathological sensitivity nurtured by his parents' circumstances, the helplessly obsessive Catharine dimly aware of love for her son, and the confused figure of Tobias bitterly resenting the unhappy results of his good deeds. Only Dorcas is a stock figure of nineteenth-century maternal goodness.

Furthermore, the events have disturbing motivations and outcomes, for Tobias's charity brings him utter emotional and spiritual desolation. His apparently paradoxical justification for what is shown to be a spontaneous deed of charity—" 'Do we not all spring from an evil root?' " (9:73)—is echoed all too disturbingly and with opposite effect in the Puritan children's "instinct of destruction" (9:92). Their upbringing has merely enhanced savage impulses that contradict any reader's easy supposition (based on Ilbrahim) that children are innocent until made guilty. Also, virtue is shown to be self-destructive—even Ilbrahim is described as the "victim of his own heavenly nature" (9:93). While the tale might wish to distinguish between what is innate and what is socially constructed in these people, this proves impossible given the various social forces shaping consciousness.

There are therefore no easy answers. Everyone acts out of the best of intentions, and this is disastrous. "Rationality," which the narrator cherishes, is not something anyone else shows signs of being able to apply to the situation. The inclusion of material (later deleted in the *Twice-told Tales* version of 1837) relating to the historical circumstances within which these characters have to operate and that structures their consciousness, only adds to the ethical and psychological confusions with its attempt to explain, though not to exonerate, the Puritan persecution of the Quakers (see 9:614–15).[14] The tale's substitution of the past perfect tense for the Biographical Sketches' invariable use of historic present verbal forms for its descriptive passages does away with that spurious immediacy that sought to dissolve the differences between the seventeenth and nineteenth centuries.

But the voice of the Biographical Sketches is also present, and the result is a strange amalgam of the sketches' conservatism with a degree of psychological and social questioning. Hawthorne uses his narrator to explore his contemporaries' apparent belief that it is possible to enclose the tale's material safely within a nineteenth-century social order. There is the narrator always lurking in the wings, who thrusts himself in front of the characters when things get difficult and who appears shortsightedly to think he can sit in judgment on everything and turn the story into a moral fable. When he appeals to "tenderness" (9:75) or clearly points out the wrong done in executing the Quakers, he is on safe ground. However, the narrator seems to think that he can avoid the bigotry and fanaticism of these seventeenth-century contenders by evasively appealing to nineteenth-century psychology and moral imperatives of decency, duty, and rationality. This voice of the nineteenth-century moral majority floats as a smooth, oily surface over dangerously turbulent, unpenetrated depths. The two levels coexist rather than interact to produce meaning. At best the result is savage sarcasm, as in the concluding paragraph that invites us to rejoice in the safe pity of the Puritans; at worst there is either panic and evasion or an irony that is too intermittent and qualified to make an impact. The reader is made to sit on a moral seesaw.

Such rational narrational endeavors are clearly sabotaged. The anarchic mental worlds of both Puritan and Quaker, each feeding on the others' compulsions, reveal the fragility, paradoxes, and far-from-orderly origins of that social order. We see how, for Quaker and Puritan alike, their ideology enshrines and acts upon certain desires and impulses that a nineteenth-century Common Sense world order had banished to the unconscious (indeed the narrator's inadequate and partial account of Quakerism and Puritanism is a product of those Common Sense theories).

The tale, then, does not simply represent the Puritans as the authority of the social order and the Quakers as the subjective challenge

which that order cannot accommodate. The Puritans are here described as having rebelled against the English church authorities, and
the antinomian Quakers consciously insist that the sole authority
for action and evaluation rests in the individual's supposedly innate
moral feelings. Both parties struggle to create a moral and social
order that sanctions certain desires and drives, and censors others
that seem to threaten that order. It is true that the Puritans appeal
to what are apparently more objective standards (actually, of course,
Bible-based ones), but their great fear of the psychic "wilderness"
(hence the bolted door, the drum call to worship, the armory in
the meetinghouse) suggests the vulnerability of this new society
to the pressures of individual needs and desires that the Quakers
remind them of and onto whom they project their own self-fears.
Both Quaker and Puritan live physically and psychologically in half-
cleared forest.[15] The tale, then, captures a historical moment when
the social order has not quite solidified into fixed forms (insofar as
it ever does) and focuses on the interface between that order and
those desires.

The psychical life that erupts onto the social stage has certain
elements that the narrator thinks can be safely condemned ("bigotry," "fanaticism," and "hatred"), while "passion," "enthusiasm,"
and "imagination" are all negatively charged. However, other aspects
suggest that matters cannot be put so easily in a moral pigeonhole. It
is difficult in the tale to distinguish the source of the Quaker "command of the spirit" (9:69)—which, for example, drives Catharine,
"the apostle of her own unquiet heart" (9:87), away from her son—
from the "speaking of an inward voice" (9:75) that prompts Tobias's
"heart" to take Ilbrahim home. There is a terrible irony in this
good deed having such desolating consequences, and further irony in
the phrase describing the congregation's "sympathies" being merely
"involuntary virtue" (9:85). It is difficult also to distinguish between
a "superfluity of sensitiveness" (9:89) on the one hand and "tenderness" (9:75) on the other, especially when Ilbrahim's disastrous
kindness to the sick Puritan boy is explicitly likened to his adopted
parents' action toward him. To desire a "more fervid faith" (9:94)
might seem understandable, but it may lead to the "heart's anguish"

(9:85), or self-doubt ("the instigation of a mocking fiend" [9:98]), or a "flood of malignity" (9:82). On the other hand, Puritan certitude can breed in some people "self-suspicion" (9:94—the internalized judge), and in others an "unbridled fanaticism" and the lynch mob.

Although the unassimilable unconscious thus overwhelms the social and moral structures of this tale, the challenge of the story is superficially avoided by making Ilbrahim, rather than Tobias or Catharine, the object of easy, all-engrossing pity that fallaciously suggests that blame might be easy to allocate. The choice is then between distortion, pain, and madness or a compromising capitulation to a demonstrably inadequate orthodoxy. The tale ends with a final ironic image. The child is restored to its mother's breast (image of primal harmony before the entry into the social order and the consequent division of the self), but that child is dead. Thus the tale ultimately discourages identification with one particular character; instead the different points of view are brought into unresolved collision or contradiction, with no final coherent or unified position.

▼

"The Gentle Boy" is, then, an early sign of a hornet's nest of entangled, irresolvable contradictions. Although this tale was susceptible of a conservative reading based on sentiment and in this way became probably Hawthorne's most popular work in the general reading public's estimation for the next ten years, the other *Provincial Tales* stories stir up further those confusions in inassimilable ways and, as a result, constitute a far more ambitious and corporate enterprise. Unlike "The Gentle Boy" and "The Gray Champion," Hawthorne chose not to reprint these tales until the 1840s and 1850s, when he was writing less conservatively than he was at the time of *Twice-told Tales* in 1837. The other stories in *Provincial Tales* focus even more on the individual subjective world, but unlike those in *Seven Tales* they do this in relation to external conditions, and unlike "The Gentle Boy" they do not attempt to retain for long the nineteenth-century rationalist and patriotic narrative voice of the Biographical Sketches.

The tales' approach to this material is an extension of the basic strategy of "The Hollow of the Three Hills." The setting is the controlling and expressive framework within which the situation of the characters at a particular moment in time can be explored. The recurrent pattern of the setting in all the *Provincial Tales* stories is striking: two or more different worlds are set in opposition. At its simplest and sharpest, the contrast is between wilderness and settlement. More elaborately, the settings play off Puritan Colonial America against Royalist England, port against ocean and frontier (the metaphor of the sea is used for the wilderness in "Roger Malvin"), farm against metropolis, home against street and public buildings. Obviously these oppositions are not all versions of a single conflict—indeed the tales reject any simple division. Instead they represent the many-sided and shifting interactions between what are conceived to be different aspects of psychic and social identity.

Crucially, however, these sets of oppositions indicate that the interactions are experienced as conflict, contrast, and difference. The stories locate themselves on the interface between opposing elements. They occupy a middle ground—a threshold, window, paths and journeys, a forest clearing, times of flux, unrest, and choice in a country's history, moments of actual physical confrontation between opposing forces. The tales are striking in their concern to explore the connections as well as the conflict between different areas of experience, although, from the protagonist's point of view, he or she is placed where things are seen to clash rather than where mediation and negotiation are possible.

What these settings provide is a topology of self that can then be explored through physical scene, concrete situation, and dramatic incident. The tales thus develop the crude opposition of the dreamer and the socially integrated person of Hawthorne's earlier work, and begin to argue more clearly for two equally important and distinct dimensions to human identity. The tales seek to elucidate the origins of the apparent division, the nature of the relationship between these two dimensions, and the continuing interactions between them.

"The Wives of the Dead" is a good example of all this. If, as seems likely, it was written late in the collection, then it benefits from the work of the earlier tales in clarifying the basic structures of identity. It has clear parallels with the more obviously problematical *Provincial Tales*, but its lucidity and high degree of control can help us to grasp their difficulties better.[16]

The narrator begins by acknowledging the unimportance and ordinariness of his plot. Action is minimal, the central coincidence is played down, and instead, the setting is described at length and with marked precision. This provides the "premises" for the thematic argument. The central theme is the fragile and confusing interlinking of individual subjectivities and the material world external to them. The women's identity is constructed of several different social and sexual roles and relationships (sister, wife, neighbor, former suitor); and the social network constructs the mental world of each character. Thus, while the tale seems dreamlike because of its introversion, these characters are different from the dreamers of Hawthorne's first phase, because their dreaming world is clearly constituted by the social network.

There is no unified self in this tale, but rather at best a delicate and fragile balance within each person between interrelated but possibly conflicting elements. Identity is shown to be a continuing process. People change with time and circumstances, though memory constituted of past relationships resists this. The tale, however, moves toward a final, seductive possibility of an integrated self. This is achieved by making the protagonists women: both are presented as sisters and sisters-in-law (mirror images of each other), and as wives wholly identified with their husbands ("another self" [II:194]). Thus the nineteenth-century readership can more easily imagine them offering to each other and their spouses a relationship that stresses cooperation, connection, and similarity rather than difference and competition. This is predicated, as in "The Hollow of the Three Hills," on a conventional, predefined, and restricted place for the women within the social order. In "The Wives of the Dead" she may try to capitalize on this loss of individuality and, in spite of some continuing inner feelings of separation, seek to merge with others. So although the tale mostly deals with the women's separation from one another where the network of relationships, far from bonding people together, instead makes each subject a unique complex of shifting and conflicting positions, and although it is concerned with the limits of possible knowledge of people and events and the unspoken gulfs between them, it moves unusually for one of the *Provincial Tales* stories toward reintegration as the fragmented spheres reform and interconnect.

Goodman Parker's lantern "gleamed along the street, bringing to view indistinct shapes of things, and the fragments of a world, like order glimmering through chaos, or memory roaming over the past" (II:196). These images suggest links between external and internal processes (the lamplight representing circumstances external to the individual, and memory suggesting the power of consciousness to create a meaningful pattern of disparate experience). These links are slow to be achieved. The sense of separation is actually intensified when Margaret's joy at her restored wifehood makes her "involuntarily unfaithful" (II:196) to her role as sister to Mary, and her door shuts. Mary then has a parallel experience of both reconnecting with parts of her life and separating even more from another part, yet this parallelism of their experiences augurs final reunification. Mary wakes to find calm moonlit weather to match that of the "deep lake" of her sleep, and looking out on a precisely detailed scene forces her to recognize and respond to a world beyond her thoughts. The selfless, empathetic joy of the once rejected suitor Stephen makes a further bridge over the gulf of separateness, and the final illusion is paradoxically, and yet at another level appropriately, dispelled when Mary's tear of misplaced and loving sympathy falls on Margaret's face.

"The Wives of the Dead" played two individual subjectivities against each other and against the social order and external circumstance. The remaining stories in *Provincial Tales* concentrate on a single individual, the mind of a young man journeying alone from one area of experience to another. The narratives focus primarily on the protagonist's subjectivity—that is, the way his sociopolitical context is reflected in the shape that his inner life takes and how his psychic self responds. The narrator's tendency to ask the reader to "dispense" with the historical background that introduces "The

Wives of the Dead," "Roger Malvin's Burial," and "My Kinsman, Major Molineux," is not intended as a dismissal of the importance of the social in that individual's life; rather it suggests that the subjective dimensions of one particular person are to be foregrounded. Nonetheless that context is necessary for us to see that his subject position within the social, political, and cultural context crucially shapes his psychic life, even though the individual, entangled in the net of his inner life, may think the external world with its momentous public events is peripheral.

These stories do not, then, escape far from the intense introversion of *Fanshawe* and *Seven Tales*, and mostly they are more enigmatic than "The Wives of the Dead." The wives had experienced silence and isolation, but their dreamworld was not regarded as problematical probably because of the way that the tale constitutes sisterhood and marriage. In the remaining *Provincial Tales* stories, despite their protagonists being placed in a carefully established physical and cultural setting, the element of private fantasy is stronger. This is because fears and desires, the customarily unsaid and unseen of a particular culture, have transformed the object world into something strange for the disturbed and silenced individual. As Rosemary Jackson has argued, fantasy is not a self-produced and self-contained world, but reveals the effect of a particular phenomenal world upon the individual.[17]

The coexistence and interdependence of the fantastical and social reality is central to these tales' meaning. The fictional world of these tales can never be merely concerned with mimetically reproduced surfaces and objectively real events, nor can the psychic world be entirely "unreal." Rather, there is doubt about what "really" exists and what is "really" happening, because this is a culture that wants to deny publicly the existence of those fears and desires. It is hardly surprising if the tales' events seem hallucinatory, or if the self, instead of being the unified "character" of nineteenth-century realist fiction, is splintered into many contradictory facets.[18]

Hawthorne's interest in theories of the psychical life is evident from his extensive reading course in Scottish Common Sense philosophy in the late 1820s and early 1830s at the same time as the composition of *Provincial Tales*. But the psychological theories available at the time would have been of limited use to him since, as Allan Gardner Smith has shown, they "concerned themselves little with individual ontology," and often would have explained neither the mental processes Hawthorne was writing about nor the nature of his protagonists' sense of isolation. While these Common Sense psychologies did recognize certain aspects of the irrational and the unconscious, such as intuition, obsession, monomania, fantasy, associationist thinking, and dreaming, they believed that the disordered mind was caused merely by a lack of will power, and that the disturbances of dreaming would easily be dispelled if only the conscious mind were allowed to deal with them (a view that bears similarities to Puritan processes in "The Gentle Boy.")[19] Their attitude was therefore that all problems were innately solvable—a view that *Provincial Tales* challenges.

The Common Sense psychology with its emphasis on rationality and a divinely ordered phenomenal and human world willfully blinded itself to mental areas that were disturbing. For all its materialism, it did not use any theories about the relationship of the individual to social systems to analyze aspects of the unconscious. Furthermore, while some of its theories about dreams are not at odds with Hawthorne's tales—in particular the close connection between the physical world of waking reality and the sleeping mind trying to order sensation, and the way dreams give the impression of being "real"—Common Sense philosophy did not provide an analysis that could account for the way subjectivity is depicted in these tales. On the other hand, Romantic conceptions of the self were not much more adequate. Their emphasis on the primacy and substantial nature of the mental world might be a useful counterargument to these materialist Common Sense theories, but the Romantic idealistic belief in an autonomous self who is the origin of meaning and action and who is set in opposition to a world conceived as external to itself, failed to recognize sufficiently the sense that Hawthorne's work at this time suggests of the individual as a subject within society and constituted to a considerable extent by it both consciously and unconsciously.[20]

From this it will be clear that the tales are somewhat at odds with both the more generally accepted psychological notions of philosophers like Thomas C. Upham, who taught at Bowdoin, and much of Romanticism's quest for selfhood. Hawthorne's explorations push to the margins of current mainstream thought. It is Hawthorne's fictional struggles with his Common Sense and Romantic inheritances that is of particular interest—that is, not only does the basic material of the tales challenge received ideas but also Hawthorne has to find the literary means to handle this challenge.

The Common Sense psychologists, with their belief in the divinely created faculty of the will as the answer to all disturbances of the mind,[21] would have seen the kind of problem Reuben Bourne faces in moral, indeed religious, terms, but Hawthorne's tale presents instead a sequence of events that cannot easily be seen in terms of an evil "heart" or a failure of an inborn moral will. The tale identifies the psychological moment in which subjectivity comes into being and why. It captures wonderfully the way moral imperatives do not exist in a sanctified vacuum but are subject to the complexities of a situation and the individual mind. It demonstrates that while these imperatives may appear as absolutes to the participants, they are not fixed in any transhistorical way. The resulting picture is bleak and not capable of resolution.

The tale is, then, not a study of actual guilt, since the "wrong" lies not in some essential and innate human nature and action but in the particular set of circumstances that dominates the individuals within the tale. A quarter of the tale is devoted to Reuben's decision making in order to reveal the stalemate of conflicting claims and the fluctuation of many powerful unconscious and biological motives that subvert rational discussion of moral responsibilities.[22] Social sanctions are also undercut by referring to that community's perceived duty of burying the dead as "an almost superstitious regard" (10:344), peculiar to a particular period and culture. Reuben may have a sense of having offended against a socially established moral code, but his sense of guilt has no other transcendental basis. Several times in discussing Reuben's motives, the tale absorbs the language of morality into the language of psychology: "conscience, or something in its similitude, pleaded strongly with him to return" (10:346); "a continual impulse, a voice audible only to himself" (10:350); and "instinct" (similar to Catharine's in "The Gentle Boy"), which makes him shoot Cyrus because "[u]nable to penetrate to the secret place of his soul, where his motives lay hidden, he believed that a supernatural voice had called him onward" (10:356).

In this way Reuben is detached from his own and Hawthorne's original readers' assumptions and judgments, and we are made to concentrate on the subjective experience of his dilemma and the social influences on these psychological structures. Much as the tale's setting presented us with duality as its controlling pattern, so the human subject experiences himself in terms of division. This split is internal. Reuben's sense of confusion, guilt, and madness is created not by actual wrongdoing, but by the accidental gulf that opens between his public image, social role or actions, and the self that cannot be given utterance in the social order. It is not a matter of Reuben having done something wrong—we know his father-substitute Roger urged this course of action on him.

But Reuben knows unconsciously that existing social discourses have no place for his actions. The unrepresented self (Reuben's unconscious impulses as well as conscious guilt) is therefore born out of society's ignorance and ideological limitations. The tale gives a precise description not just of the psychic-social structure of such a division, but of the very moment at which this subjectivity came fully into being. It demonstrates that this happens only in response to social discourses and ideologies, as the individual attempts to take up a position in society. This happens at the bedside, not in the forest: Reuben defends himself against an "imaginary accusation" (10:347), falters, and Dorcas takes over the narration and finishes Reuben's story for him in a socially appropriate and expected manner. Reuben's projection of his own doubts onto the community is reflected in the slippery syntax that momentarily seems to present Reuben's internal self-condemnation as the external narrator's judgment: "Reuben felt it impossible to acknowledge, that his selfish love of life had hurried him away, before her father's fate was decided" (10:348). The elision that the reader experiences of character and narrator here parallels the difficulty Reuben finds in realizing that his ideas are generated from his view of what his society requires.

Reuben on entering adulthood has been allotted certain positions in the community—soldier, son-in-law-to-be, husband, farmer, father and, most disturbingly, hero. These constitute his identity. But this identity contrasts sharply with other aspects of his inner life that the settlement denies. This is expressed by the use of images of wilderness, especially when the actual wilderness was the site on which Reuben was forced into consciousness of apparently antisocial elements of himself. The wildness, gloom, unlit hollows, rocks, withering tree, snow, and wind of the setting are each picked up and used as metaphors for Reuben's psychic state. In the settlement Reuben fell silent, and his dissenting dumbness was then interpreted only in terms that the community could recognize and for which it had an available vocabulary. The unrepresented self can be described by the tale only in terms that embody everything that the settlement believes is not itself—wildness and darkness.

The community unwittingly silences Reuben (thus condemning him to internal division and conflict), because the ideology of heroism and the burial rituals, which have been built up to fight a fear of the wilderness and its inhabitants, inhibit a complete understanding of society's full conditions of existence. There is a general attempt to see or make people's behavior fit an expected heroic mode (as in the legend that the actual colony historically made out of Lovell's Fight). Any contradictions and omissions are smoothed over by the community.

The consequences of this suppression must eventually be breakdown. The community, Reuben, Cyrus, Dorcas, and even the reader are all presented as dreamers waking to violent tragedy or death and oblivion. These dreams are the product of a social ideology that has shaped their lives. This ideology of the preeminence of "civilization" over wilderness (rationality, altruism, orderly social forms and family), though real and powerful for it governs how they conduct and view their social relationships, is revealed at this point to be also imaginary, although it has the apparent truth of the communally shared. It is "imaginary" in the sense that it is a construct, an idealizing fiction with an inherent tendency therefore to eventual challenge and breakdown.[23] The dreaming young Reuben of the opening becomes a "sleep-walker" (10:355); American society dreams of a heroic Lovell's Fight; a shot disturbs Dorcas's day-dreaming supper in a "wild and romantic" hollow (10:354) and she finds Cyrus, hope of the race, lying now "dreamless" in death (10:359). The otherwise unexplainable digression on the "daydream" of a "wanderer in a world of summer wilderness," dreaming of love, freedom, wealth, home, race, and fame (10:352), links the readers' private dreams with these historical and fictional ones.

But breakdown of the dreamer does not mean resolution of the conflict. There is no possibility of arriving at a "true self" in the Romantic fashion, and the stark oppositions of the tale make it clear that there will be no reconciliation. The various attempts to link the two worlds merely try to escape a sense of division; the undivided self is lost forever and Reuben cannot find a noncontradictory subject position. Escape is impossible because this is not a simple conflict between Reuben and the colony, but a conflict within him, so that he takes the settlement with him in his journey back through the forest: for example, the Almanac's "arbitrary divisions of time" (10:354) continue to pain Reuben with reminders of the date of Roger's death.

The ending is brutal. The dead child means there will be no future except the settlement's compromised one. Under pressure from being given incompatible and contradictory roles, Reuben has now sought out a position that at some level brings together the conflicting elements of his life. But for him it cannot be the simple discarding of unfounded guilt feelings (the product of a now demonstrably destructive ideology). His unconscious makes use of the vocabulary of another ideology inherited from the settlement, that of Christian repentance, penance, and absolution, to give meaningful structure to his pain and confusion, and thus he traps himself in another dangerous "dream." The tale ends not in understanding but in madness as Reuben prays to a god that he has created perversely out of Christianity, and whose savagery reflects his own self-hatred.

"My Kinsman, Major Molineux," like "Roger Malvin's Burial," is a fictional challenge to forms of ideological repression. The previous tale grew out of the way Lovell's Fight was laundered into an acceptable national myth; in this tale heroic notions about the noble origins of the American Revolution, central to the ideology of Hawthorne's contemporary society, are severely and overtly disturbed.[24] "The Gentle Boy" had shown how the seventeenth-century colony had institutionalized violence, but in that tale the narrator's irony had faltered and he had preferred to push the unpalatable into a safely remote past so that some readers could go on believing that reason and love win the day. Such illusions do not survive in "Major Molineux," because the violence is not hidden but becomes a public ceremony involving, actively or passively, most of the citizens.

"My Kinsman, Major Molineux" is more directly concerned with social structures than some of the other *Provincial Tales* stories, with its narrative focus on one very socially directed individual. It deals head-on with issues about the nature of power structures and ideologies that were explored more indirectly elsewhere through the subjectivities of self-divided individuals. The social analysis that was implicit in "Roger Malvin's Burial" and "The Gentle Boy" and even in the graveyard scene in "Alice Doane" is made explicit here. Its central concerns are not hard to grasp, but their importance at this particular phase of Hawthorne's career must be emphasized: the tale constitutes a significant step in his thinking about the nature of social structures, and it makes social aspects of *Fanshawe* and the more conventionally minded tales and sketches of this present phase seem flimsy. Its vision is quite clear, but it offers no solutions and will be superseded presently and for a time by other ways of thinking and of representing social structures.

What the tale shows is the nature of power in society, its origins, and how it is maintained. Culturally valued ideas about individual liberty and personal responsibility are exploded. Ancient authority was suspect, but democracy is mob rule, and respectability and rationality are tattered cloaks over sadistic savagery. Violence is ubiquitous and both old and new social systems are predicated on it. Nor is it ever to be entirely censored because everyone has some investment in it and no one will quite condemn it (laughter rings throughout the tale). The family that Robin left at home and imagines at evening prayer presents the conventional image of domestic bliss, Christian charity, and just authority that is supposed to stand as a paradigm of wider social structures. In this tale it becomes a sentimental dream in which family, religion, traditional forms of work, and community are revealed for the unreal ideological constructs that they are, another socially shared fantasy life.

Robin's complicity in all this, for all his passing bewilderment and helplessness, is important. Outsiders like Leonard Doane, Catharine, Tobias, Reuben and, as we shall presently consider, Goodman Brown, are in reality part of the world they feel so separated from, but they never realize this nor experience it in this way. Robin on the other hand is eager to be part of the structures of power; he hammers on the door of preferment. Far from feeling a dissenter, he is all too well adjusted to the social formation, an apparent conformist demanding his position in it in an undivided manner and untroubled by that society's evident inequalities. True, for most of the story he is forced to remain outside this world of power, status, privilege, and money, but that is because he has wrongly identified who is in power and because he is also still a disciple of the view that sees society as rational and unproblematic. He joins the dominant party of power as soon as he finds which it is.

This is a clear critique of that Revolutionary and Romantic inheritance, the ideology of self-determination and self-realization. All these *Provincial Tales* protagonists cling to a notion that they ought to be acting autonomously even though, as we have seen, their situations suggest that this has never been possible. Robin, the most secure in this view, feels only one kind of internal division—between the cozy set of values he has been reared in and the experience of cruelty, armed struggle, and pain, presented here as inextricably part of the roots of American individualism and civilization. That rural idyll survives only as a romanticized dream. The procession seems dreamlike, indeed nightmarish, not because it is unreal, but because it is totally other than society's normal self-image of freedom, fairness, and sweet reason. Robin's cudgel is a better indicator of how one achieves one's hidden desires and hungers in a competitive society. The procession emerges from the anarchic desires of individuals, which are here institutionalized and constitute the unacknowledged foundation of society. As a result a "man" may indeed have "several voices" (II:226). The most startling image of division in the tale— the black and red face—does not offer a set of mutually exclusive alternatives, but asserts the dual reality of the human subject within the social order and the inherent instability of society's apparently firm ideological structures.

Shadow

What matters for this present study is the significance of this tale's vision in relation to *Provincial Tales* as a whole and the accompanying Biographical Sketches. Though contemporary with "The Gray Champion," it presents a diametrically opposite version of a similar kind of Revolutionary movement. Once past its introductory appeal to democratic principles and the need to oust tyrants, we are pitched into the middle of Robin's story much as we are in many of the other stories in *Provincial Tales*. Indeed we are told to do without the kind of "long and dry detail of colonial affairs" (II:209) that the Biographical Sketches liked to give us—such an abstract and generalizing approach to the social context will not illuminate the matters this tale is concerned with. The narration, by focusing on Robin, limits the reader's perspective. Without the reassurance of the conventional narrative voice of the introduction with its familiar value judgments, the reader undergoes a revolution in understanding, parallel though not identical to Robin's. The heavy emphasis on perception throughout highlights the sense that this is an experience that is unmediated by traditional wisdom and where all authority is questioned and even a new language spoken. The ending is as abrupt and unresolved as some of the other *Provincial Tales* stories, and as disturbing. Freed from mere convention and false consciousness, Robin finds himself in a moral vacuum. The laughter is either a retreat from feeling or a recognition of absurdity, but it is neither catharsis nor fellowship.

"Young Goodman Brown," which was probably written after "My Kinsman, Major Molineux," seems to pick up where that tale ended. The street procession is reenacted in the forest, but with disastrous outcome. The laughter becomes that of despair. Again it is made clear that the unconscious is created in a distinctive form as a result of a person assuming his or her restricted position in a particular society. Like the other stories, this tale attempts to connect two worlds that are sharply opposed in the protagonist's mind, and this apparent division lies at the root of all the other questions the tale raises. Theological matters are recast as sociopsychological issues. "Evil" is not some innate depravity or corruption of the innocent, but is the product of the disjunction between these two states of being. Traditional explanations for evil (for example, the notion of "Original Sin") are shown to be an attempt by the culture to interpret a sense of division experienced by its subjects, in this case the polarized opposition between the human subject's construction within the cultural order and all those desires and drives which that order has banished. Thus censored, these are perverted into family murder and sexual abuse and are never spoken of out of fear of punishment (they are "dreamed" of instead).[25] It is clear that the structure of the unconscious is determined by a particular cultural order (just as it was differently structured in pre-Revolutionary Boston in "My Kinsman, Major Molineux," or in the Indian massacre community of "Roger Malvin's Burial").

Brown hardly needs to go to the forest to find that split—it exists already in the settlement, even within women whom *Provincial Tales* normally present as undivided creatures: "A lone woman is troubled with such dreams and such thoughts, that she's afeard of herself, sometimes" (10:74). The tale occupies a no-man's-land between warring elements both in Brown and in his society and culture; it begins with an argument across a threshold and then it is entirely taken up with Brown's journey to bring the two levels of being together. As Judith Wilt has argued, it is characteristic for the Gothic (and this tale transforms essentially Gothic images back into historical ones) to explore the "terrors of the separated one," faced with the "hard-core 'unknowable' in individuals and communities" and searching for reunification.[26] Brown's quest, however, has the opposite result, and an unbridgeable rift breaks open between social appearance and the mental world. He cannot accept that human beings are neither nice and simple, nor integrated wholes. The delicate vision of the different states of being of "The Wives of the

Dead" is distorted into Brown's very simplified view of human beings as whited sepulchres—a meaningless surface and a violent, depraved unconscious. The only integration of which he can conceive is that of the forest meeting where everyone is reduced to a uniform evil. Faced with the failure of his quest for knowledge of self, Brown tries an act of will to resolve matters, but resistance is pointless, because the "devil" is ineluctably part of him and everyone else, the consequence of the acquisition of one's social identity. His confrontation with this hidden, suppressed part of his culture brings connection and insight, but he sees this "sympathy" only as a "loathful brotherhood" (10:86).

The method of narration itself mirrors this state. It ensures that the reader lacks firm knowledge of Brown—much as he lacked it of his fellow villagers. All action emanates from this single man: people are seen and heard as soon as he mentions them, others' arguments seem to have sprung from himself, his yells merge with the sounds of the wilderness. Nonetheless the reader, who is never given any other view of events, also never gets completely inside Brown, and there is much we do not know about how he feels. But the narration is also constructed so that we cannot be detached from him either; there is no objective assessment of events. The reader may wonder but cannot, like a detective, answer the question that is asked about the "reality" and "truth" of Brown's dreamlike experiences. The text, when combed through painstakingly, turns out to be able to sustain simultaneously two mutually exclusive versions of events, one suggesting the physical reality of the meeting, the other making it a dream. On the very rare occasions when the narrator appears to give his own view of events rather than report Brown's actions and thoughts, he seems to be pulled into Brown's dark world.[27] It is a view substantiated after all by the tale's explicit reference to historical atrocities, the whipping of Quaker women and the massacre of Indian women and children, both of which "The Gray Champion" had flinched from pursuing, and the Salem witch-hunts that, though unmentioned like much else in this culture, shadow the events. This narrator does not have total authority over his story.

The effect of this focalization technique is to plunge the reader into a mire of unanswerable questions. One wonders if this tale has progressed at all from the troubling vision of "Alice Doane," which initiated this train of thought. Brown, like Leonard, confronts himself, and the experience, even if imaginary, is a terrifying one. This time, the demonic double is Brown's father, and the hell-bent villagers in the graveyard of "Alice Doane" are replicated in the forest meeting. But at least the later tale has recast matters so that the structure and dynamics of the situation can be grasped, even though they cannot apparently be changed. The reader, too, is persuaded of at least the subjective reality of the situation (this is one meaning of "sympathy"), and a debate is engendered between different notions of the "real" and how these interrelate.

▼

Thematically and stylistically, "The Wives of the Dead," "Roger Malvin's Burial," "My Kinsman, Major Molineux," and "Young Goodman Brown" are distinct from both the Biographical Sketches and from "The Gray Champion" and "The Gentle Boy" (the two tales that did not wholly escape the mode of these sketches). Their protagonists experience the moment of self-division and the creation of the unconscious on entering the social order. Insecurity, fragmentation, and disaster result. In addition, the tales leave the reader in hardly a better position than their protagonists. The simple if conventional structure of "The Hollow of the Three Hills" has here evolved into a more complicated narrative form in which situations are explored rather than opinions demonstrated. The settings that are the only element to shape events do not evolve into allegorical patterns of moral significance, and instead retain their material substance and dramatic function. The marked emphasis on the heightened senses in many of the tales, inherited from "The Hollow of the Three Hills" and "Alice Doane," also stresses immediate, inassimilable experience. Any preconceptions or foreseeable conclusions are soon lost in the initial dilemmas and in the twists and turns of events, as the narrator journeys with his characters ever further from known positions. These tales move toward a plurality of meaning rather than toward the didactic conclusion that his contemporary audience would expect from writings that were not merely sensational tales.

How this is achieved stylistically needs to be shown. The point of view of these stories in *Provincial Tales* is focused on that of a single, isolated figure ("Wives of the Dead" with its twin viewpoints is identical in effect) and the plot itself is generated by changes in that single, even passive, protagonist. The fictional world created this way in the mind of the central character appears fragmented because of his or her confusions; there is no reliable or stable viewpoint, and the reader is largely left to fill in and interpret. Although the characters have a greater individuality and depth of focus than those of his first phase, this emphasis on those individuals' consciousness of the worlds that they inhabit means that those worlds, although important, are vivid or distanced depending on his or her changing states of being. The reader is shut off from the reassurances of familiar social structures and their usual models of intelligibility.[28]

The sketch "The Haunted Mind," written in the 1830s, seems a retrospective comment on *Provincial Tales*, describing both this kind of introverted experience and the imaginative response to it—a somewhat sardonic response from a later perspective, but nonetheless useful here for the way it frames the experience. Picking up images to be found throughout *Provincial Tales*, the "heart" is here a "tomb" and a "dungeon" filled with grief, remorse, and memory. The sketch's narrator resembles the *Provincial Tales* protagonists lying helpless at midnight: they cannot control the events that fill their consciousness, nor see very far beyond their own subjective experience. The imagination, however, also has a role to play:

In the depths of every heart, there is a tomb and a dungeon, though the lights, the music, and revelry above may cause us to forget their existence, and the buried ones, or prisoners, whom they hide. But sometimes, and oftenest at midnight, these dark receptacles are flung wide open. In an hour like this . . . the mind has a passive sensibility, but no active strength; . . . the imagination is a mirror, imparting vividness to all ideas, without the power of selecting or controlling them. (9:306)

The imagination here, though incapable of interpreting and judg- ing, is depicted as seeing clearly things hidden to the casual or conventional eye, and responds intensely in an emotionally sympathetic way by making experiences of others vivid to oneself and others— a view that Hawthorne's current reading of aesthetics would have encouraged.[29]

However, the degree to which this can also be the experience of the reader faced with these stories in *Provincial Tales* is determined by their narrator, whose presence prevents the reader's experience from being simply identical with the protagonists' experience. We have to distinguish between the focalization of the tales, which is through a single character, and the narration, which is given by some invisible figure standing outside the world of the story. Although the tale's point of view is primarily that of the central figure, there is nonetheless a difference between the person who sees and acts in the story (the protagonist) and the person who communicates the story (the narrator).

It is true that we are not made very aware of this narrator except in the sharply offset opening paragraphs, and his powers throughout seem limited, his function being more expository than analytical or moralizing. He seldom introduces any other substantially alien point of view, except in "The Gentle Boy" and "The Gray Champion"; more typically, in "The Wives of the Dead" he takes the sisters' limited viewpoints alternately. No use is made of first-person narration (which had been tried briefly in "Alice Doane") or of any form of narration directly representing the characters' flow of thought and feeling.

Certain matters do certainly bring the narrator's point of view very closely in line with that of his characters. The narration follows the chronology of events as they happen; it is synchronous rather than retrospective or panchronic. The narrator, for all his basic externality, is concerned with inner feelings as well as external events, and his narration is more oriented toward a description of the characters' emotions than toward interpretation. The use of free indirect discourse allows the narrator to blend his consciousness with that of his characters without losing his own point of view completely. Sometimes, as Schlomith Rimmon-Kenan has pointed out, the "double-edged effect" of this kind of discourse creates a certain ambiguity about who is speaking (narrator or character)— an effect seen most notably in "Young Goodman Brown," but also evident in other tales such as "Roger Malvin's Burial" and "My Kinsman, Major Molineux."[30] As a result, the form of narration is able to offer a slightly wider perspective than "The Hollow of the Three Hills" and avoids both the chaos of "Alice Doane" and the obscurity about Fanshawe's motives and desires. Here the narrator can at least record the experiences of his occasionally inarticulate characters, and faced with the strange and irrational can attempt to give a clear description of events, slipping in and out of events without necessarily being able to explain matters.

But this cool voice cannot resolve the problems the tales confront. The ending of each of the tales presents a major problem of interpretation. They finish abruptly without explanation or moral tag (unless it be the desperate irony of the original "Gentle Boy"). It is small wonder that Oberon in "The Devil in Manuscript," the later satirical 1830s portrait of the artist as a young man, dismissed his writings with the remark, " 'and behold! it is all nonsense, now that I am awake' " (II:175).

The endings do not seem to be the product of controlled ambiguity or a settled viewpoint. Meaning eludes one because the tale's events have destroyed any simple belief in people's capacity to participate happily in the symbolic order. The narrator merely falls silent in the face of great catastrophe or an amazing climax, and the reader is left both cut off from any adequate interpretative discourse and wholly, or perhaps even more bewilderingly, only partly, within the mind of one uncomprehending character.

This kind of ambiguity is inherent in free indirect discourse. Rimmon-Kenan has commented on the difficulties, when this discourse is employed, of reconstructing an author's implied attitude to characters and events. The reader either is left distanced and skeptical if the narrator is interpreted to be very separate from the protagonist, or conversely ends up identifying empathetically with the characters if the ambiguity is resolved by uniting the narrator's speech with the protagonists' experience.[31] A third possible response may come closest to the reader's experience of *Provincial Tales:* one may find no means of choosing between the ironic and the empathetic responses. This would suggest that the *Provincial Tales* stories invite neither judgment nor sympathy; they demonstrate the impossibility of responding confidently and single-mindedly in either of these ways.

This power to make the reader experience some of the protagonists' confusion of identity is what Hawthorne at this period begins to define and find valuable. Indeed "The Wives of the Dead," possibly one of the last written of *Provincial Tales*, takes sympathy for its subject: its first sentence pleads for attention for the apparently insignificant, and throughout the story the reader watches and waits attentively and never leaves the scene. Breaking through into the prison of the introverted self, these tales communicate the "incommunicable thought" ("Roger Malvin's Burial" [10:349]). There is a striking absence of love in these tales, neither sexual passion nor affection between friends, neighbors, strangers, or family members. "Sympathy," whether intuitive or learned, may be attractive and reassuring in such a chilling vacuum, especially where opening up oneself to one's own or others' inner lives raises feelings of vulnerability and increasing strangeness.[32]

Yet as we have just seen, this sympathetic involvement remains incomplete for both readers and characters in all the tales. Only Stephen in "The Wives of the Dead" transcends the inevitable selfishness of the introverted and breaks the impasse that made sympathy useless and joy hurtful. Robin thrusts aside pity with laughter, and in "Young Goodman Brown" neither the suspected village nor the "loathful brotherhood" of the forest suggest much hope of a community flourishing on sympathy. Terrifyingly sympathetic insight is given in that latter tale to the devil and his converts: " 'By the sympathy of your human hearts for sin, ye shall scent out all the places. . . . It shall be yours to penetrate, in every bosom, the deep mystery of sin, the fountain of all wicked arts' " (10:87). The implication here is that knowledge of others will be appalling.[33] So the tales, having gone deep where *Seven Tales* had skirted the issues, recoil from what they find. The more complex notion of the human subject has brought further dismay.

▼

In "The Gentle Boy," one of the first stories of *Provincial Tales,* the young storyteller Ilbrahim is stoned by his audience, and the old Quaker's story appalls his audience into silence. "Young Goodman Brown" and "Roger Malvin's Burial" both contain stories that are never told to anyone else, and indecipherable writing covers the rock above Malvin. Even "The Wives of the Dead" breaks off before the sisters' stories can be shared. This sense of frustration and gagging seems echoed by the author's own feelings of failure, which hang over *Provincial Tales* for all their remarkable achievement. Hawthorne's ambivalence toward the collection is suggested by the hope later expressed in "Monsieur du Miroir" (an 1830s sketch that satirizes the introverted gaze) that "my mind may not wander so vaguely as heretofore, chasing its own shadow through a chaos and catching only the monsters that abide there" (10:169–70).

As early as January 1832, Hawthorne told one publisher that "I should not wish to be mentioned as the author of those tales" (15:222)—the tales in question being "Roger Malvin's Burial," "My Kinsman, Major Molineux," and "The Gentle Boy," all recently published in the 1832 *Token.* Hawthorne also delayed reprinting several of these tales until much later in his career: "Young Goodman Brown" in *Mosses from an Old Manse* (1846), "My Kinsman, Major Molineux" and "The Wives of the Dead" in *The Snow-Image* (1851). Looking back in 1851, he sensed that they were different from his later work, "the indices of intellectual condition at far separated epochs" (11:6). We should, however, also note, for it lies at the heart of his literary development, that he then goes on to connect this past work with his subsequent writings: "In youth, men are apt to write more wisely than they really know or feel; the remainder of life may be not idly spent in realizing and convincing themselves of the wisdom which they uttered long ago. The truth that was only in the fancy then may have since become a substance in the mind and heart" (II:6). By "fancy" the older Hawthorne seems to mean imaginative access to subjectivity without full understanding of what it discovered. The pursuit of what he took to be "substance in the mind and heart" took his career in a new direction after 1830. Hawthorne had found the kernel of his work in these *Provincial Tales* stories, but his initial reaction was to reject them.

Chapter 4

"Wide Awake in a Realm of Illusions"

The Story Teller and Other Tales

1830–1835

▼ ''THE HAUNTED QUACK'' and "Sights from a Steeple" were written early in 1830 while Hawthorne was still at work on *Provincial Tales*. They herald a change of direction for the decade's work ahead, ushering in a puzzling mass of tales and sketches whose relationship with *Provincial Tales* is not immediately evident. Indeed, "The Haunted Quack" mocks the scenarios of guilty and haunted dreamers characteristic of some stories in *Provincial Tales*. Here the dreamer wakes up happily to tell his story, mysteries prove illusory, and the nightmare that makes young Hippocrates cry out in his sleep like a *Provincial Tales* figure has no connection with actuality. Those grandiose parallels with Faustus and Cain (forbidden knowledge and unremitting guilt) dissolve into comedy and the restoration of the fugitive to the bosom of his community. The apparently intractable difficulties of *Provincial Tales* material are here resolved by being made into an absurd entertainment with a professional con-man as narrator and his audience only a bored traveler. In its minor way the tale simultaneously reflects an impatience with both the problems thrown up by *Provincial Tales* and the kinds of bland writing expected by the *Token* reading public (like "Sights from a Steeple," "The Haunted Quack" appears to satisfy publisher Goodrich's request for shorter pieces for this album).

With "Sights from a Steeple" we see, too, attitudes about the isolated self and community beginning to change, moving toward a simplified desire to belong to that society. Simultaneously, however, there is a disabling sense of the superficiality and contrivance of that social world and a coldly detached perspective on it. His desire to be a "spiritualized Paul Pry" (9:192) could mean losing his painful self-awareness in a process of empathy, but this new writer-narrator declares this access to subjectivity (first raised in *Provincial Tales*) to be impossible. Though standing on the steeple, he has no divine powers of understanding or action, and his circle of vision is limited. Skepticism is his only strength.

These two tales prove a foretaste of work to come. In their explorations of how the individual is expressed (or not expressed) to her or his fellow human beings, the succeeding tales and sketches will be more concerned with social networks, or will adopt a perspective more exterior to the inner drama of *Provincial Tales*. Here we are to be presented with the waking from these nightmares and daydreams to become, as "The Haunted Mind" sketch expresses it, "wide awake" in what now seems a "realm of illusions" (9:304) which that sketch parodies. These "illusions" are not only mental but also social—the ideologies of community, work, and family.

So although these works, in placing characters in a contemporary world, seek a less problematical relation with those social structures that privilege quotidian social interaction as the true "reality," this easier relationship is found only at the price of simplifying the idea of the human subject. The intricate *Provincial Tales* psychological model eventually becomes a simpler conception of a mind disturbed by what may be merely delusions that can fade into seeming unreality. However, the creation of a detached narrator figure, only vaguely present in *Provincial Tales* and to be more fully developed in subsequent works of the 1830s, becomes a means toward skeptically exploring and testing possibilities rather than merely assenting to the social system.

▼

It is striking that the majority of works written before 1835 are concerned in some way with the artist, books, or the creation of imaginative fiction—in no other phase of Hawthorne's career is this such a predominant theme. The project that dominated his work at this time was *The Story Teller*, conceived in June 1832 as a collection of tales told by a young itinerant public storyteller whose own life and travels would form a frame around his stories.[1] These stories about Oberon, the Storyteller, had been preceded by "Sights from a Steeple" (where the narrator appears to be a writer) and "The Haunted Quack" (a story told to another traveler), as well as by "The Seven Vagabonds," an early version of the *Story Teller* idea that brings together several kinds of artistic entertainer. These works were then followed by a considerable number of tales on the subject of the writer, his audience, literary aims, and creative processes.

The subversive elements of *Provincial Tales* had implicitly raised questions about the social role of the artist. Suspending now that exploration of psychic response to social and ideological oppression, Hawthorne begins an anxious yet skeptical search for a less uncomfortable relationship to social structures both for the individual and for the artist. The preponderance of material on artistic matters seems a deliberate response to this fresh task of negotiating a different place within the social order.

The works of this period attempt to steer a path between two opposing popular conceptions of the artist: the solitary writer concerned with the workings of the imagination (the figure has evolved from Romantic, mostly Byronic conceptions of the artist); and the didactic artist whose work will serve the people by demonstrating and inculcating a righteous conformity to the social mainstream. As Lawrence Buell has observed, there were two trends in the vocation of authorship in nineteenth-century New England: "a movement toward the sense of a specialized vocation, partially countered by the persistence of a generalist ideal of cultural coherence, and a movement toward commercialization, partially countered by the persistence of the ideal of art as a form of cultural service."[2] These trends have here been simplified and polarized, though the need to mediate between them is evident. What seems to be happening is that the earlier *Provincial Tales* artistic perspective, which had recognized the psychic and the social as interlocking realities, is beginning to fracture under stress. The two notions of the artist reflect two mutually exclusive elements of subjectivity resulting from that fracture, for behind this dual conception of the artist lie changing notions of the human subject. We are faced with an opposition between an art that is seen on the one hand as merely fantastical productions of a freak mind or a culpable introversion, and on the other as the articulation of certain ideologies, the collective vision of the writer's society. The split was prefigured in the previous phase where the Biographical Sketches, minor though they were, sat side by side with *Provincial Tales.*

Both formulations are here criticized, sometimes within the same tale, so that each of these artistic possibilities seems to cancel out the other. For instance, the stories of failed artists in both "Fragments from the Journal of a Solitary Man" and "The Devil in Manuscript" are narrated by a skeptical friend who is himself clearly either limited in understanding or divided in his response. Certain of these self-absorbed figures confront an unimaginative and limited New England world—Oberon in "The Devil in Manuscript," and the unnamed central figure in "The Ambitious Guest," who, though not an artist, is similarly concerned with the public recognition of his unique qualities of self (indeed his existence would have gone unknown but for this tale, which gives him prominence where Hawthorne's source story makes no mention of him).[3] There is continued criticism of a certain kind of poet whose imagination is detached from experience and serves only to gratify his own needs: the lonely, compensatory fantasies of "The Village Uncle" and "The Vision of the Fountain," and the satirical portraits of the poet in "The Canterbury Pilgrims," "The Great Carbuncle," and "Graves and Goblins." It is to be noted, however, that the rejection of these figures is not total: the main narrator of "The Great Carbuncle," like his characters, is drawn to seek the stone as a poetic subject, and "The Village Uncle" and "The Vision of the Fountain" find no satisfactory substitute for their protagonists' fantasies.

The public figure of the moralist is as much questioned as his opposite, the introverted artist. "The Minister's Black Veil" deals with the disastrous effects, both individually and communally, of the "artist" who attempts to be a public moralist. But here, as with so much else in the works of this phase of Hawthorne's writing, there is ambivalence. While "A Rill from the Town-Pump" particularly objected to the virulence of the temperance reformers, in Pastor Hooper we are presented with the kind of preacher whom the pump would prefer—not a thunderer but one who relied on "mild persuasive influences" (9:39), the imagination of his auditors, and the sentiment. Though all this is similar to an appeal to the readers' "feeling," which we shall examine later in other works of this phase, even this kind of moralist is subject to criticism, and Hooper's participation in the administration of Governor Belcher allies him to a harsher Puritanism, for all his apparent mildness.4 A moral vacuum is created in the tale: we cannot trust either Hooper as moral exemplar or his parishioners' views, but the narrator's interpretation and attack on the veil does not have any greater authority.

One of the earliest tales, "The Seven Vagabonds," is least divided in its sentiments: the narrator refuses to buy sermons, and feels closest to the "free mind" and "open spirit" of the traveling entertainers on their way to cheer up a camp meeting. A clergyman brings the news that aborts their plan. The same tug-of-war between personal expression and a conformist moralism is fought in the later "Fragments" between two different persons, the artist with his private journal and his disapproving friend who is editing it for public consumption and draws a "penitential" (II:322) moral from the story. While this editor is almost certainly a later addition after the breakup of the *Story Teller* collection and is equally under scrutiny, nonetheless it is the chastened Oberon who laments his rejection of what he conceives of as normality and common values, and the reader is left to judge to what extent this recantation is a merely sentimental dream of a dying man or a sentiment the tale endorses. In "Little Annie's Ramble" we get a similar double message: the carefree child, bored with the everyday world, is told to ignore the narrator's dominant and rather conventional moralizing. A similar ambivalence colors "The Haunted Mind," where the narrator, hovering between the mind and the external world, does make moralizing patterns but feels them to be only a "doubtful parallel between human life and the hour which has now elapsed" (9:309). "A Rill from the Town-Pump" sends up quite explicitly the rhetoric of temperance pamphlets and by implication other forms of didactic literature, so its concluding sentimental, domestic images must also be suspect.

The opposition between a moralistic approach and one that retreats from moralism for aesthetic or individualistic reasons is represented by the contrast between clergyman and merrymaker. In "Passages from a Relinquished Work," the successor to "Seven Vagabonds," where these figures first appear, the young storyteller runs away from Parson Thumpcushion to achieve greater success in the theater than his traveling companion and preacher Eliakim in the neighboring schoolhouse. "The Canterbury Pilgrims" is set on a road between the puritanical Shakers and a more morally varied world. In "The White Old Maid," however, the clergyman is entirely peripheral to the main action: the young women exchange promises before he comes, and in old age he is merely a witness to events whose secret remains unspoken and whose participants arrange themselves in ways that may seem emblematic but are indecipherable. "Alice Doane's Appeal" contrasts a sober narrator with a merry audience and a blinkered present with Puritan moralism gone mad.

"The May-Pole of Merry Mount" is clearly the most important example of the topos that opposes clergy and merrymaker, and is a critical reconsideration of Puritanism and its literary implications. It explores, most searchingly of all the tales of this phase, the compulsions and dangers of didacticism. The tale suggests that the fate of America is to be morally serious, and the narrator himself seems implicated in such an approach to life. Like both parties in the dispute, the narrator is guilty of forcing the recalcitrant fabric of existence into a rigid theory, and he appears to capitulate to a demonstrably inadequate orthodoxy as a solution to an otherwise insolvable conflict. The narrator's presence makes for a certain short-sightedness and reluctance to let go of apparent certainties to seek a more adequate understanding. He works in clichés, caricatures, and tired adjectives, writing almost wholly emblematically, deliberately polarizing the debate in an effort to make things clear. It is as if a *Provincial Tales* story had been told by a combination of Oberon the Storyteller and a preacher/moralist. In his attempt to control and order disturbing and unmanageable material, the narrator prefers to limit rather than extend the enquiry.

In contrast to and mediating between these figures of solitary poet and public moralist stands the artist as storyteller. His art is public: his engagement with his audience is immediate, but he must please it with narratives that are kept within generally acceptable boundaries. The act of storytelling is a recurrent motif, and the presence of an audience is an important element in these works' exploration of relationships between individuals and the world of which they find themselves part.[5] Storytelling is built in some way into a striking number of tales: "The Ambitious Guest," "The Great Carbuncle," "The Canterbury Pilgrims," "The Haunted Quack," "The Seven Vagabonds," "Wakefield," "Mr. Higginbotham's Catastrophe," and "Alice Doane's Appeal." As well as *The Story Teller*'s frame, audiences are imagined in "The Village Uncle" and "Seven Vagabonds," and audiences turn away in "The Minister's Black Veil." Even where the audience is not built into the plot, the reader's presence is evoked.

It is "The Canterbury Pilgrims" that pushes beyond both polarities of the quasi-Romantic artist and the writer of the merely didactic tale in its attempt to redefine storytelling, its provenance and purpose. The emphasis on moonlight upon the scene draws attention to the transforming process of the imagination—the artist does not passively mirror external reality. The image of the spring filling the cistern suggests an alternative art to three other artistic productions of the tale: the artifacts of the failed aesthete poet in the tale, the works of the sternly moralistic Shaker community clinging to a past age, and the utilitarian "parable" (II:130) that the travelers' lives seem to present and that the lovers and the narrator reject. The cistern that refreshes all travelers on the road is called "[t]he work of neat hands and considerate art" (II:120)—an art that is useful, communal, involved in shared ordinary human experience. Its "continual gush of water" (II:120) gives the impression of natural energy channeled into social forms, and there is an acceptance of change and the possibility of equipoise in the face of this (the cistern fills and empties without ever overflowing). This image of art, however, remains only an ideal, unrealized by these early 1830s writings.

"Alice Doane's Appeal" is the most substantial consideration of the public storyteller, and is especially important given its parallels with Hawthorne's own career (though the narrator is best not seen as Hawthorne in propria persona but rather as a character invented to explore certain issues of importance to him). It works out the artist's present response to *Seven Tales* and *Provincial Tales,* both in relation to their effect on an actual audience and in terms of his public purpose as a writer. *Provincial Tales* had struggled with stories that resisted conventional meanings, but the contents of "Alice Doane's Appeal" challenges its narrator's initially stated admiration for a historian of the Salem witch-hunts whose "wisdom . . . draws the moral while it tells the tale" (II:267). Historical events of his culture turn out to be almost as resistant to rationality, moral interpretation, and general public acceptance as his imaginative fictions. History turns out to be not a "truth" simply to be relayed to a contemporary audience; instead, a supposedly factual story turns out to be as much a construction of the human mind as the narrator's first Gothic fictions.[6] From this tale it seems that the role of the storyteller offers a rather less than simple answer to the desires of the narrator of "Sights from a Steeple" to participate more directly and fully in his contemporary world. The investigation of the artist is not completed with this tale.

A debate about the ways in which a writer can engage with the world surrounding him is also revealed in a preoccupation with the processes of literary composition to be found in the works of this phase. For example, whereas *Provincial Tales* refuses extended consideration of the tales' historical circumstances in order to focus on the lives of its imagined individuals, here the writer's concern is with his source material (most notably in "Old News") or on the choices a writer makes in fabricating a story from it. The self-consciousness with which such matters are approached is notable in many of these works. All the "Sketches from Memory" (the surviving descriptive frame from *The Story Teller*) contain elements of this, most of all "The Canal-Boat," where the narrator, watching another passenger by means of a mirror and imagining the contents of the man's notebook, finds himself observed in that mirror and is hence made highly conscious of his own self taking mental note of the scene. Here the mirror, being used to help record the world of objects, also becomes an image of self-awareness for the artist. "Wakefield" is the most sustained example of self-conscious narration as it goes about filling in the outlines of a "true" story, but hints of similar self-referentiality are to be found in "An Evening Party among the Mountains," "The Wedding Knell," "Mr. Higginbotham's Catastrophe," and "The May-Pole of Merry Mount." Furthermore, since a realistic art is one that makes many unstated assumptions about the nature of the world, the presence here within the tales of a detached, even dissenting artist figure inevitably helps to undermine those socially inculcated assumptions.

Hawthorne's writing in the 1830s has for the most part been seen by commentators as an espousal of Common Sense values, the discovery of an audience, the rejection of the past, the denial of the haunted mind, and the celebration of domesticity. But to see the works in these ways suggests either a rather simple-minded or evasive about-turn on the part of the author of the *Provincial Tales,* or a skewing of his writing toward popular publishing trends and public taste in desperation, cynicism, or a desire to write "more rational and conservative fiction," that is, "socially legitimate work that would bring him public esteem."[7]

However, within the tales themselves a different, more complex and less rosy picture presents itself that contradicts any critical notions of an optimistic embracing of "ordinary" life. The narrator within the tales remains an outsider and may fail with his audience, as in "Fragments from the Journal of a Solitary Man," "The Devil in Manuscript," and "Alice Doane's Appeal." The Gentle Reader at times seems a polite fiction ironically used,[8] since gathering crowds can become threatening in a considerable number of these tales— see "Mr. Higginbotham's Catastrophe," "The Devil in Manuscript," "The White Old Maid," "The Wedding Knell," "Wakefield," "The Minister's Black Veil," and "Fragments from the Journal of a Solitary Man." True, Fanshawe's individualistic devotion to a narcissistic life of the mind is being rejected, but not in order to espouse moralism. We now get the failures of both the Puritan artist ("The Minister's

Black Veil") and the failed anti-Puritan artist. The subject of "The Canterbury Pilgrims" is the failure to thrive in the social world, a failure that extends not only to the poet in the tale but also to those who, having experienced material loss, seek to make an admonitory parable out of their life story only to have it ignored by those whom they seek to warn.

There has also been a temptation to read many of these works as barely fictionalized autobiography, a temptation exacerbated by Hawthorne's own later adoption of elements from their scenario of the reclusive artist in appealing pictures of himself presented to his fiancée, Sophia, in his love letters. But that love letters persona is yet another character created by Hawthorne's pen, in certain important ways a fiction.[9] The use of material from Hawthorne's own life in Oberon's story in "The Devil in Manuscript" is better read as self-criticism that has been turned into a more generally applicable examination than as self-pitying autobiography. The artist figures of the early 1830s are more critically presented than the later love letters persona; their views are tested and their poses not necessarily validated.

These narrative figures are personae adopted as deliberate exercises in point of view, much as the narrator in "Old News" opts to tell the last part of the sketch through the eyes and voice of an old Tory. This strategy is further developed in the sketches in particular, which set out to explore how the scenes would look through different people's eyes: for example, Ticonderoga is presented through the eyes of a lieutenant engineer, an old veteran, and the writer-narrator; "The Notch of the White Mountains" and "My Visit to Niagara" offer different travelers' reactions; Merry Mount is imagined through the eyes of various onlookers from the forest; and the many onlookers' different interpretations of the black veil are an important element in the tale of that name. Yet again we find these works pulled in two directions—toward bringing the characters imaginatively closer to the reader, or alternatively (as in "The Minister's Black Veil") demonstrating irreconcilable diversity.

To sum up, the works of the first part of this decade can be seen as explorations of certain socially current versions of what the psychic and social life are like. It is clear these are cultural constructions to be critically tested, and in that sense *Provincial Tales* is not rejected or forgotten, but casts a questioning shadow. The tales of this period are not actually as conventional in subject and attitude as they have seemed to some commentators; they are instead *about* commonly cherished ideas about love, career, social responsibility, and art.[10] The writer is skeptically and critically "wide awake in the realm of illusions," and those "illusions" turn out to be not only individual, private ones, but also shared public attitudes. Like a foreigner, Hawthorne is learning a new language—the speech of belongingness—and he questions its expressive strengths and moral limitations. A self-conscious chameleon in his world of contemporary New England, he seeks with skepticism and irony a role in the community he lives within. It is an artistic practice to be found elsewhere in New England literature at the time. Lawrence Buell analyzes certain literary modes as originally "an instrument for guiding and interpreting the collective conscience by didactic expression of public values, rendered in conventionalized forms," but latterly used to "express a restive dialogue between the creative imagination and the stylistic and ideological norms to which the writers generally continued in some measure to adhere." It is that mixture of conformity and deviance that Hawthorne exemplifies— what Buell sees as "a partial assimilation of cultural norms, which helped provide the creative irritants" for their work.[11]

"Wakefield" is a good example of the exploration of these issues for the artist, and both plot and narration point to this critical project. The narrator (a version of the storyteller) and his protagonist, both being very self-conscious watchers on the scene before them, adopt outsiders' perspectives on that more usual system of social relations and institutionalized norms within which they nonetheless inevitably live and become part of. The narrator's project—the self-conscious creation of a story out of a mere outline of facts— parallels his hero's own actions: the latter's were an attempt to create a new life out of a single deed, while the narrator seeks new meaning out of meager objective facts. But the sketch has already disabused any reader who might assume that the narrator of a story has access to "truth"—much as *Provincial Tales* had shown that a full explanation of the subjective movements of a story and their social meanings are not to be had. The writer's refusal to assume a godlike knowledge of his fiction is an act on the part of the artist that is potentially as subversive as Wakefield's own stepping outside the comfortable, accepted societal structures of home and marriage. It opens up a host of possibilities. Finally, however, alarmed by the implications of the experience, both Wakefield and his narrator retreat to safety, Wakefield to his home and wife, and the narrator to a cautious acceptance of the necessity (though not the rightness) of the social system. This conclusion parallels Hawthorne's own movement from the potential radicalism of *Provincial Tales* to a tentative and skeptical rapprochement with the social order.

So Hawthorne's career is assuming a somewhat unexpected shape. Reynolds characterizes the career patterns of canonical writers of the period as "early experimentation with popular modes followed by self-conscious mixture of the modes, then stylization of the modes in highly complex literary texts."[12] Hawthorne's earliest works are in some ways his most radical in their implications, if not their mode, and yet, as we shall see, he will move even closer to conventional values and forms in the second half of this decade before beginning to move away from these. Hawthorne said subsequently that writing *The Story Teller* was like "talking to himself in a dark place,"[13] a remark that no doubt primarily reflected his current sense of rejection and dejection. But talking to oneself can also be constructive, a chance to investigate what he needed to do in the somber aftermath of *Provincial Tales*. Given the high productivity of this phase in the development of his work—nearly thirty pieces in around three years—there seems little doubt about the energy Hawthorne put into this enterprise. These works of the early 1830s do not simply turn their backs on the troubled world of the *Provincial Tales* characters to embrace the community. True, some tales do have narrators who deny the reality of inner turmoil and advocate Common Sense values, but their views are created as a means of investigating and negotiating a relationship with that world rather than of submitting to it. They must therefore be read as a skeptical experiment.

▼

We have at this point to take on board the problem of dating these works and reviewing the possible contents of the projected collection. *The Story Teller* did not survive in its complete original form, and so our picture of Hawthorne's writing at this period can only be built up from the surviving pieces with their recurrent themes, motifs, and techniques. We do not know exactly when *The Story Teller* manuscript was submitted to Goodrich, but it was sometime between mid-1833 and mid-1834. After Goodrich rejected the collection, it was handed over to the *New England Magazine,* which began to publish it in serialized form late in 1834. When editors changed, the project was abandoned, broken up, and published in separate fragments in several magazines over the next three or so years. Reconstructions of the work have been attempted, most notably by Alfred Weber, but there is no way of telling how much failed to survive, how much was later rewritten (quite a bit, given both inconsistencies between the tales and the improbability of certain works, for example "Wakefield" being told aloud to a live audience), and finally which works of this period do belong to this enterprise.[14]

One interesting problem in trying to reconstruct *The Story Teller* is the impression created by the works of this period of variety and experiment rather than the focus and single-mindedness one would expect of an integrated project. Hawthorne maintained that the collection had more unity in its original form: he is reported as saying "he cared little for the stories afterwards, which had in their original place in *The Story Teller* a great degree of significance."[15] Alternatively, one might speculate that *The Story Teller* may never have had much cohesion and failed to survive intact precisely because of this. However, rather than speculate on the nature of the lost *Story Teller,* I prefer to direct my efforts to establishing which works belong to this period in general and, having established this, to look at what the surviving fragments, in conjunction with other contemporaneous works, suggest about Hawthorne's preoccupations at this time. Unlike the *Provincial Tales* period with its handful of outstanding tales, each of them making a distinctive contribution and surrounded by related minor works, the early 1830s present us with more than thirty pieces, few of which stand out from their contemporaries. Here an overall sense of this period can best be arrived at by focusing on recurrent themes, images, key words, value judgments, and formal structuring. Rather than select a mere handful of tales to discuss, the rest of this chapter and the next attempt to identify key characteristics of this apparently motley collection of pieces. My emphasis will, therefore, be on the overall patterns; these seem to be what are important rather than the individual works in these two phases.

But first we need to review the likely contents of the collection. There has been evidence for some time that probably all the pieces published by the *New England Magazine* and the *American Monthly* between 1835 and 1837 were part of *The Story Teller* and that they were mostly written in the autumn and winter of 1832–1833 and 1833–1834. Weber argues that some of these works may not be part of the collection and could have been submitted prior to Hawthorne's quarrel with Park Benjamin, the *American Monthly* editor: this is likeliest in the case of "Old News," which is based on material borrowed from the library in October and November of 1834, only a month before serialization of the collection began. The *New England Magazine* published what was later entitled "Passages from a Relinquished Work," "Mr. Higginbotham's Catastrophe," "The Gray Champion" and "Young Goodman Brown" (these two were in all probability kept back from the rejected *Provincial Tales*), "My Visit to Niagara," "Wakefield," "The Ambitious Guest," "Graves and Goblins," "A Rill from the Town-Pump," "The White Old Maid," "The Vision of the Fountain," "The Devil in Manuscript," and "Sketches from Memory" ("The Notch of the White Mountains," "Our Evening Party among the Mountains," "The Canal-Boat," "The Inland Port," "Rochester," "A Night Scene"). The *American Monthly* published "Old Ticonderoga" and "A Visit to the Clerk of the Weather" in

1836, and "Fragments from the Journal of a Solitary Man" in 1837. There have been speculations that "The Threefold Destiny," published by the *American Monthly* in 1838, may have been a *Story Teller* tale. However, Hawthorne's relations with Benjamin, though stormy, had sufficiently improved by 1838 with Benjamin's favorable review of the volume of the *Token* in which Hawthorne's pieces had appeared (see 9:509n), and Hawthorne may well have submitted a newly written tale in addition to the sketch on Fessenden, which we know was written and submitted to the magazine shortly after Fessenden's death in November 1837. Besides, there are notebook entries written after the aborted publication of *The Story Teller* that offer considerable parallels for this tale (8:53, 166).[16]

Seymour L. Gross then provides convincing arguments that "The Wedding-Knell," "The May-Pole of Merry Mount," and "The Minister's Black Veil," which all appeared in the 1836 *Token,* are also likely to be part of *The Story Teller.* Goodrich possibly skimmed off tales from the collection before it was dismembered. Although this does not necessarily mean that the composition of these three tales is contemporary with other works of the collection, they do seem to have been written in the early 1830s.[17]

The eight tales included in the following year's *Token* (dated 1837) present problems. At least five were written after *The Story Teller* because they make use of material from the notebooks, started in May 1835: "Monsieur du Miroir," "Sunday at Home," "The Man of Adamant," and possibly "Mrs. Bullfrog" (though the notebook parallels are less strong). Library borrowings suggest dates after the submission of *The Story Teller* for "The Prophetic Pictures" and "Fancy's Show Box."[18] The notebook parallels to "Fancy's Show Box" (8:29, and possibly 25) could suggest either a later date of composition or simply a continuing interest in the theme, and so in the face of divided evidence I have chosen to discuss it in the context of the early 1830s work that it resembles in material and point of view, while recognizing that it may be instead a later survival of early 1830s preoccupations. Although there is no external evidence for the date of "The Great Carbuncle," it seems a strong candidate for *The Story Teller,* given the full reference in "Our Evening Party among the Mountains" to the legend and the promise to write it up. There is no evidence either way for dating the remaining tale of this group, "David Swan." I have assigned discussion of it to the chapter on the work of the later 1830s only because of formal and thematic parallels with that later material. Finally, there is "The Ontario Steamboat," published in the *American Magazine of Useful and Entertaining Knowledge* (AMUEK 58–64) but probably an original part of the project, given its parallels with "The Canal-Boat" and "The Inland Port."[19]

There are other tales written in this period that were apparently not part of *The Story Teller* project. Hawthorne spent the autumn and winter of 1830–1831 trying to complete *Provincial Tales*, but by 1831 he appears to have accepted that it would not be published as a collection because he let Goodrich take certain tales for the *Token*. He announced his plan for *The Story Teller* in June 1832, having let Goodrich have "The Seven Vagabonds" and "The Canterbury Pilgrims" in late spring 1832 for the 1833 *Token*.[20] These tales were probably rehearsals of the *Story Teller* theme.

Contemporary works also include "The Haunted Mind," "The Village Uncle," "Alice Doane's Appeal," and "Little Annie's Ramble" (the first three were published in the 1835 *Token,* and the last in *Youth's Keepsake* of the same year). They are generally not considered part of *The Story Teller,* though Weber makes them part of the collection's frame along with "Night Sketches," "Graves and Goblins," and the other Oberon pieces. "The Village Uncle" is linked to Hawthorne's visit in 1833 to Swampscott, where Hawthorne met a young woman whom Elizabeth Hawthorne later identified with the Susan of the story.[21]

The nature of Hawthorne's response to the breakup of *The Story Teller* is disputed. George E. Woodberry quotes Horatio Bridge's statement that Hawthorne as a result stopped writing for the *American Monthly* (the *New England Magazine* having merged with it at the end of 1835), and that the editor "begged for a mass of manuscript in his possession, as yet unpublished, and it was scornfully bestowed." Woodberry comments that "the manuscripts he [the editor Benjamin] carried to New York could have been but few and slight, unless they were burned in the fire which destroyed the archives of the 'American Monthly Magazine' not long afterwards." Woodberry therefore argues, "It may fairly be thought that he had emptied his desk of its accumulations, though a few tales may have been reserved for Goodrich." Other commentators assume without clear evidence that Hawthorne had disposed of all manuscript by December 1834, and that he stopped writing from the time of the breakup of *The Story Teller* until toward the end of 1836.[22]

This supposition needs to be challenged. Hawthorne started his notebooks in May 1835, and it is likely that at least some of the tales for the 1837 *Token* (ready in late spring 1836 and making use of notebook material) were written in the autumn of 1835. His six-month stint on the *American Magazine of Useful and Entertaining Knowledge,* which kept him frantically busy after January 1836, made for a hiatus in this new creativity. We do not know when the plans were first mooted to publish *Twice-told Tales* (the collection published in 1837 from tales already published over the years in magazines and gift books).[23]

It has been argued that the publication of *Twice-told Tales* marks a new phase in his work, but I would argue that this change began slightly earlier in the second half of 1835 after the failure of *The Story Teller.*[24] I shall argue in the next chapter that the work that Hawthorne then went on to write in the second half of the decade is different from the earlier works under consideration here. Although there was no sudden break and some works of the early 1830s appear to be forerunners of the later phase, nonetheless there are important and clearly discernible changes taking place in the group of tales and sketches written after mid-1835.

▼

The transition from *Provincial Tales* toward a different kind of writing can be represented by the shift observable in these tales from the figure of the self-absorbed mirror gazer to the image of the public highway, that is, from introversion to interaction. As the many examples of the mirror motif at this period show, it is a change full of complications and hesitations, and not a matter of simply rejecting the former posture. Oberon in "Fragments" certainly does suggest the lifelessness of a *Fanshawe*-like introversion when, looking in the mirror, he imagines himself dead, his beauty safe from aging. In his dreams, a shop-window mirror reveals him wearing a shroud, as if the commercial world regards his inward-turned life as tantamount to nonexistence. This kind of self-contemplation is presented as "unmanly," the turning toward mirrors being represented in these tales as conventionally feminine—we find mirror gazing regarded as a typical, even instinctive female gesture in "The Ambitious Guest," "A Rill from the Town-Pump," and "Little Annie's Ramble." Its implication is that a male gazer is excluded, like women in mid-nineteenth-century America, from public spheres of action.

However, the tales of this period do not propose that one should simply turn from the mirror. Parson Hooper, like Oberon, sees himself in pools and mirrors shrouded in a black veil, but in turning from these the protagonist is averting his eyes from a mirror that reveals not only an intolerable self-image but also what he deems a truth about social relations. Hooper's vision—whether of secret sorrow or sin or simply a self unrepresented by social forms—is a starker version of the *Provincial Tales* portraits of an intricate interrelationship of divided subjective and social identities. Intense self-contemplation (a kind of mirror gazing) has made him aware of some unidentified part both of himself and, he assumes, of others, which is not normally expressed in social interaction. The veil publicizes the presence of this hidden self: it is a public image of a private fact.[25] To turn away from this particular kind of mirror image is no solution, but is rather a rejection of both that psychic reality and the hope (through the symbol of the veil) that it might be expressed to others. As a result, his moving from the mirror does not bring openness to community, but instead evasion and painful exclusion.

Where the creative imagination is associated with the mirror, there is a similar ambivalence. The mirror is not rejected out of hand. The mirrorlike imagination in "The Haunted Mind" (9:306) is shown to be visually vivid but impotent in the world of social action, yet the mirrorlike show box (9:224) in a parallel sketch about self-contemplation, "Fancy's Show Box," remains a more constructive instrument of self-revelation, though that revelation remains private. Examining oneself and exploring external conditions have become mutually exclusive alternatives when the narrator in "Little Annie's Ramble," a would-be detached observer of the world around him, avoids looking in the mirror and takes to walking the streets. "The Canal-Boat" questions these polarized alternatives: the narrator, who fancies himself a detached observer mirroring the scene, is instead thrown back onto himself by an actual mirror and discovers that he has been only projecting his own imaginings upon the scene, rather than objectively recording it. So, in these works of the early 1830s, the imagination remains primarily a mirror that reveals the psychic life (as also in "The Vision of the Fountain," and in "The Village Uncle," where reflections in sea and rock pool constantly dissolve into the actuality of the artist's face in the looking glass above his desk generating his own fantasies), and as yet it can only partially record the social scene.

There is some movement outward from mirror to the image of the highway, from asking who am I, to asking who others are and what are the stories of their lives. This moving out psychically and morally into the world is a different kind of mental and physical travel from those journeys in *Provincial Tales* that sought a bridge between inner and outer realities and a unification of the self. The image of the young dreaming artist is not new, for its roots lay in *Fanshawe*, but the present image of traveling is different. The artist becomes the wanderer without fixed destination and with an open mind, whose home is the highway. An early version of *The Story Teller* idea, "The Seven Vagabonds," is set in a "house on wheels" (9:350) at a crossroads. Another early tale, "The Canterbury Pilgrims," has travelers telling their stories as they rest beside the public highway, thus placed between the open road and the Shaker community's extreme stasis and profound conformity to the rules of their order. Its conclusion is open-ended, a commitment to the "untried life" (11:131). Even Little Annie, tired of the clean, wide streets of her hometown, wishes to visit the traveling circus. So the highway is more than a discovery of the world beyond the mirror; it symbolizes a rejection of what is presented as contemporary norms of social living.

But another set of equally strong images counterpoint these highway images that seem to promise varied social intercourse. The young writer, having ventured onto the road, now returns to sit alone in his room without family or social relations or recognition of his talents. "The Seven Vagabonds" contrasts its principal images of freedom with those of toil, sleep without hope, dirty streets in a somber New England, a life to which the clergyman at the end of the tale may again consign the writer. In "Fragments," the writer-narrator leaves for the open road only to return to die at home; "Little Annie's Ramble" ends with the return of the girl to her parents. The more romanticizing artist figures remain stuck in their rooms, as in "The Devil in Manuscript" and "The Village Uncle," where it is the seamen who are the real traveling storytellers. "The Vision of the Fountain" ends with images of the narrator rescued from his narcissistic imagination, but sitting in the totally dark and silent sitting room. In "Graves and Goblins," the restricting home of the poet ghost is literally a grave.

Not only writers but also most of the solitaries who frequent the tales of this period tend to be presented as trapped in a narrow place or unsuccessfully seeking home and marriage, rather than freely wandering the road. The escape from the mirror to the highway leads back only to further confinement, not this time in nightmare but instead either in a domestic world where nothing of significance happens or in a social limbo where, unlike the *Provincial Tales* characters with their intimate connections with the world around them, the protagonists are merely disconnected from ordinary social experience. It turns out that journeys and wanderings fail to give significance to ordinary domestic existence. Wakefield's journey (initially a "frolic" [9:133] like "The Seven Vagabonds") takes him from his marriage to solitary life in one room in the space of a few streets. The wanderer in "The Ambitious Guest" can only disrupt and destroy the family. "The Great Carbuncle" is more ambivalent, still hankering after the stone while validating a very simple conception of married life (it is ideal, rather than realized) as a way of avoiding the "Ambitious Guest"–like ambition of the travelers. Other figures exist in limbo or have desperate recourse to marriage: "The White Old Maid," with its neglected empty house on a busy street and two women whose whole lives have been bound up with one dead man; "The Wedding Knell," where marriage is set up as the preferred alternative to solitary scholarship (a reversal now of *Fanshawe*); and "The Minister's Black Veil," with its protagonist imprisoned in the midst of a village community (the tale starts in the busy street) and dying unmarried, in painful isolation in the midst of a crowd.

In all this there is little sense of belonging to a community or being successfully part of the comings and goings of a shared social existence. Nonetheless, the journey is directed toward this kind of life, which the writer posits (at least from time to time) as the "real" world. It is only the earlier written tales of this phase that have simply a goalless journey or the image of traveling at random.

The way in which this definition of the "real" is built up can be seen in the tales' handling of "poetry" and "history"—formulations shown to be problematic, constructed of social illusions. Under the influence of Common Sense formulations (without necessarily accepting them) and of popular prejudice against poetry,[26] some of *The Story Teller* pieces set up an opposition between a Romantic, elitist "poetry" and a materialist vision based on a notion of "ordinary" New England life and morals. "Poetry" is defined as the aesthete's rarified vision of the sublime or the picturesque. This notion of poetry is criticized through a number of figures: Oberon; the Village Uncle; the caricatured poets of "The Canterbury Pilgrims" and "The Great Carbuncle"; the "earth-clogged," spiritually yearning lover in "Graves and Goblins" (ii:289); and the suspect narrator of "The May-Pole of Merry Mount," who wants to make a "poet's tale" (9:60). The similarly "poetic" anticipations and ridiculous hesitations of the narrator in "My Visit to Niagara" supposedly teaches him eventually that he should try to look at what is actually there (ii:285).

The treatment of "history" similarly stresses the primacy of the present-day and ordinary. The narrator of "The Wedding-Knell" disclaims all knowledge or interest in verifying the historical basis of his story. The basic historical material of *Provincial Tales* now becomes merely old newspapers, and the past seems dreamlike and full of phantoms (II:157). Only a lover of antiquity, remarks "Old News," regrets the modern scene; the emphasis is on change and ephemera: "In this world, we are the things of a moment, and are made to pursue momentary things. . . . All philosophy, that would abstract mankind from the present, is no more than words" (II:133). "The Rill from the Town-Pump" reduces history to a few reminiscences, and the Shakers in their century-old costumes are made to seem quaint. While "Old Ticonderoga" is interested in how history is constructed out of individual interests, the emphasis even here is on "the lapse of time and change of circumstances" (II:191), the countryside as farmland.

But this emphasis on the present and ignorance of the past is seen as a problem; "Alice Doane's Appeal" tests these assumptions that "we are people of the present and have no heartfelt interest in the olden time" (II:267). Woodwax covers the Gallows Hill in an illusion of green fertility, so that a deliberate effort has to be made by the narrator to call back the past. "The May-Pole of Merry Mount," the tale of this period that possibly most resembles the historically based *Provincial Tales,* demonstrates well the differences between these two phases of Hawthorne's writing. The narrator's attitudes are what are under scrutiny. He is not interested in creating a dramatic story of individual lives; instead his "philosophical romance" (II:54) is intent on offering a theory about the origins of present-day America. This attitude to the past is characteristic of the Arminian-Unitarian branch of history writing, which emphasized general progress from a remote past to an improved or at least improving present.[27]

The representation of what is purported to be ordinary social reality is problematic. Life is conceived as something that is publicly shared—the highway image evolves into many village and city streets. This image is taken up in moralistic metaphors: "ordinary avenues," "highway of human affairs," "the beaten path of the world," "the common path." Quite a number of works include detailed descriptions of these street scenes from an outsider's viewpoint (for example, "Rochester," "Little Annie's Ramble," "Fragments," "The White Old Maid," "The Minister's Black Veil," "Wakefield"), as if description was a way of laying hold of an unfamiliar, indeed strange, world. In at least ten of these tales and sketches, unelaborated images of houses and the domestic hearth as the center of this supposedly normal existence also thrust themselves into the narrative in unimaginative repetition.

But there is little sense of this "reality" being based on an experiential sense of a solid, substantial world. The desire to be settled within such a reality is all the stronger because that wish has not been realized. Heavy moralistic phrases pile up—"great and serious aim" (II:326), "the living world" (9:308), "sober duties" (II:326), "serious business of life" (II:316) (so serious that "The Wedding-Knell" absurdly promotes marriage to a man dressed in his shroud)—but this heavy-handed insistence on the "reality" of the domestic and social worlds has at times the shrillness or unthinking doggedness of a short-circuited argument or a much needed simplification in the face of the unresolved complexity of *Provincial Tales* where psychic and social realities had collided in the protagonist. In those earlier tales the failure of social institutions to accept or even recognize certain aspects of the self led to the experience of inner division, but now this conflict has evolved into a simple proposition that the social institutions of marriage and work (involving labor but not otherwise threatening to one's peace of mind) are "real" and the rest illusion. This is the ideology tried out in these works.

The word "reality" comes laden with unsupported value judgments and is used lavishly as a panacea for all ills without amplification, explanation, or representation: the "real passion" of doom and troubled joy in "The May-Pole of Merry Mount" (9:58); the "consciousness of the reality of life and love" of the young married couple in "The Great Carbuncle" (9:158); the "Wedding-Knell" condemnation of the widow's wedding party that appeared more like a "bright-colored picture, than any thing real" (9:31); the contrast in "Fragments" of "deep and warm realities" with "merely skimming the surface of life" (II:314); the insistence in "Fragments" on "real necessities" (II:316), which are paralleled by the "realities of life" in

"The Devil in Manuscript" (II:172); and the "real world" of "The Village Uncle" opposed to its shadow (II:311).

What becomes increasingly clear is that this "reality" is a domestic dream created by marginalized figures and a troubled narrator, and is the consequence of a feeling that their present solitary existence is illusory and dreamlike. Hawthorne's consciousness of this is shown in the way these images have so much of the merely notional and clichéd about them, a "moral sedative" supplied by Common Sense philosophy on which these notions are based.[28] "Fragments" most fully articulates this myth of domestic "reality." It is as much a part of the subject's fantasy life as his dreams of fame or freedom (indeed, for him the domestic is an unstable reality that can at any moment seem a dream in his mind, and his imagined world become a reality).

The treatment of women, necessary but unscrutinized props in this fantasy, is evidence of its hypothetical nature. With the few exceptions of Hooper's fiancée, Elizabeth; the schoolteacher in "Mr. Higginbotham"; and the working women in "Old News"; they are not granted autonomous status. The erotic is stripped of any dangerous actuality by appearing in this fantasy only in the form of adolescent girls dancing, a flirtation with a passing young foreigner, a ghost without a body, or the very newly wed and still sexually shy couples in "The Great Carbuncle," "The Canterbury Pilgrims," and "An Evening Party." In "Sights from a Steeple," the narrator is safely distanced from the courting couple in the street below, and in "The Canal-Boat" the women passengers undressing behind a curtain are deemed an acceptable object of sexual fantasy because they remain physically invisible. Sexually experienced women make brief appearances only as the conventional "fallen woman" in "The White Old Maid," "Fancy's Show Box," "The Wedding-Knell," "The Haunted Mind," and "Graves and Goblins." The purely conventional duality of virgin/whore shows up in "The Haunted Mind," where although the personifications of Sorrow, Disappointment, and Sexual Error are all in female form, the narrator can imagine a wife who, unlike him, sleeps peacefully (the haunted mind being presumably a purely male preserve). Although "The Vision of the Fountain" offers itself as a critique of this masculine thinking about women, the tale (and

Hawthorne himself) is not quite disentangled from the seductive rhetoric of female idealization.

The narrators' inadmissable and therefore guilty sexual feelings are neutralized by safe, stereotyped fictions of the domestic woman. The wife and mother are the ideal—for example, the narrator approves of the mother who fails to look at Niagara because she is worrying about her children (Hawthorne's satire here being as much directed at the narrator's attitude). The unambitious mothers and wives of "The Ambitious Guest," "The Great Carbuncle," and "Wakefield" are sisters of this figure. The few old women in these works are treated with hostility because they are unavailable as material for this domestic fantasy (see "The Wedding-Knell," "The Haunted Quack," and "The Ambitious Guest"). "The May-Pole of Merry Mount" attempts to find a way of fitting the sexual into the fabric of Puritan work, marriage, and state, but only by polarizing and stereotyping the opposing forces in a naively moralistic way.

Some of the tales themselves explicitly recognize and criticize this fantasy of the "real" world rather than merely rehearse it for the reader to ponder. "The Village Uncle," which provides the lengthiest portrait of family life at this period, finally reveals that it is only the solitary author's fantasy that produces such pictures, and in "The Haunted Mind" the happy images of children, bride, hearth, and dancers are deliberately culled by the narrator from the possibilities of his world in order to console himself. The early "Seven Vagabonds," which is not drawn to this domestic option, talks of the "routine of artificial life" (9:365), and "Old News" speaks of "the whole system of things" (11:156), reminding us of its artificiality and restriction. It is "Wakefield" that most fully explores this sense of the artificiality in normal social arrangements. It is about the destruction of domestic bliss (which is itself treated with a certain irony [9:130]). It reveals the tremendous fragility of daily structures that are so easily breached: "Amid the seeming confusion of our mysterious world, individuals are so nicely adjusted to a system, and systems to one another, and to a whole, that, by stepping aside for a moment, a man exposes himself to a fearful risk of losing his place forever" (9:140). "The Canterbury Pilgrims," also an early tale, shows that the supposedly simple life of work and family can fail. "The Minister's Black Veil" presents us with a happy village scene, but given what follows, it is clearly introduced as the conventionally pretty surface that hides much pain and fear. Parson Hooper may be wrong in his vision of secret sin, but the mobbing and ostracism that the congregation inflict on him are sufficient in themselves to undercut in another way the opening happy picture. There is no sense of a living community in these tales—witness the mob in "Mr. Higginbotham's Catastrophe." "Alice Doane's Appeal" deals more fully with that mob in its account of the witch trials; "Old News" handles the question of slavery in a manner that is revealing of community cruelty and moral blindness, personified in its narrator.

▼

What stories can the storyteller tell to such an audience that, recoiling from the haunted mind, substitutes only an ideologically based fantasy of domesticity and an unsubstantiated dream of community? What plots does he find to give such lives some significant shape (plot being important to Hawthorne's contemporary readership),[29] and how is subjectivity to be represented in these tales?

Looking at what these tales say about story-making as well as at the range of actual narratives contained within these tales, it appears that their writer-narrators' imaginations are not drawn to what their society regards as ordinary, everyday existence. The main interest in "Rochester," the narrator avers, is not the falls, but the legend of Sam Patch, which will become "poetical" with time (11:301). Comments on Indian legends in "An Evening Party" suggest that the qualities he seeks in stories are "romance, or poetry, or grandeur, or beauty" (10:429). "Mr. Higginbotham's Catastrophe" succeeds in telling a good story, but its excitements are entirely mendacious, while we can gauge something about the way the narrator's creativity works in "A Night Scene" by his reaction to some Irish laborers by a fire who, he comments, "might have been transferred, almost unaltered, to a tale of the supernatural" (11:305). "Alice Doane's Appeal," though concluding that "we are not a people of legend or tradition" (11:267) and proposing "a trial whether truth were more powerful than fiction" (II:278), fabricates instead a melodramatic narrative of the Salem Witch Trial victims.

The reason for these attitudes is clear when we look for narratives made from the material of common life. There is a blank: as the would-be storyteller of "Fragments" remarks about the crowd in his village, their "days were all alike, and a long lifetime like each day" (II:325). "The Ambitious Guest" demonstrates that the domestic scene has no "story" (9:333) until an unusual catastrophe occurs and legends can be made of it. If the characters in that tale had remained in the house, they would have survived, but there would then have been no story; indeed, to create narrative interest Hawthorne added the young man to the facts he had been given, and the tale thrives on might-have-beens and conjecture (as do "Mr. Higginbotham's Catastrophe," "The Great Carbuncle," "Wakefield," "The Village Uncle," and "The May-Pole of Merry Mount"). In "Wakefield," the story only exists because the uneventful domestic routine is disrupted, and the events of "The Village Uncle," the apotheosis of domesticity in this period, are only of interest because they are pure fantasy.

This makes a considerable contrast with *Provincial Tales*. Here is no catastrophic interaction between the human subject and societal structures. The psyche mostly does not emerge in external drama. The major point in "Fancy's Show Box" is that there are no external events to write about; instead, within the mind, there is a drama of unrealized acts (9:225–26). In "The Ambitious Guest" the young man encourages his hosts to put into words their unexpressed and unacted-upon desires. Other images also emphasize the internalized quality of these characters' stories: veils, masks, prison, rooms. This hidden life remains mostly unexpressed and therefore unknown. Unlike in *Provincial Tales,* we know very little indeed about what happens subjectively.

Occasionally a story focuses on events where at least some aspect of the inner person is expressed in public ritual: the marriage ceremony in "The Wedding-Knell," funeral processions in "The White Old Maid," and the wedding, burial service, and sabbath service in "The Minister's Black Veil." Mostly, however, the community does not offer the means of expressing the hidden self, and even the participation in those ceremonies mainly strike the majority of people as merely freakish ("freak" is used of Wakefield [9:130]). Although the tales' narrators often demur, these characters' actions are on very many occasions simply dismissed as insanity by bystanders: Hooper (9:48), Wakefield (9:138), the Salem witch-hunts (11:278), the Seeker of the Great Carbuncle (9:150), Oberon's journal in "Fragments" (11:318), the White Old Maid (9:372), and Mr. Ellenwood (9:28) are all deemed "mad."

So the characters remain largely mysteries to the reader. In "The Minister's Black Veil" the narrator's questions (9:39) show that he is not privy to Hooper's motives. While the motive for Wakefield's action derives from a compulsion that, the narrator argues, we feel is common to all of us though unadmitted in our self, Wakefield is unique in choosing to act upon it and is isolated in consequence. Paradoxically, his acting out of a common compulsion does not bring him closer to the general reader, but distances him. Hooper makes a deliberate attempt to communicate, his unique gesture being an acting out of what he takes to be a whole community's desire to conceal themselves from each other, but because Hooper does not directly express his own personal feelings that lie beneath the veil and his assumed quiet demeanor, there is no open contact with others.

The fiction of this period undoubtedly is mostly still concerned with events located in the mind—dreams, hauntings, visions—but the point of view from which it is examined has changed. "Dream" is the recurrent term used for the psychic life but it no longer carries the *Provincial Tales* sense of being involved with the unexpressed of the culture. Instead, this image is used to convey a sense of unreality in the inner world and hence its discontinuity with waking activity. Such a model of identity sets up two elements, the psychic and the social, in opposition, rather than seeing the causal relationship between them. The inner life of dream, insofar as the reader has access to it, still seems more vivid and full of incident than the uneventful, externally viewed world of social living, but its separation from the external world brings a sense of impotence, mystery, lack of choice, and the impossibility of realizing ambitions. "The Haunted Mind," "Wakefield," and "Fancy's Show Box" in particular illustrate this. Notably all three sketches are not dramatized narratives—the inner events are never fully constructed as a story of external happenings. It is seen as imperative to wake from this "unreal," though vivid, world: waking from a dream or struggling with a dream on waking is a recurrent motif in "The Haunted Mind," "The Haunted Quack," "The Vision of the Fountain," "The May-Pole of Merry Mount," "Old Ticonderoga," "The Devil in Manuscript," and "The Village Uncle." Only in "The Great Carbuncle" and "My Visit to Niagara" do dreams lead to the desired object.

All in all, there is in these tales an impoverished sense of subjectivity, and a certain distance in the way it is handled. The point of view adopted is that of the external bystander as in "The May-Pole of Merry Mount"; "The Minister's Black Veil"; "The White Old Maid," where the bystanders watch uncomprehendingly from the street; and "The Haunted Mind," which deals with its potentially interesting subject, the space between sleeping and waking, with a self-conscious use of metaphor and a generalizing and increasingly cliché-ridden approach.[30] Although "The May-Pole of Merry Mount" does propose to investigate how societal systems are formed from inner compulsion, it focuses on the world of objects and codes, on the mode of living in a community or state, and shows no capacity simultaneously to deal with the inner world and make this social analysis. Indeed, the Puritan efforts to control and order anarchic impulses are paralleled by a narrative that forces its material into a rigidifying frame.

A recurrently expressed desire to be imaginatively part of something despite this sense of separation and distance leads to a notion of "sympathy." Sympathy will become a key term in Hawthorne's developing ideas. Here, however, "sympathy" has a more limited meaning and appears rather as a substitute for that more complete knowledge of an individual that the artistic figures in these tales had wanted and failed to achieve: in the words of one, the artist's capacity to "see deeply into the hearts of mankind, discovering what is hidden from the wisest" (II:327). This ambition we find in the narrator's faculty in "Seven Vagabonds" of "throwing myself mentally into situations foreign to my own" (9:352) and the secrets-knowing fortune teller of the same story, and it is close to the desire of the narrator of "Sights from a Steeple" to be a "spiritualized Paul Pry." The narrator of "The Canal-Boat" with his mirror literally becomes this kind of artistic spy in his attempt to achieve this knowledge.

But although the characters within the tales and sketches talk about their ability to penetrate and express imaginatively what they find,[31] this is not actually achieved either for themselves or for the reader. Indeed, "The Minister's Black Veil" suggests the impossibility or possibly delusory nature of this attempt to see into hearts, even if some parishioners do respond wordlessly to his action. In view of that tale's pessimism and peril, this project becomes something merely wished for, an ideal notion. In its place there is merely repeated mention of "sympathy." There is something intrusive about the word because it does not lead to insight and real community, as it might if it were the sympathetic imagination espoused by Adam Smith in *The Theory of Moral Sentiments* (to be discussed fully in later chapters). Instead it becomes a substitute for knowledge: the image of knowledge as sight is replaced by this vaguer discourse of feeling.

"Sympathy" is regarded here as being a reaching out to another who is in some way distant or separate. For example, "there is sympathy" between little Annie and her middle-aged companion (9:122), and the old Tory is "worthy of our sympathy" (11:159). In "The Great Carbuncle," "the natural sympathies" (9:149) suggest a notion of an innate capacity, a common denominator for the artist to draw on. "Wakefield" also posits this in talking of an "original share of human sympathies" (9:138) that the protagonist retains without having a reciprocal influence on others (he resembles a failed artist without an audience for his expressive act); Hooper, too, cannot be reached by "love or sympathy" (9:48).

At the center of this idea of "sympathy" is a frequently expressed belief in the efficacy, indeed primacy, of "feeling." Both "Wakefield" and "The Minister's Black Veil" indicate the narrator's horror at the thought of being cut off from this emotion. The narrator in "My Visit to Niagara" will "know, by my own feelings" (II:285), and in "The Wedding-Knell," Mr. Ellenwood (another cold figure like Hooper and Wakefield) and Mrs. Dabney come to a better understanding of themselves and their situation by "true feelings": "one true feeling," "truth of feeling," a "gush of human feeling," and "a swell of exalted sentiment, in those who felt aright" (9:29, 36, 32, 36). The writer-narrator of "Alice Doane's Appeal" works through "feeling": "[w]ith such eloquence as my share of feeling and fancy could supply" [II:278]. He comments, "I had reached the seldom trodden places of their hearts, and found the well-spring of their tears" (II:280). Both the rhetoric and manipulativeness of this suggest that the narrator has to some extent latched onto a language of emotion, which goes unexamined to a large extent, partly because it is more hoped for than realized.

"Feeling" here appears to be more emotional and imaginative than Common Sense "right judgement" (that god-given internal moral sense) and undoubtedly owes something to notions of an innate affective sympathy, reaching back to Shaftesbury. Adam Smith, as we shall see, had also argued that social intercourse depended on the operations of sympathy.[32] However, "sympathy" as it is being used in this present phase of Hawthorne's writing, though clearly cognate to those ideas, seems too undeveloped and undefined in its operation. It is closer to more general critical notions, current at the time, about reader response. The contemporary view of the novel reading experience was that it was a profoundly emotive one: as Baym explains, a combination of catharsis and a "Shaftesburian sense that deep emotion called up on another's behalf was morally unlifting." Novels were deemed "healthy" if they avoided "misanthropy," and suggested the lovability and ethically admirable qualities of human nature.[33]

Furthermore, in the *Story Teller* texts, the insights that more vaguely sympathetic feelings bring tend to draw the outsider back into the conservative common fold, rather than make for radical exploration of alienation and extreme moral states and an understanding of others different from oneself. This appeal for "feeling" thus becomes linked to desire for some commonly acceptable moral stance. Home and community also exert their ideological pull to enhance this effect. It is because of this that, although we have seen a definite wariness of moralism or at least a hesitancy about aligning the texts with what are deemed to be commonly held sentiments and judgments, nonetheless, in the face of the failure of more individualistic alternatives (represented by the mirror and the highway), the tales and sketches do seem to lean slightly and ambivalently toward those publicly held assumptions. As I have argued, these ideological positions are being tested, and a heavily moralistic response is still rejected in the majority of cases. It is only under pressure that the tales and sketches make tentative gestures toward current ideologies of work and home. That ideology blankets out the pain and protest, but blankets are comforting.

But we must not give too much weight to this. True, at the end of "The May-Pole of Merry Mount" the Puritan soldier throws a rose wreath over the newly wedded couple who, cropped and redressed, will be entering the sober community that is to generate nineteenth-century New England, but "The Great Carbuncle," the tale that most purposefully and explicitly of all the works of this phase promotes the values underpinning conventional notions of the social fabric (marriage, home, and work), is an investigative exercise to establish the close connection between that ideology and a particular kind of didactic writing. The tale is stylized to the point of caricature to underline this. It shows how ideology, given its factitious nature and its slender basis in actuality, needs such moralistic writing not merely as reinforcement but also as an essential confirmation. Reynolds discusses pious domestic fiction of the time that "valorized the home, good works, stylistic clarity, and Christian virtues such as submission and endurance." These, he points out, were "rhetorical constructs in which the troubled social and philosophical climate of antebellum America was deliberately meliorated and an alternative world of village pastoralism and victorious exemplars were offered as mythic correctives for thorny realities."[34]

Most of the other works of this period do not have such a closed meaning as "The Great Carbuncle." In "Passages" the storyteller protagonist offers his ideal: tales that are open-ended, varied, and not preconceived: "I cannot remember ever to have told a tale, which did not vary considerably from my pre-conceived idea" (10:417). (His opposite, Eliakim's providential view of life, would lead to a literature of moral symbolism [10:414–15].) True, few of the subsequent stories match this ideal of openness, yet neither is the slight yearning for some gently uplifting moral conclusion satisfied. In some places this moral simply does not fit. The narrator of "The Village Uncle" asks which of several contradictory "morals" he should select for his tale, finally choosing one whose espousal of "chaste and warm affections, humble wishes, and honest toil for some useful end" (9:323) does not fit obviously with the story. The end of "Wakefield" teases the reader who may have expectations of a moral even for as chance-ridden a story as this, by a sentence that seems to offer less and less as it proceeds: "He has left us much food for thought, a portion of which shall lend its wisdom to a moral; and be shaped into a figure" (9:140). In "The Wedding-Knell" the storytelling narrator does not impose the moral. Instead, the moral is generated on a more individual level than the clergyman's tradition-based "sad, but profitable moral" (9:32). "Fancy's Show Box" is called a "morality," but the agent of judgment is not society but an individual conscience whose standards are far more exacting than orthodox judgments. "The Canterbury Pilgrims" rejects the "parable" that the travelers' lives present to the lovers and ends on the open road, leading to several possibilities (though admittedly all within the sphere of marriage, home, and work). Offered a choice between a safe, predictable retreat and the uncertainties, passions, and customary troubles of a workaday existence, the story celebrates a deliberate turning to a life of battling against ordinary economic adversities and the acceptance of difficulty.

The use of the sketch form itself suggests an experiment in finding other ways of constructing meaning in a narrative. As Jonathan Arac has argued, the inventing of the "overviewing eye"—the technique of narrative generalization—was a "crucial imaginative act" for the nineteenth-century writer attempting to define her or his place in society.[35] The next phase of Hawthorne's career can be seen in terms of finding formal techniques that will open his narratives not only to insight grounded on sympathy but also to interpretation and social judgment.

In this, "Wakefield" is of considerable importance in the search for artistic solutions for handling his material. Instead of a dramatic fiction, there is a meditation on events, and characters are merely sketched out and summed up in the first paragraph. The structural outline is very obtrusive throughout. Much as the audience was present in some of the tales about storytelling, so too the reader is invited here to participate in the attempt to understand Wakefield; we are free, the narrator states, to "shape out our idea" of the man, to expand the "fact, thus abstractly stated" (9:131, 130). While the self-conscious voice of "Old News" addressing the (gentle) reader still seems a somewhat ironic testing of the formal and analytical possibilities of the sketch form, "Wakefield" has material with a subjective interest that takes the sketch, in spite of all its rather crude, even self-mocking, narrational directions and its abstracting and theorizing tendencies, beyond a certain experimental neutrality and yet not into merely the expression of ideologically sanctioned mores.[36]

In this, Hawthorne is moving away from an exploration of individual experience (as in *Provincial Tales*) and toward a more deliberately conceived collective vision of human lives (Wakefield represents possibilities one suspects in many others, he says). Nevertheless, the author still refuses the role of spokesman for the ideologies of his contemporary culture. These pieces' concern is still with individual subjective needs rather than with the community's judgments, but those needs are set in a social context and examined from an external point of view. This is a different kind of engagement with the social world. These works mark a transition in his thinking, tentatively, even obliquely, establishing a new direction, without wholly securing it.

Chapter 5

"Not . . . Altogether a Chameleon Spirit"

The Work of the Later 1830s

1835–1842

▼ I N J A N U A R Y 1 8 3 6 Hawthorne became editor of *The American Magazine of Useful and Entertaining Knowledge,* and for six months he produced factual material to accompany whatever illustrations the magazine's publishers selected. This was unredeemed hack work—his letters show him scrounging for any copy he can lay his hands on, and approximately a quarter of each issue was copied directly from other books.[1] Although 1835 had seen the publication of some remaining *Story Teller* pieces in the *New England Magazine,* this new editorship seems a self-destructive response of a disappointed author cynically satisfying the only audience prepared to read him. He appears to have hated every moment of it—indeed on Hawthorne's return to Salem, his friend Horatio Bridge feared suicide. His first extant notebook shows an early preoccupation with death, ruin, misplaced circumstances, and the lack of a place in the world.[2]

Nonetheless, in beginning this notebook in May 1835 Hawthorne had made a gesture toward a continuing creative life: "Four precepts;—to break off custom—to shake off spirits ill-disposed—to meditate on youth—to do nothing against a man's genius" (LN [21]).[3] After the failure of *The Story Teller,* Hawthorne did not stop writing. *Twice-told Tales* was published in 1838, and sometime between August 1836 and August 1837 he recovered enough to note with double underlining the unelaborated statement, "In this dismal and squalid chamber, *fame* was won" (LN [25]).

Once composition dates are identified, it is clear that Hawthorne's writing in the second half of the 1830s is distinctive in containing, with a few important exceptions, a striking preponderance of sketches and fables. These tales see the completion of that earlier gradual withdrawal from the exploration of individual subjectivity. Here narcissists, solipsists, egotists, and dreamers get short shrift. The artist is envisaged as social spokesman and public moralist, and many of these works are morally deterministic narrative structures with emblematic events and stereotypical characters. Such moralistic preoccupations are, in a sense, entirely characteristic of New England literary culture at the time. As Lawrence Buell comments, "Altogether, before 1865 no New England writer of any consequence argued for the position that the moral dimension of art was unimportant."[4] But what is unexpected, given Hawthorne's earlier writing, is how very few works go beyond a relatively simple formula or construct any fully developed ironic stance or complexity of response.

All this does not, however, represent a wholesale takeover of the artist by the majority. Instead, Hawthorne's interest now is in how identity is socially constructed—a self "regulated" by others (9:298 and 180) in the sense that it has social roles and its life is ideologically determined. These works allow him to see how these structures operate by rehearsing their ideological underpinnings. The democracy presented here is paradoxical: it purports to be based on and assist individual freedom, but it is a system in which subjectivities are completely contained by the social order with only occasional faint awareness of elements of the person not formed by these forces. The "democratic" ideal is here that of a collective fate, and the individual is not the origin of her or his meaning. Introversion is attacked, and more secure structures of meaning are sought in the contemporary democratic ideologies of "duty . . . prosperity, and happiness" (9:482), shored up with the Christian promise of heaven.

But within these nineteenth-century allegories of equality, community, progress, and self-determination lie painful images of lack of choice, isolation, conformity, suffering, and death. Though the tales never fully unmask those public illusions, the accommodating surface conceals residual resistance to its stated vision. In addition, many of the tales and sketches, with their morally very conformist content and narrative self-consciousness about both audience expectations and the forms of literary didacticism, show a conscious concern with certain conventional ways in which a work's meaning is conveyed and with the encoding, within the text, of an audience purportedly drawn from the moral majority. Out of this understanding of the way in which the human subject is constructed by ideology and discourse comes a knowledge of subjectivity and of political structures that will be vital to new directions in his work in the 1840s.

Evidence that there is some residual detachment on Hawthorne's part from the stated concerns, tastes, and values of this fiction can be found in several places: the experience of producing *The American Magazine of Useful and Entertaining Knowledge* with its blatantly conventional moralizing ("We have endeavoured to fill our pages with a pleasant variety of wholesome matter" [AMUEK 224]); the disparity between so much of the notebooks and his published works at this time; and the ideologically conformist children's work *The Whole History of Grandfather's Chair* at the close of this period.

The notebook voice in particular is very unlike that of the sketches, some of whose material is drawn from experiences recorded in the notebooks (for example, "Foot-prints on the Sea-shore" from 8:162–65). The so-called *American Notebooks,* written throughout this period, are not sentimental or moralizing. They reveal at times the unself-conscious enjoyment of an interested observer in the scenes around him, particularly in the North Adams notebooks (8:32–151): "I talk with everybody" (8:66). His attitude to people is imaginatively sympathetic rather than merely curious or censorious, while in the contemporaneous fiction published at this time, character creation, even when given a certain idiosyncratic gloss, leans instead toward the emblematic. The notebook might propose, "To think, as the sun goes down, what events have happened in the course of the day—events of ordinary occurrence" (LN [34], a proposal that the *American Notebooks* subsequently goes on to satisfy in a few of its entries, for example 8:156–58 and 171–72), but the fiction and sketches of this period are concerned instead with fitting this sort of material within a framework of contemporary New England ideologies of American democracy, Christian hopes and resignation, and commercial, professional, or domestic work within the community.[5] Whereas the early notebooks show for some time a liking for oddities and paradoxes, ironies and upsets, and recognize the effect of unforeseen causes or inexorable fate, the imaginative work Hawthorne writes at this time seeks instead to establish more secure structures of meaning and would not relish seeing normal notions of cause and effect being thus upset. Indications in the notebook of a similar desire for things to assume a significant shape emerge only later.

So detachment coexists with accommodation in the published work of this period in spite of the closed systems within which they operate. The ventriloquist knows he is the concealed producer of the entertaining voice. One has only to see the discrepancies between Hawthorne's private portrait of his acquaintance Jonathan Cilley and the published memorial sketch of this senator the following year to see both Hawthorne's sense of the actualities of power in a democracy and his ability to write within publicly determined structures.[6] We shall find that generally, in Hawthorne's work at this period, a certain distance is maintained, and slight contradictions and hesitations sabotage the moral power structure. Irony flickers   35 at the edges of the texts, and a certain darkness of vision shadows nearly everything. Here there is no safe haven; Christianity alone provides a frail safety net in an unpredictable world. The accommodating surface conceals a residual resistance to its stated vision, and underneath its ostensibly conventional morality the beginnings of a more questioning approach to these structures of meaning will be seen tentatively to emerge.

▼

The compositional history of the later 1830s can be constructed as follows from the available evidence. It is obvious that the eight tales submitted to Goodrich in mid-1836 for the 1837 *Token* could hardly all have been written during Hawthorne's frantic editorship of *The American Magazine*. From notebook evidence, it seems that he had a busy autumn in 1835 writing "Monsieur du Miroir" (LN [18]), "Mrs. Bullfrog" (LN [13]), "Dr. Heidegger's Experiment" (LN [18]) and "The Man of Adamant" (LN [15 and 16]). Possibly "David Swan" and "Sunday at Home" belong in this group, although these are tales with no clue to their dates. From references to source material, we know that "The Prophetic Pictures" was written in 1836.[7]

As for the works published subsequently and listed below, it is of course possible that these were written earlier and considered unsuitable for *The Story Teller*, but this is unlikely given the accommodatingly heterogeneous nature of that collection. Notebook evidence or references in his letters exist for some tales, and others closely resemble datable ones in their style. There is general agreement about these datings.[8] The one exception is "The Shaker Bridal," often believed to belong to the early 1830s for no other reason than Hawthorne's visit to the Shaker community in 1831. Though discussed frequently in conjunction with "The Canterbury Pilgrims" (published 1833), the two tales are too different to share the same composition date.[9]

The bulk of his output in this phase was done prior to or around the publication of *Twice-told Tales* in March 1837: "The Shaker Bridal," "Endicott and the Red Cross," "Peter Goldthwaite's Treasure," "Sylph Etherege," and "Night Sketches" would have had to be ready by early summer in 1837 for publication in the 1838 *Token*. "A Bell's Biography" was published in March 1837. Also in 1837 he spent the first of two successive summers in North Adams, vacations notable for extensive notebook entries (Hawthorne usually stopped writing in summer). The winter of 1837–1838 was hard for Hawthorne: "a winter of much anxiety and of very little pleasure or profit" (15:269). Nonetheless, it saw the composition of three of the four "Legends of the Province-House," arguably the most substantial achievement of this phase, and "Edward Fane's Rosebud," all more heterodox than other contemporary pieces ("The Threefold Destiny," "The Toll-Gatherer's Day," "Foot-prints on the Sea-shore," and "Time's Portraiture").

Hawthorne wrote very little in the autumn of 1838 after another summer in North Adams, except for "Chippings with a Chisel" and "Snow-flakes," neither of which could have made much demand on his imagination. Two biographical sketches on acquaintances, "Jonathan Cilley" and "Thomas Green Fessenden," were also published in 1838. There followed "The Sister Years" for the *Salem Gazette* New Year issue and "The Lily's Quest" (published in January 1839), which had the advantage of using an unusually substantial outline in the 1836/1837 notebooks). He was also planning a second, expanded edition of *Twice-told Tales*, though this was not published until 1842.

After Hawthorne took up a post at the Boston Custom House in January 1839, his creative writing virtually stopped, with "Old Esther Dudley," the last "Legend of the Province-House," being published in March 1839. Instead he wrote at length to his fiancée, Sophia Peabody. The only short story is "John Inglefield's Thanksgiving," based on a substantial story outline in his early notebooks (1835) and published in March 1840 in his friend John Louis O'Sullivan's journal under the pseudonym of Rev. A. A. Royce. Given Hawthorne's previous bitter complaints about being published without acknowledgment, it is tempting to speculate that in this case he did not wish to lay public claim to this tale, a hangover from a fictional phase that Hawthorne was by that date beginning to put behind him. Early in 1839 Hawthorne was requested to write historical stories for children—a needed project at a point when he was trying to improve his financial position so that he would be able to marry. He seems to have begun this project only in mid-1840, with *Grandfather's Chair* being published in December 1840, *Famous Old People* in January, and *Liberty Tree* in March 1841 (for details, see 6:287–94). *Biographical Stories* followed in 1842.[10]

The end to this period and the beginnings of a new phase are clearly signaled in his letters to Sophia, which directly contrast with his letter to Longfellow in June 1837 (15:251–53) at the outset of this period. Whether or not it is an accurate reflection of his life or feelings, this letter reflects a frustration in his relation to the notion of reality reproduced in the tales and sketches of the period: secluded

unintentionally, he says, from "society," "I have not lived, but only
dreamed about living." What he means by "living" and "society"
can be induced from his portrait of himself as unmarried and
unemployed, an anonymously published writer, who can therefore
only produce "shadowy stuff" because of a "lack of materials."

The radical shift in the letters to Sophia from this socially constructed "reality" is yet further evidence of the lack of any real
commitment to the heavily socialized value system reproduced in
those later 1830s works, even though the love letters are also in
some ways a fiction prepared for a particular audience rather than a
necessarily accurate representation of his private feelings and beliefs.
Life in the Custom House is rendered "dreamlike" by loving Sophia
(15:437), so that there would need to be, he says, two journals to
match these dual lives: "Nobody would think that the same man
could live two such different lives simultaneously. But then, as I
have said above, the grosser life is a dream, and the spiritual life
a reality" (15:395). The letter to Sophia in 1842 after revisiting that
"lonely chamber" in Salem of the 1837 letter to Longfellow is the
most striking example of a rewriting of his past: the world is no
longer preferable to solitude and only Sophia may come within the
"circle of my loneliness" (15:383). These letters herald a different
perspective on self and the world to be explored in the stories and
essays begun after his marriage in July 1842.

▼

A good indication of the changes in progress in the later 1830s
can be found in the new handling of an old theme in "Monsieur
du Miroir," one of the earliest published tales of this phase and
Hawthorne's most extended exploration of the mirror motif. Its tone
is public, detached, and mocking rather than contemplative. The
sketch amounts to a rejection of that sense of a separate, hidden self.
Self-examination is futile; here only the mirror's surface is knowable.

This direct attack on narcissism, solipsism, and self-chosen soli-
tariness is typical of his work at this period. "Sympathy," a notion
about relationship still offered in some of the early 1830s tales,

becomes here the butt of humor (10:161–62), and the world of the *Provincial Tales* is decisively discarded in the resolution to stop "chasing its own shadow through a chaos, and catching only the monsters that abide there" (10:170). Self-mockingly sending up the "perplexities of this dark investigation," the narrator states a preference for "fact" (10:159). These transitions are not, however, without problems, for finally the sketch admits briefly and without irony both to underlying pain and bewilderment and to a wish for a universal solution—a desire for a shortcut to certainty and explanation.

Following that resolute refusal of psychic exploration, other tales and sketches go on in effect to dispose of earlier conceptions of an introverted life. The early 1830s trend away from individual consciousness continues; the dreamers of this period are condemned. In "The Threefold Destiny," Ralph, like Oberon, returns home, but this "wild dreamer" (9:481) wakes up to be a village schoolmaster, smallholder, and husband. Another self-absorbed Oberon-like figure, Mr. Bullfrog, comes close to marrying his own image in the looking glass (10:130); instead, his intimate married life is grotesquely spilled out onto the public highway. The prostitute Prudence in "John Inglefield's Thanksgiving" has a dream of home that is reminiscent of "The Village Uncle," but her final viciousness gives the tale a sharp moral twist (though the early notebook entry on which the tale is based took a more benign view: see LN [17]). Although it is actually Sylph Etherege's betrothed who destroys her by jealously manipulating her dreamworld, she seems in any case doomed by her introversion, much as are Lilias, who dreams of perfect happiness on earth in "The Lily's Quest," and Walter, the madman in "The Prophetic Pictures." The arch solipsist, the Man of Adamant separates himself from a benign community to die of isolation in a self-built sepulchre in the wilderness. Other images of self-enclosure linked with death are found in "Peter Goldthwaite's Treasure" and in the sickroom setting within the "tomb"-like Shaker settlement and shroudlike clothes of "The Shaker Bridal" (9:425). The gutting of the inside of Peter Goldthwaite's house is a good symbol of this phase's lack of interest in individual subjectivity. Some of the other sketches ("Foot-prints on the Sea-shore," "Sunday at Home," "Snow-flakes," and "Night Sketches") do appear to persist with a degree of self-contemplation, but the character of their narrator is very much that of a public person. The narrator throws stones at his own shadow (9:461), and the experiences he writes about are presented as common and shared by his readers, and always close to social norms.

Images of mirrors continue to appear in quite a number of works belonging to this period, but there are two significant shifts in how the image is handled, which together suggest a connection between the depiction of what purports to be the material world of common, public experience and the need to place this in a frame of publicly accepted morality. Firstly, where the mirror continues to be used to represent narcissism or private fantasy, a moral frame is now placed around it that censors what is now presented as an antidemocratic rejection of the life of the majority. The feminized Mr. Bullfrog with his curls and face lotion so apparently like his wife is a comic example; Sylph's miniature of her dream lover is a disastrous mirrorlike reflection of herself. Dr. Heidegger's guest's conventional female vanity is merely confirmed when his study mirror reflects her transitory transformation; she is then harshly punished by the same mirror. Unlike the other guests, the antidemocratic Lady Eleanor in "Legends of the Province House" does not look in the mirror—she is too self-absorbed to need to do even that—but her smallpox is a classic punishment of the narcissistic woman. Peter Goldthwaite's dusty mirror in which he mistakes his own image for his dead ancestor is designed to show the illusory nature of his pre-Revolutionary monomania. Similarly, the fantasies in the Loyalist Esther Dudley's mirror are seen as an introversion and isolation caused by a refusal of revolutionary social change.

Secondly and in relation to the above, mirrors are now used as an image of artistic representation of the social world, especially the public and political realm with its explicit ideologies of democracy and Christianity. Far from embodying an independent inner life, these mirrors make clear the social construction of the subject. "Endicott and the Red Cross" makes an explicit parallel between the sketch form itself and Endicott's armor, which literally reflects and causes the material conditions of the colony (9:434). This breastplate mirror simultaneously indicates the militant morality of that society and the embattled subjectivity that this morality creates. It is not a neutral mirror, but a cultural artifact. "Lady Eleanor's Mantle" makes similar connections between mirrors and the representation of a self that is socially constructed. This mode of representation is here given a didactic point—an ideological frame is added to the mirror to suit the conventional view of Hawthorne's mid-nineteenth-century audience, and this now links narcissism with "incorrect" political attitudes:

> The altered taste of the present day—a taste symbolic of a deep change in the whole system of society—would look upon almost any of those gorgeous figures as ridiculous; although that evening the guests sought their reflections in the pier-glasses, and rejoiced to catch their own glitter amid the glittering crowd. What a pity that one of the stately mirrors has not preserved a picture of the scene, which, by the very traits that were so transitory, might have taught us much that would be worth knowing and remembering! (9:277)

This emphasis on representation, especially on accuracy of physical representation and its social significance, is found also in the use of portraits in this phase. The pre-Revolutionary masqueraders in the Province House pretend to be portraits (which are "as true as in a looking-glass" [9:251]), and Howe confronts a mirrorlike simulacrum of himself in an unveiling moment of self-recognition. This has its deliberate parallel (though without any actual mirror images) in the moment in "Edward Randolph's Portrait" when Governor Hutchinson is faced with the symbolic representation of the tyrant he is about to become.

These mirrors, then, represent something more than surface realism: costumes, expression, and gestures are used to apply a general political and ideological message to an individual case—a message that, though not necessarily fully endorsed by the tales themselves, is offered by the narrator for the public good rather than to reveal some individual psychological insight. Peter Goldthwaite's mirror functions similarly, linked with the money he seeks and the coronation medal he finds, products of a corrupt or unstable economic and political system. The message is that Peter cannot go on refusing to be a subject in his contemporary social order. The many historical biographies that Hawthorne found himself producing at this time for both *The American Magazine of Useful and Entertaining Knowledge* and the three children's books he wrote in 1840–1841 (*Grandfather's Chair, Famous Old People,* and *Liberty Tree*) demonstrate a similar tie-up, this time between historically placed literary portraits and the presentation of a clear ideological message on politics. In general, then, although mirrors may initially suggest a desire for factual representation, the didactic and ideological element is clear: " 'Keep my image in your remembrance,' " urges Lady Eleanore (9:281).

▼

Given the mix of social accommodation and residual detachment in these works, the various images of the artist found in tales and sketches of this period not surprisingly indicate a never fully resolved tension between the artist as public moralist and the more individualistic, critical, and inner-directed creators. Sometimes standard ideological positions are merely confirmed, sometimes a more critical stance is assumed.

This tension shows up early in "The Prophetic Pictures," again using the mirror: that "natural gift of adapting himself to every variety of character, insomuch that all men—and all women too, Elinor—shall find a mirror of themselves in this wonderful painter" (9:166). Written in 1836, the tale faces two ways, back to both Hawthorne's earlier attempts to write about his characters' consciousness and the now abandoned pose of itinerant storyteller, and forward to the later 1830s, which will test out moralism and conformity. The tale offers, but does not examine, a powerful dichotomy in the artist between on the one hand insight into the individual psyche, and on the other hand a moral concern that is linked with the mass of society.

The tale begins with an account of the artist attracted by the unusual rather than the "sleek and comfortable" (9:168). Emotion, not established morals, is his concern. Halfway through, the tale switches to a critique of the painter in terms that had been evolving in the early 1830s and that will become characteristic of the latter half of the decade: he is "insulated from the mass of human kind" (9:178), his heart is cold, he has "pryed into their souls" (9:179), he has "the semblance, perhaps the reality, of a madman" (9:180). This criticism is hard to assess—after all the painter does turn out to be the perceptive prophet he fancies himself to be. His insights are quite unrelated to his being a useful member of the community, but if it had been possible to "regulate" (9:180) himself by others, he would have then lacked that insight. On the other hand, no one is deterred by his work. The tale is broken-backed.[11]

Later tales increasingly privilege didacticism and a notion of communal experience. "Sylph Etherege," published a year later, is unambiguous in rejecting art that embodies individual consciousness, in this case the miniature that gives material form to Sylph's ideals. Picking up the "Prophetic Pictures" theme of the potential misuse of artistic power, it offers a simpler scenario and hence a clearer judgment on the role of the artist as it is now being conceived. Neither is the moralist, Dr. Heidegger, the preferred type of artist because the subjects of his experiment, as in "The Prophetic Pictures," carry on regardless. But what is gradually emerging is the sense of the artist as one engaged with social issues rather than with the individual psyche—in this tale it is a critical engagement. The Fountain of Youth in "Dr. Heidegger" is part of the New World myth of regeneration, the ideology of liberation from the past and of individual freedom and self-gratification. The doctor's magic mirror may flatter the beholder with apparent wish fulfillment, but the actuality that it goes on to reflect amid the myth-created illusions is irreversible age, imminent death, and the pointlessness of all human action, whether sexual, political, or mercantile. This view is reiterated by "The Sister Years," in which the allegorical figure of the Old Year is presented as a kind of artist recording the suffering and waste of human energy in politics, war, and technology, despite the official ideology of onward, upward progress of humankind.

Most of the work of this period, however, presents a moralistic face more confidently and to some extent more blandly than this, and successfully espouses a notion of a commonplace world where, unlike in *Provincial Tales* or *The Story Teller*, the "truths and realities of life" are given moral meanings. In "The Man of Adamant" the disturbing legend of the less acceptable side of that Puritan past, so lauded by the patriotic "Legends of the Province-House" narrator, is safely buried by the more progressive American family. In other tales the marvelous and puzzling is dissipated in the "realities" of money ("Mrs. Bullfrog"), the village ("The Threefold Destiny"), and the commercial streets ("Peter Goldthwaite's Treasure," "Night Sketches," and "Snow-flakes," as well as "Legends of the Province-House"). "Night Sketches" even states its rejection of the "unreality" (9:427) created by imaginative writing. "The Toll-Gatherer's Day" welcomes the "realities" (9:206) of the early morning after dreams of night; "Sunday at Home" cuts down any flights of fantasy; and "Foot-prints on the Sea-shore," though indulging in some fantasies, finally returns gratefully to ordinary material comforts. The doppelgänger motif is given material explanation in "Monsieur du Miroir," the magic water of Dr. Heidegger is a temporary delusion, the Gothic horror tale in "Mrs. Bullfrog" is safely domesticated, and best of all, in "David Swan" (a would-be fairy story), nothing ever actually happens to ruffle the surface of an ordinary, modest existence.

These attitudes to imaginative writing are also expressed in Hawthorne's first literary review, published in February 1836 at the same time that he was battling to find copy for the *American Magazine of Useful and Entertaining Knowledge*. There was surely a certain degree of irony in urging the following advice on Samuel Goodrich, author of the collection of poems under review. Goodrich had not only rejected *The Story Teller* but also given Hawthorne the hated *Magazine* job: "We think that he might safely trust to homely nature and sober truth, and not etherealize so much. Imagination, unless of the very loftiest order, should keep near to earth, and clothe itself in earthly forms; for if it soar too high, it is almost certain to be transformed, in its flight, into cold and glittering Fancy."[12]

"The Threefold Destiny" provides the image of the artist at this period that is most successful (within its own terms). It converts the dreamer into the practical schoolmaster of the unchanging New

England village, dedicated to the "sphere of duty, of prosperity, and happiness, within those precincts, and in that station where Providence itself has cast their lot" (9:482)—a favorite image of the American social ideal at the time.[13] The opening paragraph functions to establish clear, deliberate parallels between Ralph's discoveries of the mundane at the root of the romantic, and the narrator's attempt to blend fairy story with the depiction of the commonplace. The tale's allegorical elements are then given "life-like warmth" by a fairly stereotyped realism purporting to show "characters and manners of familiar life," though the narrator remains aware that this is not "a story of events claiming to be real," but a moral parable (9:472).

The sketches—"Sunday at Home," "Night Sketches," "Foot-prints on the Sea-shore," "The Toll-Gatherer's Day," "Chippings with a Chisel," and "Snow-flakes"—in which the writer usually occupies center stage throughout, offer further images of the artist as public moralist of what is deemed to be common experience. They purport to describe the ordinary world of his readers, but unlike the notebooks that focus on description, they foreground the narrator's responses as a mere onlooker on life (a motif in all of them). But this position and process are highly self-conscious, making us aware of the author's imagination and writing work. So the sketches, for all their ostensible personal pose, are highly public. The "gentle reader" is addressed (9:26), even asked to "walk" with the narrator. There is also greater sympathetic engagement with the social scene ("Sunday at Home" provides a clear contrast with earlier "Sights from a Steeple") and a constant attempt to relate what the narrator is seeing to people's lives. So for the most part public sentiment, not the individual imagination, is being articulated here.

It is, however, in these sketches with their hint of the personal that we can detect a residual element of dissent from this accommodation to the collective. There is a difference between on the one hand these writer-narrators and on the other the tombstone carver who is truly the popular artist with his entirely conventional repetition of simple old clichéd rhymes, and the toll gatherer, another simple pseudowise moralizer. Several of the sketches set up a stark opposition between the private imaginative life in the writer's study and the New England scene outside, and most show that writing is actually an essentially solitary activity (9:344). This is despite the sketches being written as if the activities and scenes were happening as he writes and the reader were sharing the experience. Consequently, while these works do express public sentiment, often (though not always) there is a residual sense of something being held back. The narrator offers himself partly, and not wholly, to the reader: "Not that mine is altogether a chameleon spirit, with no life of its own" (9:431). In the "crowded streets," he goes on, "I shall walk among men kindly and as a brother, with affection and sympathy, but yet shall not melt into the indistinguishable mass of human kind. I shall think my own thoughts, and feel my own emotions, and possess my individuality unviolated" (9:461). If the tone of this seems somewhat forced, it is because its terms are those of the society to which impossibly the narrator wants to belong and yet be essentially unaffected by.

For the most part, however, the sketches show a highly adaptable chameleon with practically nothing to distinguish his thoughts from thousands of others. The way the narrator uses the image of the chameleon disturbingly suggests a denial of the artist's individual creativity and a problematic and impoverished sense of the possibilities of the sympathetic imagination.[14]

The chameleon's camouflage is not total, however. The reader is kept aware that the narrator is playing a game that verges on the parodic. The moralizing is limp, lazy, and entirely conventional, reducing individuals to stereotypes and evoking awkward or graceful clichés indiscriminately. Large claims are made for wisdom gained from trivial objects in "Chippings from a Chisel," while "Night Sketches" plays safe, never venturing into the darkness beyond the town streets, yet treating its consoling sentiments with a certain degree of mockery. There is often no sustained argument and little structure. The endings are prosaic, even self-contradictory, offering several possible conflicting views so that the ostensible moral is undermined in a gesture of indifference to the whole piece: for instance, a final statement of dislike for tombstones after a whole essay on them; the advocacy of faith from a self-confessed nonchurchgoer; the solitary seaside rambler finally enjoying company better than all the solitary pleasures he has previously hymned; the night wanderer going out to share the world when nearly everyone else is wisely sheltering at home. Such sabotage remains covert, however, and the surface of the text accommodates itself to normative standards, much as it seems to do in many of the tales of the period.

By the time "Legends of the Province-House" was written toward the end of this phase, images of a socially relevant art had developed into something more complex and contradictory. The effect is of a palimpsest, layer on layer of storytellers, artists, audiences. Each varies our sense of the story and of history itself. In an interventionist attempt to liberate both her country and her art, Alice Vane "restores" politically relevant New England images for her pre-Revolutionary audience and asks, "'And yet . . . may not such fables have a moral?'" (9:262). Popular traditions are given explicit Revolutionary meanings by a number of people: the masquers of "Howe's Masquerade"; the restorer of Edward Randolph's portrait; Helwyse; the Doctor who interprets Lady Eleanore's embroidered mantle; and the several different tellers of these stories. These "artists" oppose antirepublican versions of sociopolitical reality. Their voices are orchestrated by a patriotic narrator who, "hoping to deserve well of my country by snatching from oblivion some else unheard-of fact of history" (9:256), appropriates these events for the establishment's construction of history and social values and legitimizes these views.[15] The narrator of *Grandfather's Chair* and its sequels has an identical voice. The deaths of both artists of the aristocracy, the mantle embroiderer and the story-telling Esther Dudley, ostensibly testify to the evident corruption of the regime they were caught up in.

Nonetheless, none of these voices has final authority, not even the main narrator, whose taste for supposedly factual narrative done up with a little purely decorative fantasy is neither satisfied nor adequate to the complexity of his material. There is something disturbing about the complacency with which the narrator contemplates the way those Revolutionary challengers to the old authority's grip on social reality have themselves become the new authority. The reader is thus made aware of how these political fables rewrite events and push characters into representative and symbolic ideological positions.

Having said this, we must, however, note that the tales never fully unmask these public illusions. At one level the patriotic pageant inevitably plays on. Readers are reckoned to have much invested in it—even literally so, as the tales' effect on the commercial success of the tavern and on increasing property values makes clear. But the tales' politically engaged artists are shown to be limited and as impotent as the Painter of the Prophetic Pictures to change the Loyalists to whom they address their masques, portraits, and interpretations. The material of the tales increasingly sits uneasily within its republican frame—"Lady Eleanore's Mantle" is heavy-handed, and Esther Dudley refuses to be a mere counter in the ideological game. Although the narrator had planned yet another story, he ends "Old Esther Dudley" with the resolution never to return. We are told instead that the Province House may be gutted like Peter Goldthwaite's house and fitted with a wholly modern interior. Telling stories about the past in this way is shown to be inadequate and finally to be abandoned.

A growing unease about merely assenting to the existing social order shows up again in the only two tales to follow "Old Esther Dudley" (itself written much later than the previous three "Legends"). "The Lily's Quest" and "John Inglefield's Thanksgiving" are exceptionally conventional in material and form, but they introduce themselves almost parodically, one as an "Apologue" (a unique term for Hawthorne with hints of a pun on apology), and the other as a clergyman's composition. The days of writing dutiful homilies are nearly over.

▼

The tales also set themselves questions about the presence of didactic moral argument in a literary text. True, compared to the work of the early 1830s, there seems to be less wariness about this kind of moralism, less reluctance to play the spokesman's part, and a certain accommodation to what are presented as generally received opinions. Insofar as there is explicit exploration, it is mostly not at the level of the thematic content but rather a trial of the various methods (such as allegory, moral fable, and essay), through which these codes are conveyed within a literary text. The workshop methods of "Wakefield" are being applied for a more limited didactic purpose. This shows up in a self-referential narrative voice, conscious in particular of the way these works are being shaped to meet a perceived requirement that a text should exemplify generally agreed values of its society—see, for example, the introductions to "The Threefold Destiny" and "Edward Fane's Rosebud" where narratorial intentions are elaborated.

It is possible that this experiment commits itself even as far as to the serious adoption of these moral views as a way of reaching an audience, but it is hard to gauge here the degree of commitment on the part of the writer. There may be irony, and there is certainly an element of detachment created by the self-referentiality of the narration. What we can say is that some accommodation is taking place, whether out of commitment, or necessity, or as an experiment. This may reflect what Buell calls a "symbiosis of respectability and deviance" in New England writers of this time. Buell further comments on the way writings at the margins of conventional moral discourse could "problematize the dogmatic structures that gave rise to them by operating in the crevices between outright conformity and outright dissent."[16] However, with very few exceptions, there is no radical questioning in Hawthorne's work at this time, although some of the material suggests an awareness of questions that could be begged. The intellectual quests of *Provincial Tales* and even *The Story Teller* have come to a temporary halt, and these new tales adopt, for a time, conventional or commonly accepted values, an orthodoxy that expects assent and conformity without any need to justify or explore.

The apotheosis of this is the publication of *Twice-told Tales* in 1837, for which it appears Hawthorne selected tales and sketches that would most appeal to popular taste for sentimental, "refined" tales that repetitiously stressed their moral, counseled Christian resignation, saw virtue rewarded, and offered no untoward thoughts or expression. In 1839 Hawthorne also extensively revised "The Gentle Boy" to highlight the sentimental portrait of Ilbrahim. Typically, reviewers of *Twice-told Tales* praised him for his "delicate taste," his "beautiful simplicity and elegance of style," his "quiet and cheerful humour," "tone of pensive feeling," and his "fine moral tone."[17] As Hawthorne comments in a letter to friend and editor O'Sullivan: "It makes me smile to see what a mild, gentle, and holy personage the reviewer makes of me—living, one would think, in a heaven of peace and calm affection. I fear you would take rather a different view of me" (15:279).

These tales and sketches express an ideology of community life that is based on home, business, and church, and traces its origins, as the historical tales of this phase demonstrate, to the foundation of democratic forms of government. It exerts an underlying pressure to conform, since it presupposes not only that experiences of work, family, and country are shared by all but also, implicitly, that people have a common voice and beliefs that will therefore command everybody's assent. Meaning is determined by the victors, as "Legends of the Province-House" shows. The tales' demonstration of the need for common sympathies and social regulation (to use recurrent terms of these tales) is as much an insistence on conformity as a vision of sharing. The new definition of "evil" is to set oneself apart from others (in contradistinction to notions of "evil" as fragmentation within the human subject that have been encountered at earlier periods of Hawthorne's career). Existence is envisaged as a shared fate and involvement in social forces.

"Peter Goldthwaite's Treasure" is the exemplary text here, expressing an ideology of circumscribed and unindividualized social interaction: "His brief glimpse into the street had given him the forcible impression of the manner in which the world kept itself cheerful and prosperous, by social pleasures and an intercourse of business. . . . It is one great advantage of a gregarious mode of life, that each person rectifies his mind by other minds, and squares his conduct to that of his neighbours, so as seldom to be lost in eccentricity" (9:400). "Monsieur du Miroir" had expressed the same sternly self-disciplining resolution based on "masculine" action within the social order.

The isolationists are heavily criticized: the lives of the Shakers, though materially prosperous, are attacked because they are not rooted in common domestic experience, and the Man of Adamant's bigotry is overtly rejected. It is as if "Young Goodman Brown" has been rewritten in this latter tale to provide unambiguously benign images of the settlement that obliterate the forest revelations. The fullest, most confident definition of the "sin" of isolation is given several times by the protodemocratic characters in "Lady Eleanore's Mantle," thus making clear the provenance of such values: "She seeks to place herself above the sympathies of our common nature, which envelopes all human souls" (9:276). Duty, prosperity, and happiness are the goals of the right-thinking man and woman, and each seeks a "place," that is to say, a role in the community. "The Threefold Destiny" shows the successful achievement of this. "Sympathy," the early 1830s link between people, has shifted a little in emphasis to become an occasional active benevolence and a greater insistence that it is "natural" for one to feel akin to others—"a glow of kindred feeling" (9:481). The Shakers are criticized for overcoming "natural sympathy with human frailties and affections" (9:424). True, there is not much evidence of this in other works, though feelings "gush" and "glow" in "The Threefold Destiny" (9:480, 481), and Mr. Brown shows a benevolence to Peter Goldthwaite that overrides his common sense and financial considerations.

But all is not inevitable progress and the pursuit of happiness in these tales, and when faced by problems posed by failure and suffering, ideology maintains itself both by censorship and if necessary by creating further ideological layers. Any contradictions are ignored. These tales do not realize that early 1830s domestic dream; their domestic narratives are painful. The home is no longer that secure haven, pleasant stereotype, or consoling fantasy. Marriages do not take place as the bride dies or is rejected and cast into an emotional limbo ("Dr. Heidegger's Experiment," "The Shaker Bridal," "Sylph Etherege," "The Man of Adamant," "The Lily's Quest," "David Swan," "Edward Fane's Rosebud," "The Toll-Gatherer's Day"). Women also may betray men, and may even be poisonous to them or monstrous ("Lady Eleanore's Mantle," "John Inglefield's Thanksgiving," "Endicott and the Red Cross," "Mrs. Bullfrog," the young girl's grave in "Edward Fane's Rosebud" that causes an epidemic). "The Threefold Destiny," which sets fair for marriage at the end, can now be seen as an exception. Two tales that explore marriage beyond betrothal and wedding day end either in attempted murder or turn the marriage bed into a deathbed ("The Prophetic Pictures" and "Edward Fane's Rosebud"). "Chippings from a Chisel" suggests that love changes both in marriage or death. Rose Grafton is the most elaborated and extreme example: her bitter tears on her wedding day, her suppressed sexuality, her marriage a "tomb" (9:467), her "home" (9:469) only in the sick chamber. This domestic gloom is part of a wider sense of a suffering world of wrongdoing, sickness, pain, and death. Rose sums this up: she is "the handmaid of human infirmity and affliction" dealing with "all that is saddest in the doom of mortals" (9:470), without any possibility of happiness.

But gloom and doom are held at bay by another set of established beliefs, those of a superintending Providence. This Providence, seen also guiding the nation in its struggle for political independence, guarantees eternal happiness in heaven after the death that darkens so many of these works. So in the most public of the sketches, "The Sister Years," while the official belief in progress is still expressed, happiness in eternity alone offsets the general effect of waste, stagnation, and trouble. "A Bell's Biography" again tells a history of change, revolution, and republican growth, where only eternity can offset the individual histories of death, anxiety, toil, theft, and despair, as well as the bigotry and desecration that are part of the bell's more public past.

"Night Sketches," "Chippings with a Chisel," and "The Toll-Gatherer's Day" all relish these heavenly sentiments, though here their highly clichéd expression so draws attention to their merely conventional nature that it undermines confidence in this Christian safety net for all who fall off the high wire of national progress. It is virtually meaningless to say simply that "dark shadowing of life" is as comforting as "life's joy" (9:418). If the narrator finds it consoling to see all homes united in suffering and death, then he is using the democratic idea of equality and the sharing of experience in a facile, even absurd way to palliate and not probe. "The Lily's Quest" is devoted to the same paradoxical conclusion, expressed in clichéd images. "Monsieur du Miroir" points out that "Divine Intelligence" (10:171) does not unveil its mysteries; instead one must blindly assent to an existing order. "David Swan," the tale coming closest to exploring the idea of Providence, ties itself in moral knots trying to produce a safe conclusion that allows for some human foresight even though our hero has slept through the entire tale. Only "The Threefold Destiny" provides providential images of happiness in this world. The underlying argument of "The Shaker Bridal" is instead that it is wrong to try to evade the experience of sin and sorrow.

The tales, however, do not ponder the relationship between this "democracy" of suffering and death and the other democracy of universal progress; instead these two conflicting worldviews coexist without apparently causing conflict. Ideology, after all, always contains contradictions held in suspension. Forms of the Christian religion, as the other socially established belief system, provide a way of avoiding these difficulties. Nor do these works explore another tension that grows out of that opposition between suffering and progress: the contradiction between the republican belief of self-determination and the tales' majority view of fatality. The Man of Adamant can be seen as "self-doomed" (11:166) in that, like Adam in "The Shaker Bridal," he is offered a clear choice of return to the community. Most other characters in this period are either trapped by personal traits over which they are shown to have little control ("The Prophetic Pictures," "Sylph Etherege," "John Inglefield's Thanksgiving," "Dr. Heidegger's Experiment," which deals with the helpless repetition of past errors, and "Peter Goldthwaite's Treasure," where "fatality" [9:385] ties Peter to his birthplace), or they are pitched into situations they cannot change ("Monsieur du Miroir," "The Shaker Bridal," and "The Lily's Quest," in which the whole human race is doomed). In "Edward Fane's Rosebud," Rose's destiny is the result of rejection and a world without choice, and even Fane is forced against his will. Rose's claim of kinship with death is the ultimate in this. The sketches present us with a decidedly passive figure who lets things happen, pointlessly shouting at the sea or waiting for the traffic jam of life ("The Toll-Gatherer's Day") to sort itself out.

No explanation is offered. The very notion of Providence seems not to be a living faith, but a substitute for either investigation, or nonmetaphysical explanation, or protest; it merely palliates the feeling of living in a world without choice. The tales embed themselves in the status quo and the ideology that defends it. The writing is conventional not because there is certainty about values, but rather because of a great deal of insecurity.[18]

Not surprisingly, didactic structures are closed in meaning, and the tales wrapped in a homiletic straitjacket. This working within an ideological system contrasts with the relative openness of the preceding phase of Hawthorne's work. Even Dr. Heidegger's experiment is not really an experiment for the tale's narrator, who retells events merely to demonstrate a foregone conclusion. Most of the tales do not even fulfill the "Threefold Destiny" ideal of combining narrative and moralism. Where the dominant mode is narrative with characters and actions with an attempt at naturalism, as in "Peter Goldthwaite's Treasure" and "The Shaker Bridal," there is little sense of exploring new ideas, nor likelihood that the tale will open up to other possibilities than the assumed necessity of reintegrating oneself into the wider community of supposedly common life. At best we get hints of subjectivity: Peter opening the window with snow-dazzled eyes, or Martha's final desolate agony.[19]

"The Lily's Quest" ("An Apologue") is an epitome of this kind of writing. Its characters are irrelevant to the action, mere counters to be moved from point to point. The typology is explicit, and their lives are merely as conscious participants in a "parable" (9:449). "David Swan" has a similar morally deterministic narrative structure. "Edward Fane's Rosebud," though it goes on to develop a more speculative examination of the human subject, starts with similar didactic elements: "it is no unprofitable task, to . . . set fancy resolutely to work" (9:463), and "deep lessons of thought and feeling" are to be found from which "profit might be derived" (9:464). Interestingly, it is only when the narrator admits that he cannot fulfill this intention that exploration can begin. "The Sister Years" and "Time's Portraiture" are, as one would expect from their occasion, conformist allegories.

Looking at "The Threefold Destiny," "Peter Goldthwaite's Treasure," "Dr. Heidegger's Experiment," "The Shaker Bridal," "The Man of Adamant," "The Lily's Quest," and "John Inglefield's Thanksgiving," it would be hard to argue that these should be read ironically, yet an element of detachment from their stated views and intentions persists.[20] It is not a matter of overt dissent from the tales' messages, but rather the effect of the self-referentiality of this writing.

"Legends of the Province House," because of their layering of narrators and complex relationship of present to past, are the exceptions to this. They question, rather than just watch, the act of shaping persons and events into moralistic images. They come to explore that compulsion not only to see material within a "correct" ideological framework but also to inculcate a lesson from it. Here it is the characters who self-consciously voice these didactic views, and the tales as a whole do not necessarily wholly endorse them: "'Now, were I a rebel,' said Miss Joliffe, half aloud, 'I might fancy that the ghosts of these ancient governors had been summoned to form the funeral procession of royal authority in New England'" (9:249). The simpler "Man of Adamant," by turning a living being into an admonitory human stalagmite, also suggests an awareness of the rigidifying aspect of didacticism, even though on the surface the tale merely affirms the statue's message.[21]

"Endicott and the Red Cross" is an exception among the tales of this time in that it does have to be read ironically. The story raises questions on matters absolutely central to the work of the later 1830s, namely the nature of moral and political authority, in particular the constitution of democracy (which popular ideology traced back to Puritan protests like Endicott's, as we see in *Grandfather's Chair* and its sequels [for example, 6:33, 76, 138, 151]), the nature of freedom and communality, and problems around ethical judgments and the judiciary (the "engine of Puritanic authority" [9:434]). It achieves this by a return to a fuller history in fiction after less interest shown in it in the work of the early 1830s. It is a return that, in comparison to the bland "Man of Adamant," brings with it complexity. "The Man of Adamant" merely presented Digby as something grotesque from a remote, unconnected past.

In "Endicott," the historical sources at Hawthorne's disposal are adapted to make the debate about authority clearer though safer and less disturbing on the surface. Williams is made into a moderate and a reassuring counterweight, while Endicott goes uncensored, an undimmed hero in a false history that nineteenth-century readers will love (indeed they are explicitly implicated—"Our forefathers" and "our history" (9:433, 441).[22] The tension between proto-Revolutionary revolt against the civil authority of England and the individual revolt against Puritan moral laws (the adulteress and the gospeler) lies at the center of the tale, even if the ironic question, " 'Call you this liberty of conscience?' " (9:439), remains unanswered. There is also the disturbing implication that, if the nineteenth century can match the seventeenth in sins (as the tale suggests), there must be contemporary social repression to match the seventeenth century too.

Although the sketch itself is compared to Endicott's breastplate, it does not share Endicott's views. Irony creeps in with the separation of the Puritan point of view from that of the narrator's and that of the narrator's from his readers'. The chauvinistic, moralistic frame is being manipulated to write a more subversive tale. On the surface, the reading public is being given the patriotic tale that it might be supposed to desire, but the tale as a whole moves beyond the moral pieties of its culture. The contradictions between the official view of the situation and what is actually happening are obvious and unresolved. Since its implications are taboo, the attack on the complacent self-image of post-Revolutionary American society remains covert. Indeed, this need for secrecy and the availability of an orthodox reading of the tale serve to underline how authoritarian, conformist, and insensitive that social order can be. There is a link between the situation of the half-detached, half-accommodating author of those mainly rather conservative moral tales of this phase of Hawthorne's career, and the coexistence within "Endicott and the Red Cross" of the official portrait of events and the more painful and disturbing actuality. But irony is uneven here, and only intermittent elsewhere.

▼

Beneath the fatalism of these characters' lives and the moral determinism of the tales themselves lies a potentially deeper determinism—these works create a sense that the human subject may be wholly constructed by the social order. The preoccupation in this whole phase of Hawthorne's work with social interaction, discourses, and ideologies leads in a few tales, mostly toward the end of this period, to a deliberate and more overt exploration of this model of the subject. Most other tales and sketches, for all their orientation toward the contemporary social scene, somewhat obscure an understanding of the issues both by the democratic ideology of individual choice and the nonpublic focus of their fictional world (the "private" domestic scene). In the "Legends of the Province-House," however, the only substantial work of this period, it becomes clear that it is false thus to separate the political and the personal into discrete categories: the political determines the personal. Lady Eleanore's pox is sexually devastating for individual lives (it is implicitly venereal), but also it affects the history of the country (the epidemic "left its traces . . . on the history of the country, the affairs of which were thrown into confusion by its ravages" [9:282]). The Province House itself is the joint symbol of a political system and of its inhabitants; Esther Dudley's condition is paralleled with that of the Province-House.

These four tales investigate the power structures of American society, involving those who hold administrative power, others who challenge this and are potentially the real power holders in the country, and those who have no power at all within existing structures. The works are quite unlike *Provincial Tales*, where the primary focus had been on the experience of private persons. They are set almost exclusively in public rooms, but ones that hint also at the domestic (the stateroom housing the governors' families, and the tavern as a public form of sitting room). They take as the main part of their subject matter major events or influential figures in the country's history in order to explore the political origins of present-day America. The overt debate is about contemporary democracy and the relationship of the individual person both to this and to the previous colonial order in which monarchial forms of government and elements of self-determination had uneasily coexisted.

However, although the modern Republic sees itself as self-determining in ways in which it deems the preceding British colony had not been, every one of the characters, whether Loyalist or republican, reveal themselves to be ineluctably shaped by one or the other of these social and ideological structures. As a result, although the tales may seem on one level to be about the evolution of equality and self-determination, the characters' actions often actually imply conformity and lack of independence or choice. Lady Eleanore is made to blame herself (that is to say, the surface of the tale, assuming an appropriately democratic attitude, presents her as capable of determining her life), but there are also hints that her actions can be ascribed to the social formation of her character or to innate tendencies in her personality. Since she can hardly be said to have much control over such social influences, the ideology of free self-determination is effectively sabotaged. While "Providence" or insanity are the officially defined causes of the events of "Lady Eleanore's Mantle," the influence of a particular social order provides a more adequate explanation.

The "Tories" are the main interest of all four tales, people whose allegiances are to the forms of government and society now superseded by the Republic. Much as the tales are all situated at moments of historical change and on the threshold between the Province House and the town and colony beyond, so these figures exist simultaneously in two worlds. By focusing on characters who belong to a now defunct system, Hawthorne makes the social shaping of these figures' emotions and actions clearer for his contemporary readers than he could have done if he had tried to show the same social determinism in operation in the order presently in place in America. The tale leads the reader to investigate the decision those characters make to remain loyal to monarchical forms of society even when given

compelling arguments for aligning themselves with protodemocratic
or actual democratic values (from the point of view of most mid-
nineteenth-century readers they made the "wrong" choices), and
the tragedy of their unwilling alienation from the majority of their
country people calls on the readers' intelligent understanding and
nonpartisan compassion.

The final tale of the sequence comes to the clearest overall sense of
the forces apparently involved in the creation of the human subject.
Superficially there is a clear political bias to the way in which Esther is
still seen by both "stern republicans" (9:295) and by royalist Howe
as a symbol of a departed system, so that Esther's self disappears
beneath mere moralistic rhetoric—"palace of ruined pride and overthrown power" (9:296). But there is more to her portrait than this;
there are other empathetic and analytical elements. The original
Tory storyteller's presence at least suggests other possible approaches
than the establishment view, even though his acknowledged anger,
tears, and expressive speech are not made an active element of the
narration.

The tale shows an accurate understanding of how Esther has been
shaped by a particular social and ideological order, her consciousness inextricably interdependent on social forms: " 'Your life has
been prolonged until the world has changed around you. You have
treasured up all that time has rendered worthless—the principles,
feelings, manners, modes of being and acting, which another generation has flung aside—and you are a symbol of the past' " (9:301). This
account cuts beneath any notion of permanent values transcending
a particular society. It presents an idea of the social order as one in
which the apparently superficial elements like clothes and manners
are signs of the underlying ideological structure. She is shown "amid
the wreck and ruin of the system to which she appertained" (9:299).
"System," a term used fairly frequently in this phase, indicates a sense
of a coherent structure, and "appertained" suggests a relationship to
that order which is neither organic, intimate, nor chosen.

There are echoes of "Peter Goldthwaite's Treasure" in the comment
that "[l]iving so continually in her own circle of ideas, and never
regulating her mind by a proper reference to present things, Esther

Dudley appears to have grown partially crazed" (9:298). But Peter is assimilable into the present system because the model of the human subject used in that tale is based on the democratic assumption that people can change when confronted with present society's "correct" views of reality. Esther on the other hand lives on unaffected by the new authorities, but dies when faced with the fact that the world that created and sustained her no longer exists—she has no separate existence from it. Her mind is not an instrument for the free choice of new "proper" principles. There is a sense here of an entire culture—interlocking networks of ideology and discourse, and structures of social interaction and belief. Its effects are not superficial. The inner world of the looking glass (the image of Esther's mind) contains only shadows from the society. The painting of Edward Randolph provides a parallel example in its depiction of the torturing effect of a "People's curse" (9:269). Portrayed here is the extreme social pressure overwhelming the mind.

The four tales' plots center on moments when the individual faces a sociopolitical system that is different from the one within which they were reared; even rulers cannot avoid this. However, the nature of this confrontation is mystified in these tales by a democratic ideology that has appropriated the concept of "nature" to justify its structures. It is a mystification made very obvious. The notion of "nature" along with that of "sympathy" clearly becomes politically biased in the mouth of the Doctor in "Lady Eleanore's Mantle," and this is confirmed by both Helwyse and Eleanore: " 'She seeks to place herself above the sympathies of our common nature, which envelopes all human souls. See, if that nature do not assert its claim over her in some mode that shall bring her level with the lowest' " (9:276). The tale then undermines this argument by showing how smallpox, though a natural leveler, makes everyone afraid of human contact, and beneath the nineteenth-century moral allegory of equality, community, and self-determination lies lack of choice, isolation, and death.

The reality here is that society assigns people subject positions, whether they are conscious of this or not, and whether they agree with the principles of the political state or not. Nineteenth-century

America believed that from early in the colonies' history, it was the "people" who brought about the Revolution.[23] But this is an invented past. The public illusion is now unmasked, even though the principle narrator of these tales is still caught up in it. Although the convergence of popular imagination and the democratic ideology seems to produce a powerful "truth," it is one that excludes the uncomfortable reality (at least as far as these tales are concerned) of how we are shaped by the culture in which we live. When Helwyse allows himself to be trampled by Lady Eleanore, the narrator may draw the "proper" conclusions about this ("never, surely, was there an apter emblem of aristocratic and hereditary pride, trampling on human sympathies and the kindred of nature" [276]), but in fact the crowds around the coach applaud her display of power over the weak and poor and without rank. The underlying truth is conformity to authority, both in the present and the past. Change becomes possible only because that culture also contains the seeds of opposition to itself.

"Edward Fane's Rosebud," within a moralizing framework, also explores the way identity seems ineluctably constructed by the social order in which a person finds herself. The tale's insights on the nature of subjectivity prove to be more interesting than its intended moral or the concluding paragraph's rather confused offer of a happy heaven in which people may have a second chance. The question asked is whether anything original survives in a person whose life has been so wholly defined by social circumstances and role. Rose appears to be entirely constructed by other people (including the narrator, who initially aimed to reconstruct the young Rose from highly stereotyped notions). While there may be some "identity of form and features" (9:463) between the young and the old Rose, there is not necessarily a continuous psychic identity to complement that physical self. While Dr. Heidegger restores the youth of his friends only to discover their basic personalities unchanged, "Edward Fane's Rosebud," published eight months later, begins with the similar desire to restore youth (note the same motifs of darkening the hair and the Fountain of Youth) only to find the physical and social mask virtually impenetrable and untransformable.

Rose is defined by her relationship to men, especially her husband, the effects of whose illness define the rest of her life and doom her to an extreme version of the "feminine" role of caregiver. Her husband even finds a focus for sexual jealousy in that role. Not just her material circumstances but her whole nature is altered by this position. Because of the role she had to play with her husband, she is psychically unable to live any other life. One circumscribed area has formed her, and in this alone is she at ease, totally defined by her nursing and provided with parodic forms of "home": "By that indissoluble bond she had gained a home in every sick-chamber, and nowhere else; there were her brethren and sisters; thither her husband summoned her" (9:469). Her "destiny" (9:469) was not a free choice, and its origins lie in class prejudice.

There is, however, a hint of more to Rose than this, and in this the tale moves tentatively beyond both the Revolutionary ideology of individual freedom and the socially determined definition of identity that had arisen for Hawthorne in relation to that ideology. It is as if, having pursued social determinism to its extreme, he found that something else still survived. Though the narrator fails to reconstruct the young Rosebud, he does succeed in describing the shape of her mental world. Private, erotically based feelings, which the social order has banned and silenced, survive even in this most dreary of subject positions (as we see when Rose sits by Fane's deathbed). In spite of the trivial predictability of the moralizing framework, the "deep lessons of thought and feeling" turn out to be less trite, less conventionally moralizing and more focused on the emotions than that phrase initially implied. True, that tabooed self is still defined in relation to a man of power within the community, yet what matters is the glimpse of the integrity of a psychic self in the face of what seems like wholesale societal takeover.

"The Shaker Bridal" has similar material—the loss of the emotional self because of an unloving man, and the assumption of a social role that precludes personal and sexual bonding. Patriarchy has repressed a rebellious emotional self (the "heart"), associated here with the feminine (though femininity is still conventionally defined in domestic and family terms). Here again sexual feelings remain unvoiced. Asked to declare her views to the Shaker elders, "Martha started, and moved her lips, as if she would have made a formal reply to this appeal. But, had she attempted it, perhaps the old recollections, the long-repressed feelings of childhood, youth, and womanhood, might have gushed from her heart, in words that it would have been profanation to utter there" (9:423). A degree of unsocialized individuality is thus preserved in some buried place in the person, even at the cost of her life.

It seems, then, that the "chameleon" writer of this phase of Hawthorne's work has resisted taking on totally the coloring of his social milieu. Within this conformist phase of Hawthorne's writing, something else is brewing. New questions are beginning to be raised. There is a fresh understanding of the ways in which the human subject is constructed within the social order, and this is an analysis based less on the plight of unique individuals as in *Provincial Tales* and more on a knowledge of the social fabric and the nature of political structures. There is also a residual sense that something escapes this social structuring of the subject. We see traces of this in Lady Eleanore, the adulteress in "Endicott and the Red Cross," and the young girl whose diseased grave devastates a community (surely a displaced image of Rose's totally repressed rage). These are hints of forces potentially destructive to that repressive and conventional order. There is also in these last tales a possible drift away from plot (the forte of *The Story Teller*) and from the conventional, morally deterministic framework of most of the later 1830s tales, and a move toward the foregrounding of emotional lives. "Old Esther Dudley" explicitly acknowledges this; "Edward Fane's Rosebud" demonstrates this as it grows to be more than the "exercise" it set out to be (9:463): "The tale itself is a mere sketch, with no involution of plot, nor any great interest of events, yet possessing . . . that pensive influence over the mind [9:291]). The North Adams Journals, too, are consistently interested in such material (for example, the account of the lawyer soap maker [8:90–93]).

Some of the source material of *The Scarlet Letter* lies here, most obviously in "Endicott and the Red Cross," but also in "Edward Fane's Rosebud" (the young nurse wife of the old husband, denied any other role), in Esther Dudley existing "in utter loneliness" with a "chill and withered heart (9:296) in a separate physical and mental world in the middle of a hostile or uncomprehending community (it seems no coincidence that her name foreshadows Hester Prynne's), and in Hawthorne's speculations in the North Adams journal (again a work unlike the majority of his writing at this time) about the husband seeking his prostitute wife: "I would have given considerable to witness his meeting with his wife. . . . It is worth thinking over and studying out" (8:59). This apparently sterile period of Hawthorne's writing has seeded some very different material.

Chapter 6

"A Truer . . . Representation of the Human Heart"

The Concord Period

1842–1845

▼ ''DEAR LOUZE,'' wrote Hawthorne from Concord to his sister the day after his wedding on July 9, 1842, "The execution took place yesterday. We made a christian end, and came straight to Paradise, where we abide at this present writing" (15:639). Yet the questions raised by his work in the 1830s about the domestic dream linger on, even though the domestic is now strikingly peripheral in his work at Concord, even in his earliest pieces. The 1842 notebook source for "The Old Apple-Dealer" concludes with, "I should like, if I could, to follow him [the apple-dealer] home, and see his domestic life" (8:226), but the actual sketch does not realize this suggestion. Another of his first Concord pieces, "The New Adam and Eve," rejects contemporary forms of the home but offers no new conception of housekeeping. "Fire-Worship" casts modern domestic life in the image of a dangerous caged being, and "Buds and Bird-Voices" fundamentally opposes Hawthorne's Concord experience (the sketch draws from his notebooks) and the world of the fiction written while living there.

The marginalization of the domestic—that important 1830s motif—continues in later Concord works. Scientific and artistic ambitions in both "The Birth-mark" and "The Artist of the Beautiful" (written in the first and second winters at Concord respectively) exclude their protagonists from the domestic hearth. "The Christmas Banquet," far from being a family occasion, is a desolate celebration of widespread misery by strangers, presided over by a man for whom all persons, including his now dead wife and scattered children, are only "shadows flickering on the wall" (10:304). In the later 1830s work marriages had similarly failed, but that had been more or less contained by an ideological framework of democracy, progress, and providence. The exploration of subjectivity had previously been rejected. Typically "Monsieur du Miroir" had refused to chase the "monsters" (10:170) within; *Mosses from an Old Manse* will, as we shall see, deliberately pursue them.[1]

"The Old Manse" sketch seems the sole celebrant of house and home at this time, though even it excludes mention of his wife: "how sweet was it to return within the system of human society, not as to a dungeon and a chain, but as to a stately edifice. . . . [The old Manse] had grown sacred, in connection with the artificial life against which we inveighed; it had been a home, for many years, in spite of all; it was my home, too" (10:25). But Hawthorne wrote this sketch in the spring of 1846 when his views had undergone a further change while working in the Salem Custom House, and he regarded many of his Concord-held ideas as the product of "but a distorted survey of the state and prospects of mankind" (10:30). His enormous difficulty writing the sketch (see letters—16:94, 105, 136, 152) possibly arose from such tensions between that Concord vision and his later milieu.

Discussion of the place of this change of view in Hawthorne's creative evolution must wait until the next chapter of this study. However, "The Old Manse" sketch does help to suggest what his preoccupations and attitudes had been at Concord. The boat journeys up the Assabeth introduce his imaginative investigations into the psyche that challenge the status quo—"rowing . . . against the current" (10:21) into the "midmost privacy and deepest heart of a wood" (10:22). In making the riverbank "at once our kitchen and banquetting-hall" (10:24), he relocates the domestic space and redefines its purpose as dedicated to intellectual freedom "from all custom and conventionalism, and fettering influences of man on man" (10:25). This wood represents the "interior regions of a poet's imagination" (10:22), and the river reflections symbolize creative and speculative meditations on the "inner world" (10:22).

"The Old Manse" sketch is therefore a later attempt to mediate between the Concord-inspired imperatives of experimentation (situated in opposition to the house) and all that home or village life has come to embody after he had left Concord. Hawthorne attempts to recuperate his experience of "home" by making a crucial distinction between honored "institutions that had grown out of the heart of mankind" (10:26) (for example his view of his own marriage), and "all the artifice and conventionalism of life," which he questions as "but an impalpable thinness upon its surface" (10:25). So Hawthorne's own experience, thus set apart from merely conventional notions of home and family, seems to resist being written up within those customary frames of meaning. With a new radicalism, Hawthorne instead extends his 1830s sense of power structures to identify his contemporary society as an "artificial system" to be questioned.

The journeys are ranked as equal to the house in importance: the scene of Hawthorne's exploratory conversations with Channing is a place "only less sacred in my remembrance than the hearth of a household-fire" (10:25). Although Hawthorne claims that, "now, being happy, I felt as if there were no question to be put" (10:31), questioning nonetheless turns out to be an essential characteristic of this phase of his work. "Be free! Be free!" (10:25) is not a call to revolutionary action, but rather a shift in mental perspective, a freedom to question social arrangements and imagine them other than they have been customarily assumed to be: "It is only through the medium of the imagination that we can loosen those iron fetters, which we call truth and reality, and make ourselves even partially sensible what prisoners we are" (10:247).[2]

As his letter to his sister had jokingly implied, his previous mode of existence ended with the move to Concord, and his writings reflect this. What he wrote in his notebook about Christianity in August 1842 is more generally applicable: "We certainly do need a new revelation—a new system—for there seems to be no life in the old one" (8:351–52). The catalysts for change were his marriage and an increasing openness to current Romantic ideas about human consciousness, the social order, and the role of art, which his new association with Sophia's family and friends brought him more directly into contact with. Although "The Old Manse" will come to see marriage and home more as a conserving force, the initial effect is radicalizing—a personal revolution. Having supposedly found his own "place," he simultaneously opens up in his fiction an investigation into displacement, initiating an exploration that articulates a feeling of pervasive mismatching of individual desire and social circumstance: "I want my place!—my own place!—my true place in the world!—my proper sphere!—my thing to do, which nature intended me to perform when she fashioned me thus awry, and which I have vainly sought, all my lifetime!" (10:323).

In stating that there is an "innate sense of something wrong" (10:207) in the way society conventionally categorizes its members, his work at Concord suggests a reaction against 1830s ideologically based notions of social reality and the subject, and hints at the existence of something (as yet unspecified) outside that ideology, something predating socialization, fashioned by "nature" as in the above quotation. Whereas the work of the later 1830s presents characters who, with few notable exceptions, were wholly constituted by the social order, the focus here will be on a self that is presupposed to antedate this construction by the social order, or at least part of a self that remains unrealized by that order. Hints of this could be seen in a couple of the late 1830s works, precipitated out of an extreme version of the socially constructed subject. "Reality" is now defined subjectively. The tales grope toward the idea of "sympathy," other people's recognition of this inner self.

It seems likely that Romantic notions of subjectivity helped drive out the remaining legacy of Common Sense formulations that he had explored, questioned, and modified over the years, leaving Hawthorne to begin to form conceptions of his own. It is not, however, a matter of Hawthorne simply adopting the Transcendentalist notions of his neighbors and wife; he remains the skeptical seeker, negotiating a view of the subject that tries to combine the Romantic notion of an independent psychic being with other more socially produced aspects of identity.3 In asserting that "[h]uman character in individual developments—human nature in the mass—may best be studied in its wishes" (10:331–32), his tales peel back the socioeconomic aspects of identity to reveal a world of desire and to show how this desire is repressed by "circumstance." "Circumstance" is used here as a term pointing to regulating forms of social determinism, the social conditions within which desire struggles for realization. Desire is represented, for example, by the imaginary "Book of Wishes," which is "probably truer, as a representation of the human heart, than is the living drama of action, as it evolves around us. There is more of good and more of evil in it; . . . in short, a more perplexing amalgamation of vice and virtue, than we witness in the outward world" (10:333). In "The Intelligence Office" both these elements, human desire and social organization, are recorded in the "great folio" (10:331). In this way the Concord tales will be seen to be interested both in an identity that resides in desire and is unrepresented socially, and to a lesser extent in the actual social conditions of the 1840s, the world of production and convention.

Hawthorne's work at Concord spans about two years from the autumn of 1842 to mid-November 1844 when he finished "Rappaccini's Daughter." Only three works lie outside this period: "The Virtuoso's Collection," published just before his marriage; "P's Correspondence," finished in mid-March 1845; and "The Old Manse," started in April 1845 but mostly written in March and April 1846. He planned two more new tales for the collected volume *Mosses from an Old Manse* (finally published in June 1846), but struggled instead with "The Old Manse" for more than a year: "I feel no physical vigor; and my inner man droops in sympathy" (16:105). He spent the second part of the winter of 1844–1845 editing his friend Horatio Bridge's *Journal of an African Cruiser*. Nonetheless, more than twenty works were produced in a short space of time, and the order of composition can be dated reasonably accurately since the need to support his family pressured him to publish as fast as possible. Given this intensity of composition and a clear chronology, it is important to look at this period as a whole and in sequence and to explore the interrelationships between the texts—something that has not been done before—as well as plotting how this phase constitutes a major shift in Hawthorne's development.4

▼

Something of this change of direction can be charted in his first Concord works. All explore aspects of art and the artist. The first, however, "The Virtuoso's Collection," based on an 1836/1837 notebook entry (LN [26]) and published just before Hawthorne's marriage, may appear merely a continuation of the worldview of the later 1830s but is in effect a self-critique. Its over-comfortable narrator champions the "ordinary course of Providence" (10:481) and looks to heaven for escape from "error or sorrow" (10:490). He has simplistic recourse to these former solutions when faced with the evasion of human suffering and debasement of art that the Virtuoso's collection represents—a cultural tradition reduced to trivia, arranged in absurd conjunctions that strip objects of meaning. Art has become a material product to be consumed for entertainment, a trompe l'oeil substituting for reality. Any investigation into human wrong is sabotaged by the tale itself, which invests most of its creative energy in describing the collection in facile and remorseless detail—a virtuoso performance indeed on Hawthorne's part.

"The Antique Ring" (published early in 1843 and probably, though not definitely, written at the Old Manse) reinforces the need to find some other way of responding to suffering, and more obviously rejects Hawthorne's previous work. Its reproduction of a typical 1830s romantic moral fable within a self-reflexive frame ridicules those earlier literary productions and their compliant creators, pious-minded audience, and supporting publishing and critical establishment. Its "Legend" (11:341), though supposedly suggested by a dream, gives no access into the subjective world of individual desire, but turns out to be merely the product of a mind full of highly conventional, clichéd motifs. Like "The Virtuoso's Collection," the tale cynically satisfies its market, but its use of symbol contrasts sharply with the later Concord "Allegories of the Heart," which will employ the fabulous to explore subjectivity and struggle against conventional meaning.

Of all his other Concord work, only the heavily didactic children's tale, "Little Daffydowndilly," and the simple lesson on the origins of Sunday Schools, "The Good Man's Miracle," resemble the "Antique Ring" use of conventional moral fable. Their bourgeois values of decency, benevolence, and useful employment, though typical of the later 1830s, are not characteristic of most of the Concord pieces. That kind of didactic fiction has now been consciously rejected.

"The Hall of Fantasy" (finished December 1842 and published February 1843) is the "Virtuoso's Collection" companion piece on the subject of art. Here the concern is to negotiate a new relationship between the "Actual" (10:173) and "Fantasy," that is, between existing social conditions and the mind's capacity to imagine the world other than it is. "The Virtuoso's Collection" had ridiculed an art that was mere commercial entertainment; "The Hall of Fantasy" debates new artistic possibilities and suggests that "fantasy" can have substance and relevance (though in the case of this particular tale, the piece's flimsy structuring image suggests the difficulties of such a medium).

As in "The Virtuoso's Collection," a dialogue ensues between the visitor and his guide around a fantastical spectacle. The visitor-narrator's view, so characteristic of Hawthorne's later 1830s work with its apparent acceptance of the status quo with a compensatory heaven thereafter, is finally opposed by a vision of both a universally shared desire for reform in present society and the capacity to imagine what this apparently inevitable reform might be.

The Hall represents not just art but also human consciousness. The building with its contents, such as the ever-changing fountain, is the tale's image for the mind's capacity to reach beyond given circumstance, not necessarily to imagine a wholly new world (though the Hall also includes this possibility) but to view present conditions in a different light. This is the meaning of "ideal." For some people (the social reformers) this would mean envisioning structural change in society; for others it would mean some spiritual discovery, "some great moral" (10:182). For everyone here art is public and not merely private. Art employs the hypothetical, the fantastical, and the imaginary as a means of exploring this social change, and instead of the artist being either an isolate or an establishment spokesman, there is a sense of participation in a communally shared effort to change things (the original version included a long list of real-life creative writers and reformers [10:635–39]).

These possibilities are further extended in "The Old Apple-Dealer." While the delineation of the grimly factual in "The Old Apple-Dealer" may at first appear in subject and approach the very opposite of the fantastical "Hall of Fantasy," both sketches emphasize the unquietness of contemporary experience. "The Hall of Fantasy" had stressed a dual need to look at reality both through the "pictured windows" (10:180) of the hypothesizing and fantastical imagination, and also in the "white sunshine" (10:179) of a factual, naturalistic presentation of present actualities. The two approaches are complementary, not opposed (as conventionally they would be).

Comparing "The Old Apple-Dealer" with its notebook source, it is clear that, like "The Hall of Fantasy," this sketch is concerned with art. The lengthy notebook entry (8:222–26) on the old man would have needed almost no revision to be publishable, but the published sketch chooses to foreground the artistic issues raised by the notebook's penultimate paragraph: "To confess the truth, it is not the easiest matter in the world, to define and individualize a character like this which we are now handling. The portrait must be so generally negative, that the most delicate pencil is likely to spoil it by introducing some too positive a tint" (10:444).

The difficulty lies in that blank outward appearance. There is no plot, dialogue, or action to build with, and the subject's expressive movements are "hardly perceptible" (10:443). The writer must work largely in negatives, describing him only in terms of what he is not; even language itself is too definite: "He is not desperate—that, though its etymology implies no more, would be too positive an expression—but merely devoid of hope" (10:440). This exercise in minimalism pushes certain general issues into sharper focus, for the old man is not unique but an extreme representative of what Hawthorne will come to see at this period as a vast class of subjects in whom exists a great gap between the psychic self and existence within the social order. These people run the risk of being both invisible to others and impossible to describe except in terms of that social order. Much of Hawthorne's 1830s work, so silent about subjectivity, exemplifies this problem. The old man's depths are "soundless" (10:446). The resultant lack of knowledge of what he desires (as opposed to what he does) makes it impossible to "define and individualize" his "character" (10:444), that is, to express fully his subjectivity. The old man lacks consciousness of himself for the same reason.

To some extent the old man must be defined economically, his misery ascribed at least partly to lack of money. The notebook version, speculating that "his inward nature is half-frozen by the chillness of his circumstances" (8:225), emphasizes social influences. However, by drawing attention to the scanty evidence of the man's inner life, the tale foregrounds a more inwardly focused malaise, an alienation from the modern world in which he hovers. Though Hawthorne calls this frozen quality a "moral" one (10:440), he is concerned primarily with psychological rather than ethical matters. "Moral" seems to refer to an emotional responsiveness.

What the author discovers, then, is that he cannot approach his subject objectively (placing him, as it were, in "white sunshine"). The narrator's primary act of detached observation rapidly leads back to the artist, and to guesswork, assumptions, imagination, interpretation, and projection—"solitary" thought (10:446) in the busy station. Indeed, he admits that from the start he is "unconsciously" (10:439) involved in the subject. Thus the man becomes a "citizen of my inner world" (10:439), a phrase that suggests an imaginative realignment of the writer with those who suffer—a community of sympathy that is different from the American republic and in which this "citizen" has rights and connections.

Undeniably, this endeavor has a patronizing, even arrogant element to it. The sketch is ultimately moralizing and sentimental, and it mystifies the effects of the economic order ("witchcraft" [10:446]). Nonetheless, the piece is important for Hawthorne's development at this stage: it understands that, though the exterior is blank, the "mind and heart" would be "a volume of deeper and more comprehensive import than all that the wisest mortals have given to the world" (10:446). His term, the "moral picturesque" (10:439), seems to express this need of images for the processes of the subjective identity within the contemporary world.

This new preeminence of the subjective world is confirmed by "The Bosom Serpent," written four months later. Here the inner life intrudes into the social order; it is not a secret as in the *Provincial Tales,* nor is it to be safely labeled as madness. Roderick Elliston, doomed to an acute self-consciousness that the apple-dealer lacked (10:273), is an assertive "new apostle" (10:278). He is a kind of artist whose work of art is himself. His skin resembles the marble out of which his sculptor friend made a statue of Envy, and his snakelike movements enact his symbol of his subjective state—the "shadow" of his "moral system" (10:271). In keeping with his role as the future artist of "The Christmas Banquet," his purpose is to make a complacent, blind, or evasive audience aware of the hidden world of desire that lies below everyday, socially constructed relationships. This inner turmoil is no longer seen as exceptional: "He grappled with the ugliest truth that he could lay his hand on, and compelled his adversary to do the same. Strange spectacle in human life, where it is the instinctive effort of one and all to hide those sad realities, and leave them undisturbed beneath a heap of superficial topics, which constitute the materials of intercourse between man and man!" (10:277–78).

The tale clearly posits two areas of existence—"the possession of a double nature, a life within a life" (10:274)—feelings unacknowledged and unincorporated into a traditionally constituted social order. This social order is rather reminiscent of Hawthorne's 1830s formulations, and is composed of "decent people" and "the received rules of decorum" (10:278), which the Concord work now clearly challenges. Elliston is not, we are told, a "madman," but he "had habitually violated many of the customs and prejudices of society" (10:280).

Elliston's key question is, " 'Do you know me . . . ?' " (10:269). Although it is the inner "snake" that gives him "individuality" (10:273), he has become unrecognizable within normal social intercourse as the unknown psychic self has come to dominate. Traditionally, the snake symbolizes metaphysical evil and human sin; here it is redefined as psychic impulses prior to entry into the social order. Because these are deemed to be unacceptable, they are often seen in terms of "fatal error, or hoarded sin, or unquiet conscience" (10:277)—a traditional religious interpretation that Elliston must find unsatisfactory given his response to Jeremy Taylor's *Ductor Dubitantium*. Instead, his "dark fantasy" (10:283) is subjectively real, yet merely fantasy in other people's eyes. What he requires is others' acknowledgment. Unlike in earlier phases of Hawthorne's work, looking at one's face in an ordinary mirror (10:280) has not helped. His fantasy disappears when he sees himself "reflected" in his wife's face (10:283) and being thus wholly recognized, his blocked feelings are released.5

This tale, however, still dodges certain problems. The wife, Rosina, is a convenient stereotype, a mere projection of the desire for all-knowing, unqualified love. Her own subjectivity goes unrepresented. Furthermore, as one of the "Allegories of the Heart" (10:268), the tale represents a return to the "heart," indeed to the troubled psychic lives of *Provincial Tales*, but the means chosen here to express subjectivity limit its analysis: the allegory of the snake is foregrounded to the point of absurdity. The tale lacks psychological substance, and in its moral stance it faces two ways in Hawthorne's career, backward to the pieties and simplicities of much of the 1830s work and forward to exploration, complexity, and irresolution. Elliston himself as artist, although gifted with intuitive insight and speaking wryly of his "homilies" (10:282), still preaches on stereotyped topics that are familiar from the writings of the previous decade: the politician, miser, drunkard, isolate, rival author, sinning young woman, all represented by "Virtuoso's Collection"–type elaborations.

Herkimer, the sculptor who, like the "Old Apple-Dealer" narrator, is a "compassionate" observer (10:269), is also more conventional, pronouncing the tale's concluding moral in terms simply of "morbidness" and "Egotism" (10:283)—two words associated earlier in the tale (10:273–74) with a lack of propriety in Elliston's social dealings. "Propriety," that is, not just conformity to a social norm but also appropriate and effective forms of communication, is an important issue in relation to the sympathetic imagination. Adam

Smith devotes Part I of *The Theory of Moral Sentiments* to a discussion of the problems to do with the need to express our feelings with what he calls "propriety"—that is, in a way that will allow others to respond with the sympathy we seek: "If, upon bringing the case home to our own breast, we find that the sentiments which it gives occasion to coincide and tally with our own, we necessarily approve of them, as proportioned and suitable to their objects; if otherwise, we necessarily disapprove of them, as extravagant and out of proportion."[6]

"The Birth-mark," published immediately before "The Bosom-Serpent," is closely related to these foregoing tales concerning art, the artist, and the "life within a life." The gorgeous apartments created by Aylmer are another Hall of Fantasy with quasi-magical recreations of actual life. However, far from Aylmer creating "new worlds for himself" (10:36), the reality is instead a hellish laboratory. Aylmer is a failed artist/reformer, whose attempts at photographic art merely reproduce his own obsessions and whose book is ultimately a record of his disasters.

Far from making Georgiana a "citizen of my inner world" like "The Old Apple-Dealer" narrator, Aylmer projects his own fears and desires onto her. His experiment parallels Elliston's monomania, its source clearly located in his unconscious from which it emerges, like Elliston's snake, into the world of relationships or community. The tale makes a strikingly clear diagnosis of this psychic world; this is no longer dismissed as in the 1830s as an antisocial delusion:

> The mind is in a sad note, when Sleep, the all-involving, cannot confine her spectres within the dim region of her sway, but suffers them to break forth, affrighting this actual life with secrets that perchance belong to a deeper one.... Truth often finds its way to the mind close-muffled in robes of sleep, and then speaks with uncompromising directness of matters in regard of which we practise an unconscious self-deception, during our waking moments. (10:40)

Aylmer cannot help his desires; the narrator finally suggests that they are the perceptions by a spiritual man of the inevitable clash between desire and "momentary circumstance" (10:56), "circumstance" having the meaning here of the limiting conditions of the physical body. But what makes Aylmer's actions a catastrophe is that, unlike Elliston who tries to make his desires known to others and to have them recognize similar desires in themselves, Aylmer insists on the material realization of his dreams, not merely their recognition. He wishes to control; "science" is always more important than love. He fails to recognize Georgiana as a subject in her own right. Instead, impossibly, she must be both "Nature" and the "Ideal," a sexual, potentially childbearing being who must also be physically flawless, self-denying, all-loving. Aylmer cannot cope with her as she actually is: he fears her body, he throws her picture in "corrosive acid," calls her a "prying woman" who would "throw the blight of that fatal birth-mark over my labours," and he cries "rapturously" over her self-abasement as if sexually aroused (10:45, 51, 41). As a follower of Sir Kenelm Digby, Aylmer can conceive only of a scientifically defined "sympathy" that is entirely materialistic, rather than something that involves communication, understanding, and relationship.[7]

"The Birth-mark" is a more substantial tale than "The Bosom-Serpent" partly because the allegorical image is an integral, debated element of a dramatically handled tale. The tale takes the symbol itself as its subject: Aylmer failed to treat the birthmark as a sufficient symbolic expression of a nonphysical part of the human subject. Further making for a more achieved tale, Georgiana is a more fully realized character, no mere "ideal of gentle womanhood" (10:270). She does submit her will and her body to her husband, but only out of a despairing desire for a love conditional on her physical perfection. This is a woman with an independent mind, firmly answering the distraught or raging Aylmer, but driven nearly to "madness" (10:41) and suicide. She takes the potion knowing that her death will be the price of her perfection. The tale gives her a subjectivity that Rosina does not have, though what we see of this is only the product of her relationship with Aylmer. Georgiana, looking in a mirror, is shown to be aware that she, too, has come to see herself only in terms of Aylmer's distorted perception of her. This makes her suicidal—denied her being by him, she has no life. Aylmer can see the birthmark's benign "individuality" (the word was used in

"The Bosom-Serpent" too) only as mere "circumstance" and not a part of her "identity." The mirror image is reinforced when, at the experiment's culmination, she wakes to look in a mirror that "her husband had arranged for that purpose" (10:55). A person created according to Aylmer's desire has taken her place, an inanimate art object.

Eschewing the formal moralism of the 1830s work, the tale avoids taking up a simple moral stance and retains its exploratory approach, working dramatically rather than relying on the mediation of a moralizing narrator or the foregrounding of allegorical image. For example, the various attempts to make sense of the two protagonists are located in the minds of Aylmer and Georgiana, and the narrator withholds judgment until the final paragraph. So it is Aylmer, not the narrator, who ponders at length on the mark as "the fatal flaw of humanity" (see 10:38–39), and the reverence and admiration expressed for Aylmer's ambition is clearly located in Georgiana's mind and not necessarily authorized by the narrator: for instance, the narrator frames reflections on the scientist's book with phrases indicating that these are Georgiana's thoughts (10:48–49), and her exultation at Aylmer's "love" is introduced sentence by sentence by the narrator with phrases showing these to be her (and not the narrator's) impassioned ideas (see 10:52).

Unlike some *Provincial Tales*, this story does finally at least attempt the "deeply impressive moral" (10:37) it promised at its start, although the "profounder wisdom" (10:56) that eluded Aylmer is not very much more securely in the narrator's grasp. The possibility is raised that married happiness might transcend this clash between desire and circumstance, but this idea, couched in only the final two convoluted sentences, is still shrouded in paradoxes and brief abstractions that will not be more fully explored until some of the work of the next Concord winter. Nonetheless the tale, working through drama and "fantastic" image, has sought a position that neither retreats to the safe but inadequate formulas of the 1830s, nor is trapped by self-serving or futile experimentation. It is the only tale of this kind written during Hawthorne's first winter, as he now moved into other forms of experimentation.

▼

The opening sentences of "The New Adam and Eve," a tale contemporary with "The Hall of Fantasy," "The Birth-mark," and "The
Bosom-Serpent," make very clear Hawthorne's new imaginative radicalism. This tale proposes a very different conception of the social
order from most of his work in the 1830s and engages with society
in a fresh way:

> We, who are born into the world's artificial system, can never ad-
> equately know how little in our present state and circumstances is
> natural, and how much is merely the interpolation of the perverted
> mind and heart of man. . . . It is only through the medium of the
> imagination that we can loosen those iron fetters, which we call truth
> and reality, and make ourselves even partially sensible what prisoners
> we are. (10:247)

As a "system" of institutions and discourses constructed by human
beings, society is inherently open to fundamental questioning; permanence and absoluteness is an ideologically fostered illusion. It can
now be sidestepped mentally. This is what is meant by the intellectual
freedom claimed by Hawthorne for his Concord explorations: "the
chief profit of those wild days [excursions with Ellery Channing] to
him and me, lay—not in any definite idea—nor in any angular or
rounded truth, which we dug out of the shapeless mass of problematical stuff—but in the freedom we thereby won from all custom and
conventionalism, and fettering influences of man on man" (10:25).
   Hawthorne now goes on to write other works that deliberately
attempt to imagine the world from outside established discourses.
True, he cannot break free intellectually from his culture entirely:
his notion of "nature" in "The New Adam and Eve" is obviously still
shaped by current ideological assumptions, especially in relation to
gender, and gender stereotypes permeate the tale. But he is at least
partially aware of this; he knows that he cannot ever have a wholly
innocent eye. Still, he claims the imaginative latitude to invent: "The
New Adam and Eve" begins, "let us conceive" (10:247), and nearly
all the succeeding sketches present themselves quite self-consciously

as explorative fantasies, a series of mental rearrangements of social reality using the fantastic and hypothetical as their literary means. The notebooks of this period also revel in the fabulous; see many of the entries after the old apple dealer entry in January 1842 until March 1845 (8:226–54). The sketches' investigations take place (as we shall presently explore in detail) from the point of view of individual subjectivity, for it is this psychic self that anarchically challenges the apparent inevitability and stability of social arrangements and most clearly perceives their inadequacies and lacunae. So "The Celestial Rail-road" is a "Dream" (10:206), and "The Intelligence Office" is a recording of the "desire of man's heart" (10:336); "Earth's Holocaust" is a "parable of my own brain" (10:404), and "The Christmas Banquet" is the "exhalation from a stagnant heart" (10:293).

This is an art that does not merely reproduce reality like the trompe l'oeil of "The Virtuoso's Collection," nor is it the carefully patterned moral fable of the later 1830s, nor does it foreground individual character and action. Instead, these tales and sketches use forms of allegory to attempt to clarify issues in a general and constructive way. The use of various different points of view, narrators, and interlocutors aims to destabilize meaning and to some extent creates the atmosphere of debate and question.

No one single conclusion emerges from these tales, and they have no program beyond that initial sense of the artificiality of more usual conceptions of reality and a preference for imaginative revisions and explorations rather than practical reformist action. There is, however, the effort to make sense of the world he describes, even while being aware that this is well nigh impossible: " 'I seek for Truth,' " explains one enquirer in "The Intelligence Office," but the officer replies that he " 'can lend no help for your researches. You must achieve the miracle for yourself' " (10:335).

Images of both riddles or wandering and of talismans and keys to meaning can be found in many of these Concord pieces. Adam in "The New Adam and Eve" is endowed with a "natural" (that is at least to say, a deep-rooted) desire for knowledge; though Eve turns her attention in on their relationship, he insists on exploring his world. The narrator, unlike his Adam, cannot avoid the bafflement of this "experiment of life" (10:265), or ignore the people who crowd these tales. It is only "The Old Manse" that retrospectively will suggest—satirically or perhaps nostalgically—that sleep might restore "the simple perception of what is right, and the single-hearted desire to achieve it" (10:30). However, in the universe of pain envisaged by the Concord tales, there can be no "simple" perceptions. At best, sorrow is a "talisman, admitting them into spiritual depths which no other spell can open" (10:297). Out of this "rich matter" come momentary flashes of illumination, such as made "The Christmas Banquet" guests feel, " 'Surely the riddle is on the point of being solved!' " (10:297). In "The Old Manse," Hawthorne imagined that every book "may contain the 'Open Sesame'—the spell to disclose treasures, hidden in some unsuspected cave of Truth" (10:21), but of course the location of that truth remained hidden. Instead, it is investigations that matter here: " 'I have here attempted,' " is Elliston's twice-repeated introduction to "The Christmas Banquet" (10:284).

The social world investigated by these six tales is not the generalized picture of rural or small-town life found in much of Hawthorne's writing throughout the 1830s. "The Old Apple-Dealer" had introduced new images of contemporary metropolitan existence, and this concern for actual social conditions—the "objects and circumstances that surround" these city dwellers (10:249)—continues, though in a less particularized, extensive way. The utopian vision of "The New Adam and Eve" provides only a perspective on this world, not an alternative to it. In much the same way that Hawthorne had in the Old Manse preferred newspapers to literature and philosophical texts as "bits of magic looking-glass" that had "a distinct purpose and meaning, at the time, and a kind of intelligible truth for all times" (10:20), so also is his attention drawn to issues of contemporary society in his own writing.

This world and its issues are not, however, explored in a realistic way. In surveying legal, commercial, political, religious, and academic institutions, and in exploring the consequences of social inequality and reform movements, Hawthorne seems most interested in analyzing his sense of society as a "system" (the term is much repeated), that is, a construction with a conventional sign system and a series of subject positions available within it for its members. It is an approach to the social order that is a radicalized extension of the way power structures were depicted in a few works of the later 1830s.

"The New Adam and Eve" and "The Procession of Life," both works of his first Concord winter, are particularly important for establishing this view, but nearly all of these six sketches stress the artificiality of society (the notion recurs several times), its human-made stratifications, categories, and distinctions, and its purely conventional nature: for example, to select but a few of many phrases, the tales speak of the "artificial system," "artificial badge," "conventional distinctions of society," the "exemplary system of outward duties," "earthly distinctions," "external conscience" (10:247, 208, 210, 214, 383, 284). "The Intelligence Office" term, "external conscience" (10:333–34), makes these ideas strikingly clear in the implied distinction between those moral codes of a society and a personal moral sense (perhaps an "internal conscience" to parallel the "external" one—a distinction unthinkable in much of his 1830s work). The term "circumstance," also often repeated, implies a world that is in some senses external to the individual, a matter of human creation and potentially alterable.

"The New Adam and Eve" and "The Procession of Life" are both early attempts to rearrange this world, but although these works have this fairly clear sense of society as a system, they produce vastly oversimplified alternatives and as such constitute a critique of such utopian designs. "The Procession of Life" is traditional and fairly naive in the categories that it substitutes for usual class ones (the sick, bereaved, and benevolent would turn up in a number of other Christian and humanist paradigms, though it is important that this sketch wishes to stress the psychological rather than the social). The insufficiencies and simplicities of the populist apocalyptic universe of "The New Adam and Eve" are recognized even within the tale itself.

However, in doing away with "the effect of circumstance and accident" (10:215), "The Procession of Life" is drawn to what the Concord tales call the "heart." Any attention paid to the largely public realm leads increasingly toward an attempted explication of human subjectivity within the social order. Late in the first Concord winter, "The Celestial Rail-road" showed that it was misleading to conceal the "heart," to "smooth it away," like the narrator's materialist guide on the train who not only appropriates the optimistic and individualistic rhetoric of transcendentalism but also averts his eyes from the suffering psychic self in a manner similar to much of the 1830s work. The true impulses of human desire are thus ignored or concealed as "freaks of imagination . . . mere delusions . . . waking dreams" (10:196). In consequence, the "devil" of repression and hypocrisy runs the railroad, and the reality of Mr. Smooth-it-away's efforts is shown to be self-deception, ignorance of others, failure, futility, and despair. "The Celestial Rail-road" becomes a metaphor for the unavoidability of effort and pain in the search for happiness and personal fulfillment. Tophet has indeed the "metaphorical existence" (10:194) that the guide had denied it. Gervayse Hastings in "The Christmas Banquet," who is a success in the conventional terms of the bourgeois world that lies beyond the banqueting room, is also cut off from an essential understanding of the half-concealed world of suffering and desire, though he has not chosen this as the Celestial Railroaders had done. People lose their three-dimensionality and are seen by him merely as flat shadows on the wall of social reality, not fully known and conscious that they are not known.

The three sketches written in the second winter in Concord, "The Christmas Banquet," "Earth's Holocaust," and "The Intelligence Office," are increasingly concerned with this subjective world. Unlike in the early 1830s, this is not observed from an external standpoint by a puzzled observer. Instead we have the reverse: the social world—what the tales call "merest external circumstances" (10:207)—is viewed from the perspective of unsatisfied desire, a subjective reality that is more important than "external circumstance," even when unrealized and unexpressed in the material world and thus "buried in a tomb of sluggish circumstances" (10:220).[8] Both "Earth's Holocaust" and "The Celestial Rail-road" ultimately suggest the power of desire to burst through social arrangements to demand attention. Those sketches also indicate the irrelevance or inefficacy of any reformist tinkering with social structures that do not incorporate a full understanding of the nature of that subjectivity. What is called "reality" is no longer the early 1830s idea of "characters and manners of familiar life," but comes to resemble more closely that of the *Provincial Tales*. It differs, however, from *Provincial Tales* in being less concerned with how the formative and regulating social mechanisms operate on the subject to create subjectivity. Instead, "desire" is set in opposition to that order, and is possibly prior to it (for example, the innate talents of various people in "The Procession of Life"). It is something discoverable as a lack and is characterized by society as insufficiency and hunger. Nonetheless, it is of interest that "Roger Malvin's Burial," that key text of the early *Provincial Tales* phase and dealing with the birth of subjectivity, was reprinted for the first time in August 1843, and subsequently published alongside Hawthorne's Concord work in *Mosses*.

The many figures who now people these sketches are not mere "freaks" as the 1830s would have seen them, but supposedly represent the majority of the population. They suffer from a self-consciousness that the new Adam and Eve conspicuously lack until confronted with the evidence of the modern world. Learning "the soul's incongruity with its circumstances" (10:266), even these Edenic figures would have painfully become mirror-gazers, self-conscious amid the detritus of contemporary America, but for the fact that, looking in the mirror that they have found, they focus instead on each other's images: "Each is satisfied to be, because the other exists likewise" (10:248). These sketches want to draw attention to what they now call the "real nature of individuals" (10:221): "Human character in its individual developments—human nature in the mass—may best be studied in its wishes" (10:331–32). "The Intelligence Office," the last written of these six, then goes on to define these "wishes" with some assurance in a way that will be very important for future developments in Hawthorne's work (indeed, the opening sentence suggests a future project):

> It would be an instructive employment for a student of mankind, perusing this volume carefully, and comparing its records with man's

perfected designs, as expressed in their deeds and daily life, to ascer-
tain how far the one accorded with the other. . . . Yet this volume is
probably truer, as a representation of the human heart, than is the
living drama of action, as it evolves around us. There is more of good
and more of evil in it; more redeeming points of the bad, and more
errors of the virtuous; higher up-soarings, and baser degradation
of the soul; in short, a more perplexing amalgamation of vice and
virtue, than we witness in the outward world. Decency, and external
conscience, often produce a far fairer outside, than is warranted by
the stains within. (10:333–34)

A crucial distinction is clearly being drawn between what is realized
and what is not realized in the social world, and greater significance
is attached to the more complex structures of the psychic self, largely
unrepresented in the social order.

This statement from "The Intelligence Office" also avoids casting
all this into clear-cut moral categories: the good and bad, the trivial
and serious, are all mixed together in this "heart," and while it
is offered as an intriguing idea that all people are, at the level of
desire, guilty of would-be wrongdoing ("The New Adam and Eve,"
"The Procession of Life," and "The Intelligence Office" all play with
this), it is only the untrustworthy devil-like figure with dark face
and red glowing eyes in "Earth's Holocaust" who would see this
psychic self simply as a "foul cavern" (10:403). "The Intelligence
Office" offers a less simple conception of the "heart." Human evil
is only one of an array of subjective elements, and it is an analysis
of this psychic structure that is foregrounded rather than the ethical
implications. It is in this emotional sense that Hawthorne uses the
word "moral" about these persons who "wanted . . . with an urgent
moral necessity" (10:323).

Hawthorne's present emphasis can be summed up in two often
repeated words in these tales—"place" and "reality." The characters'
demand for a "place" is an expression of the individual's inability
to realize her or his own supposedly innate drives. There is "a
great multitude" (10:219) in "The Procession of Life" (itself a sketch
attempting to place people in better categories), who "have lost, or
never found, their proper places in the world" (10:218), and "The

Intelligence Office" is confronted with one who, seeking his place, "evidently wanted, not in a physical or intellectual sense, but with an urgent moral necessity that is the hardest of all things to satisfy, since it knows not its own object" (10:323). This seeker cannot know exactly what he needs because these desires are invisible to others and therefore lack definition even to his eyes: " 'I want my place!—my own place!—my true place in the world!—my proper sphere!—my thing to do, which nature intended me to perform when she fashioned me thus awry' " (10:323). For "The Procession of Life," the "great mistake of life" (10:219) is defined in terms of a mismatching of temperament and social role. The resultant sense of being split brings a feeling of unreality: he "sighs to miss that fitness, the one invaluable touch, which makes all things true and real. So much achieved, yet how abortive his life!" (10:220). The idea of touch dates back to Hawthorne's engagement letters to Sophia: "Indeed, we are but shadows—we are not endowed with real life, and all that seems most real about us is but the thinnest substance of a dream—till the heart is touched. That touch creates us—then we begin to be—" (15:495). Here this notion is widened from romantic relationships to a more general relationship of the individual to the world in which she or he lives.

Gervayse Hastings in "The Christmas Banquet" is an extreme example. The disjunction between his outward life and his subjective experience is total, and so no contact is possible with others, for he can neither feel nor be felt. Hastings, an example of "moral monsters" (10:305)—and again the word has emotional as much as ethical connotations—is the reincarnation of the emotionally frozen old apple dealer, and though the tale's narrator admits the unlikelihood of such a person being thus conscious of his mode of being, Gervayse's sense of being haunted does suggest the ability of the repressed to assert itself at least vestigially. Yet it remains a "mystery" to him, shut off as he is from his psychic self; it is what he then defines as "the deep warm secret—the life within the life—which, whether manifested in joy or sorrow, is what gives substance to a world of shadows" (10:301). When, after years of hostility from his fellow guests, Hastings tries to explain himself, his account begins by focusing on both the failure of others to understand him and his great difficulty in expressing himself:

"You will not understand it," replied Gervayse Hastings, feebly, and with a singular inefficiency of pronunciation, and sometimes putting one word for another. "None have understood it—not even those who experience the like. It is a chillness—a want of earnestness—a feeling as if what should be my heart were a thing a vapour—a haunting perception of unreality! Thus, seeming to possess all that other men have—all that men aim at—I have really possessed nothing, neither joys nor griefs. All things—all persons . . . have been like shadows flickering on the wall. . . . Neither have I myself any real existence, but am a shadow like the rest!" (10:304–5)

The "life within a life" is no longer the snake of "The Bosom-Serpent" (which used the same phrase), but something vital to existence, whether happy or unhappy.

It is not possible from these works to deduce a single explanation for why this splitting should occur. Blame cannot simply be laid at this time either on a repressive society or on anarchic individual desire, though both these elements are present. "The Procession of Life," "The Christmas Banquet," and "The Intelligence Office" all focus on aspects of the paradigm. It is evidently a complex, two-way process.

There are no solutions, neither the destruction of society as Hawthorne's readers knew it, such as envisaged by "The New Adam and Eve," nor the ignoring of the problem as in "The Celestial Railroad." "Earth's Holocaust" also offers two unsatisfactory responses: a fatalistic vision of an endlessly repeated cycle of freshly created evil from the psychic realm, or an airy proposal to change human subjectivity without explaining how this could be possible—"Purify that inner sphere; and the many shapes of evil that haunt the outward, and which now seem almost our only realities, will turn to shadowy phantoms, and vanish of their own accord" (10:404). But none of these tales constitutes a final statement; all experiment with different emphases and positions. The dominant feeling common to them all is widespread human misery because of this disjunction between "the desire of man's heart" (10:336) and "circumstance."

▼

In a situation in which there is no convincing hope of structural change socially or reformation psychologically, Hawthorne's extended image of the heart, composed in the notebooks sometime between 1842 and 1844, nevertheless suggests a constructive imaginative response. The passage proposes an exploration of a subjective territory typical of Hawthorne's Concord work, adapting here Transcendentalist images into the new terms he has been evolving:

> The human Heart to allegorized as a cavern; at the entrance there is sunshine, and flowers growing about it. You step within, but a short distance, and begin to find yourself surrounded with a terrible gloom, and monsters of divers kinds; it seems like Hell itself. You are bewildered, and wander long without hope. At last a light strikes upon you. You press towards it yon [sic], and find yourself in a region that seems, in some sort, to reproduce the flowers and sunny beauty of the entrance, but all perfect. These are the depths of the heart, or of human nature, bright and peaceful; the gloom and terror may lie deep; but deeper still is this eternal beauty. (8:237)

This imaginative journey takes him to a utopian vision of an undivided subjectivity where consciousness and externalities at last coincide in uncompromised desire. It is also an image of "sympathy," that is to say a moment of contact, recognition, and response.

The full imaginative and social possibilities of sympathy begin now to emerge. This "sympathy" is not the defensive strategy of the later 1830s "chameleon" taking the color of his surroundings. "The Procession of Life" calls it "love"—a recognition of suffering leading to action. It is akin to that "reality of their mutual glance" (10:249), created by the only two untroubled figures in all those sketches, Adam and Eve.[9] It is also what Elliston, transformed from the sufferer of "The Bosom-Serpent" to the narrator of "The Christmas Banquet," calls the "demands that spirit makes upon spirit." Elliston's "former sad experience," in an echo of the notebook allegory of the heart, has gifted him " 'with some degree of insight into the gloomy mysteries of the human heart, through which I have wandered like one astray in a dark cavern' " (10:284). The artist's role, as defined now by Elliston, is "to seize hold" (10:284) of his protagonist, and Rosina, his audience for this tale, constructs the reader's role in terms of imaginative sympathy: " 'I have an idea of the character you endeavour to describe; but it is rather by dint of my own thought than your expression' " (10:305).

These possibilities of "sympathy" were most famously formulated by Adam Smith in what has been called a "landmark of mid-century writings on sympathy and imagination," the enormously influential *Theory of Moral Sentiments* of 1759. Smith's view of sympathy can be described as "that special power of the imagination which permits the self to escape its own confines, to identify with other people, to perceive things in a new way, and to develop an aesthetic appreciation of the world that coalesces both the subjective self and the objective other."[10] It was a theory that emerged in a world that had increasingly emphasized the separateness of the individual: if individual experience was essentially private, how then do we know what others feel? Smith answered, "By the imagination we place ourselves in his situation, we conceive ourselves enduring all the same torments, we enter as it were into his body, and become in some measure the same person with him, and thence form some idea of his sensations, and even feel something which, though weaker in degree, is not altogether unlike them."[11] Crucially, sympathy is seen to depend entirely on the imagination. It is this that gives one the ability to escape from one's own imprisoning subjectivity. It is the basis of all beliefs, moral action, and social bonding. Sympathy, as Smith defines it, is not a particular sentiment, but a correspondence between sentiments.

This Smithean notion of imaginative sympathy would seem to require a particular kind of fiction to elicit such a response. Hawthorne's recent productions—rather abstract and often structured as lists—had been useful in providing a better analysis of the human subject, but were not capable of handling its "endless diversity"

(10:332) and "perplexing amalgamation" of impulses (10:333), or of evoking a sympathetic response (the Intelligence Officer is "impassive to human sympathy" [10:328]). However, over two winters those six sketches had moved steadily away from portraying mere stereotypes to more individualized subjects and particular cases (some indeed are prototypes for characters in his later novels).[12] As "The Intelligence Office" observes, "Most of them, doubtless, had a history and meaning, if there were time to search it out and room to tell it" (10:327). Hawthorne now has to find "time" and "room," a spacious enough fictional form. "The Old Manse" reveals that Hawthorne did nurture such ambitions, hoping to write a novel "that should evolve some deep lesson, and should possess physical substance enough to stand alone" (10:5).

In relation to this, the dominant artistic issue was that of character creation, a problem first raised explicitly in "The Old Apple-Dealer" and continued in "The Christmas Banquet." It is something Hawthorne is still playing with in one of the last of his Concord pieces, "A Book of Autographs" of October 1844. Though a mere makeweight and stereotyped in historical attitudes, it is built around the possibility of reconstructing a person's character from their writing and employs the same distinction between "interior" (11:364) and "circumstances" (11:365). In "The Christmas Banquet," Elliston commented to his sculptor friend that his subject " 'is such a being as I could conceive you to carve out of marble . . . but still there lacks the last inestimable touch of a divine Creator' " (10:284). "Drowne's Wooden Image," composed three months later immediately after the last of the six sketches, uses a similar image to explore this new concern with the sympathetic imagination in the representation of the human subject. This tale, along with "The Artist of the Beautiful" and "A Select Party" (composed together over four months in 1844), form a sequence exploring aspects of art and the artist, and constitute an important reconsideration of the role of art after the previous year's intensive work defining the conflict between desire and circumstance in the human subject.[13]

In realistic recreation of another through self-transcendent love, Drowne represents Adam Smith's sympathetic imagination at work.

Sympathy is closely connected with mimesis; imaginative sympathy is related to the process of imitation that gives the spectator/reader a sense of the subject. Drowne makes a simulacrum of a human being; the contemporary naturalism of his style and the admiration of Copley (a historical figure known to readers for the realism of his portraits) stress verisimilitude as a key aesthetic quality.

Furthermore, "sensibility" (a word used of Drowne [10:319]) was also a term frequently used within Adam Smith's philosophy of sympathy to indicate what James Engell calls "the susceptibility or ability of the poet to identify with his creations in a feeling way and to express that feeling in passionate and natural language."[14] This "sensibility" is linked with that key Concord image of "touch"—Drowne's "magic touch" by which "intelligence and sensibility brightened through the features [of the statue]. . . . The face became alive" (10:312–13). This touch is not merely Drowne's tools carving the wood, but his emotional response to the woman model—"stretching forth his arms as if he would have embraced and drawn it [the statue] to his heart" (10:312). His art is not concerned with creating a person, but discovering what lies hidden in her: " 'The figure lies within that block of oak, and it is my business to find it' " (10:311). In this respect this tale rewrites "The Birth-mark." Although both protagonists are compared to Pygmalion, Drowne celebrates the woman as she is in every detail and recognizes that he cannot change or possess her. His art is thus given qualities that the narrators of both "The Old Apple-Dealer" and "The Christmas Banquet" would have needed to penetrate the psychological chill of their subjects: "that deep quality . . . which bestows life upon the lifeless, and warmth upon the cold" (10:309).

This quality is radicalizing. Though a product of private desire (his efforts have the quality of "dream" [10:319]), the statue enters the public realm (Drowne refuses to sell it privately abroad) and it is this artistic achievement, rather than his personal loss, that the tale stresses. This erotic representation of a woman has a powerful emotional effect on the whole town—a figure that arouses the antagonism of its moral spokesmen, and that the Puritans "would have thought it a pious deed to burn" (10:318). She is a forerunner of

Beatrice Rappaccini and of Hester Prynne, disrupter of New England culture. She is contrasted with Drowne's usual pieces, inflexible images made to preexisting stereotypical or allegorical designs, and emotionally as well as materially wooden. In view of Hawthorne's 1830s career, the choice for the artist is clear: moralistic or conventional generalizing tales are insufficient for his present purposes.

Owen Warland of "The Artist of the Beautiful," a "being of thought, imagination, and keenest sensibility" (10:466), exemplifies the same "imagination, sensibility, creative power, genius" (10:319) that "Drowne's Wooden Image" attributed to all, but his art is very different. This tale is an important step in establishing Hawthorne's need to move away now from the "Hall of Fantasy," the art of the fantastical that had been radicalizing but insufficient in other ways. In exploring different forms of artistic creativity, this tale asks questions about how art might relate to the structures of social and sexual roles in which his audience live.

Owen is a familiar Concord-period figure, another occupant of the Hall of Fantasy, another applicant at the Intelligence Office who, like the man seeking his "proper place," is "engaged in any task that seems assigned by Providence as our proper thing to do" (10:467), another artist-scientist searching for perfection, another radical monomaniac like Elliston, whom the conventional town calls mad but the tale claims for our attention: "How universally efficacious—how satisfactory, too, and soothing to the injured sensibility of narrowness and dullness—is this easy method of accounting for whatever lies beyond the world's most ordinary scope!" (10:462). Indeed, "The Hall of Fantasy" mentions "inventors of fantastic machines" putting daydreams into practice (10:177), and "The Intelligence Office" (finished only a month or two previously) asserts that "to create an insect, if nothing higher in the living scale—is a sort of wish that has often revelled in the breast of a man of science" (10:332).

So desire and the attempt to realize it ("the impulse to give external reality to his ideas" [10:458]) is again explored in this tale. Owen's ambitions have to be seen in the context of Hawthorne's previous year's work in defining the conflict of desire and circumstance. Over and over again the tale speaks of Owen's project in terms of desire:

Owen believes that it is "the absorbing dream of his imagination" (10:453), that in the butterfly's beauty is "represented the intellect, the imagination, the sensibility, the soul, of an Artist of the Beautiful!" (10:471), and that, if unable to work on it, "there will come vague and unsatisfied dreams" (10:452). Like Drowne, he secludes himself from interaction with society to realize these desires artistically, seeking "the sharp distinctness with which he was compelled to shape out his thoughts, during his nightly toil" (10:458)—images of compulsion and night that associate his project not with commonly accepted social forms, but with irrationality and the time of the unconscious. Again like Drowne, he succeeds; this time a Pygmalion literally bestows life on the manufactured object. Owen is an exceptional figure among the Concord characters: his desire is happily fulfilled.

But his fulfillment is predicated on separation from social processes. He has to be entirely self-validating, and his escape from dependence on others is clearly highly ambivalent. The tale polarizes the beautiful and the practical (unlike Drowne's ship's figurehead). A butterfly has limited significance for others even though "the mind could not have been more filled or satisfied" (10:470). Owen has found the talisman, but his audience does not know how to use it. It is the church clock, mended by Owen, that has a beneficial effect on a wide range of lives, and if he had instead found his desire in Annie, "he might have wrought the Beautiful into many a worthier type than he had toiled for" (10:464).[15]

We cannot, however, simply reject Owen. The tale is careful to offer both points of view, Owen's and, on the other hand, Annie's, her father's, and her husband's. Perspectives crisscross so that things look different depending on what they are set against. It is debatable whether any hierarchy of meaning is established within the tale. It proves impossible to mediate between the conflicting claims of human relationships on the one hand, and on the other "the better sphere that lies unseen around us" (10:466).

However, placed in the wider context of the other Concord tales, the lack of "sympathy," the "moral cold" of Owen's life, is a familiar evil to be avoided: "And what a help and strength would it be to him, in his lonely toil, if he could gain the sympathy of the only being whom he loved! To persons whose pursuits are insulated from the common business of life—who are either in advance of mankind, or apart from it—there often comes a sensation of moral cold, that makes the spirit shiver, as if it reached the frozen solitudes around the pole" (10:459). His life is entirely inward and painful: "a long space of intense thought, yearning effort, minute toil, and wasting anxiety, succeeded by an instant of solitary triumph" (10:468).

Owen Warland does not seem to be Hawthorne's alter ego: the main thrust of the Concord tales suggests that Hawthorne did not want himself to create the "Beautiful."[16] But the radicalism of both Drowne's and Owen's art is important to him: while Owen challenges Peter Hovenden, the epitome of the conventional, the eroticism of "Drowne's Wooden Image" is potentially far more disruptive than that mechanical insect. But this art must be relevant to life within society, and Drowne's artistry comes closer to what the preceding two winters' work had identified as needed.

This move away from the Hall of Fantasy into actual conditions of social living, is echoed in Hawthorne's letter of March 24, 1844, on his first child, born while he was working on "The Artist of the Beautiful."[17] It is notable that Hawthorne's thoughts on the baby lead seamlessly into a discussion of his art and its future development: "As for myself, who have been a trifler preposterously long, I find it necessary at last to come out of my cloud-region, and allow myself to be woven into the somber texture of humanity. There is no escaping it any longer. I have business on earth now, and must look about me for the means of doing it. It will never do for me to continue merely a writer of stories for the magazines—the most unprofitable business in the world" (16:23). For Owen, the baby was the opponent of his creation—admittedly not an innocent creature but one that Annie "with good reason" (474) admires more than the butterfly. For Hawthorne, art and his own child are bound up together, and his "business" is not only a matter of life aims but also involvement in the money-making structures of his society. The markedly lengthy meditation in "The Artist of the Beautiful" on the artist's fear of death (466–68) speaks of a similar importance attached to life on earth and the material realization of the "task . . .

assigned by Providence" (10:467), something that only Owen is able finally to transcend.

"A Select Party" that finishes off Hawthorne's work for the summer of 1844 confirms this trend. The tale, itself entirely and self-consciously a fantasy about the "realm of Nowhere" (10:73), is a humorous send-up of what "The Hall of Fantasy," in a similar setting, had treated more seriously earlier in the Concord period. The figure of Posterity instructs creative writers that "the surest, the only method, is, to live truly and wisely for your own age" (10:68). "P's Correspondence," finished nearly a year later in March 1845 and Hawthorne's final piece there, reduces the Hall of Fantasy to a mental asylum, a prison in which the protagonist's imagination takes over completely from fact, presenting a disturbing vision of the creative imagination colonized by a morally banal world. Seen from the full range of his Concord work, we can see that Hawthorne is drawn to the radical, desirous of social involvement yet fearful of the conventionalizing powers of that social order.

▼

"Rappaccini's Daughter," written in the third Concord winter, needs to be read as the culmination of this period's radical exploration of desire and circumstance. The scenario recalls the darkest of the *Provincial Tales*—an isolated individual's desperate, utterly bewildering experience, with a similar emphasis on perception, cognition, and dreamlike states. Hawthorne himself, when asked about how the as yet unfinished tale was to end and whether Beatrice was demon or angel, claimed "with some emotion" that he had "no idea."[18] Some earlier Concord works had included visitors or bystanders at events; now this spectator figure is a fully drawn character, and the reader, like Giovanni, from whose viewpoint most of the tale is told, is "out of his native sphere" (10:93), confronting apparently unintelligible events. However, buttressed by the psychological and social analysis of the previous two years, the tale does not collapse into confusion. The work, as we shall see, is not a consistent allegory or moral parable—something hardly to be expected given both the way the Concord work had been developing and the evidence of Hawthorne's explorative approach to its composition—but is a dramatically handled narrative with characters more fully delineated than usual in the Concord phase.[19]

The tale does, however, retain the Concord use of the fantastic. "The Artist of the Beautiful" had revealed the need for an art more immediately relevant to existence within the social order, but while Hawthorne remained at Concord, his concern was still with a radical exploration of the psychological consequences of the disjunction between psychic need and forms of social determination and positioning, and fantasy provided the best medium for this. The enclosed garden of desire may seem, in the Preface's words, to make "little or no reference either to time or space" (10:92), but the external power structures of science, economics, class, and gender relations are shown vitally to intrude and shape the garden and the young woman and man.

It is in the inner arena that these are worked out: "those shapeless half-ideas, which throng the dim region beyond the daylight of our perfect consciousness" (10:114). The tale is packed with references to kinds of mental activity and shades of emotion, and the tale's considerable use of color, sound, touch, and smell heighten this. Desire is projected into action and scene, as Rappaccini, Beatrice, and Giovanni all live out their differing inner dramas: thus, as Giovanni enters the garden, "impossibilities have come to pass, and dreams have condensed their misty substance into tangible realities" (10:109).

Rappaccini's poisonous garden is his way of expressing desire—primarily the desire for power and for knowledge in the pursuit of power. The tale is explicit on this: the flowers are not "of God's making, but the monstrous offspring of man's depraved fancy" (10:110). This psychological reading of the poison as the projection of desire (whether erotic, or for power or knowledge) is confirmed by its use as a metaphor for Giovanni's own turbulent thoughts; a "fierce and subtle poison" supposedly instilled by the young woman "into his system" (10:105) is revealed by Beatrice to have existed instead in Giovanni before he entered the garden: "'Oh, was there not, from the first, more poison in thy nature than in mine?'" (10:127).

Beatrice's problem is literally *man*-made. Firstly, her father's desire for power contaminates her, while giving a socially weak woman unprecedented but intolerable power over others. Secondly, Giovanni is unable to operate outside oppressive, conventional gender relations and patriarchal constructions of femininity. Baglioni, the other male, is engaged in this power struggle. As the garden shows, there is nothing natural about her situation: while she may as yet have no direct experience of the external world, the garden is actually an extreme form of the coercive forces lying outside.

The poison in Beatrice, therefore, is symbolic evidence of the split between inner and outer identities. The tale is also attacking the simplicities and certainties of certain modes of apprehending reality where appearance and meaning are supposedly neatly matched. The division is not simply between appearance and reality, since both are real; neither is the division between "heaven" and "earth," nor "spirit" and "flesh," two other overly neat ways of resolving the conundrum.[20] In desperation Beatrice attempts to claim for herself a more acceptable identity by making a distinction between what people see and what she herself says, and then privileging a "true" self that does not originate in the social order: " 'Forget whatever you may have fancied in regard to me. If true to the outward senses, still it may be false in its essence. But the words of Beatrice Rappaccini's lips are true from the depths of the heart outward.' " (10:112). But, though Giovanni may momentarily see "her transparent soul" (10:112), he cannot simply ignore her physically contaminating effect on him. Beatrice's external condition and her subjective sense of herself are inextricably mixed; Giovanni oversimplifies the situation in trying to see her in binary terms of either wholly "good" or "bad."

The "poison" makes Beatrice another in a long line of Concord figures who, like Gervayse Hastings, have no "place," are not loved, and are untouchable (a central image in the work of this period, here taken literally). Although her father may seem to gaze into "the inmost nature" (10:95) of his plants to see their true qualities, he "avoided their actual touch" (10:96). The face and the act of gazing into it represent a point of contact in other Concord tales, but Rappaccini's face could never, we are told, have expressed "much warmth of heart" (10:95): on meeting Giovanni in the street, his look shows "merely a speculative, not a human, interest in the young man" (10:107). The only "sympathy" (10:101) given to Beatrice is that of flowers reflecting her physical being, rather than that human act of recognition and response that "sympathy" has come to mean for Hawthorne at Concord.

Hawthorne now investigates the possibility of romantic love as the supreme example of "sympathy." Rosina who saved Elliston in "The Bosom-Serpent" had been simply an ideal figure, but in this new tale, written just five months after "Drowne's Wooden Image," Hawthorne for the first time explores an erotic relationship at length with two equally important and substantial characters. Until now the woman has appeared as an ideal or as an unobtainable figure or as one obscured by male desire.

For the New Adam and Eve, love was the "inner sphere which they inhabit together" (10:248), but though Rappaccini's garden is "the Eden of the present world" (10:96), this world is a fallen one. So while Giovanni and Beatrice do indeed together inhabit an "inner sphere," the "sympathy" it generates proves "fearful" (10:125).[21] His body becomes identical to hers in a destructive identification of self with other that is typical of the garden where plants nod in "sympathy" with each other and the pool reflects them (10:101). This is not the imaginative sympathy of a Drowne. Under the pressure of extraordinary tensions, problems begin to show that Hawthorne will not confront fully until The Scarlet Letter. It is the wrong kind of "sympathy" for two reasons. Firstly, Giovanni does not really offer the "free intercourse" of a brother (10:113). He oscillates wildly between uncontrollable sexual desire and a sterile narcissism (contrast his mirror-gazing with the mirror images of mutuality and recognition of self in "The New Adam and Eve" and "The Bosom-Serpent"). Secondly, Giovanni is so erotically obsessed by her physicality, which he separates from what he thinks of as her sweetness and simplicity of mind, that he is unable to love this divided being as a whole. He resists this duality by finally trying to transform Beatrice's body into one like his own (another example of harmful identification).

The resulting intersubjective tensions are described with all the revelatory complexity of feeling that "The Intelligence Office" had predicted: "Blessed are all simple emotions, be they dark or bright! It is the lurid intermixture of the two that produces the illuminating blaze of the infernal regions" (10:105). "The Christmas Banquet" had demonstrated the need for feeling, contact, expression, and relatedness, but hitherto passion had been held back or expressed in action or object as in the stoical or sublimated love of Georgiana, Owen, or Drowne. Passionate encounters in his earlier work are rare, brief, and often reported briefly and indirectly or lost in an inability to feel or say anything. Here passion builds up to the intense final encounter between Beatrice and Giovanni, which moves through a great range of emotions and positions. For the first time Hawthorne has simultaneously created scene, events, two substantial characters interacting, multiple point of view, and a sense of the complexity of circumstances that is crucial to his Concord thinking.

The complicated web of circumstances and compulsion thus woven contains moral questions of freedom and responsibility: in this medicinal garden what healing is possible? is Giovanni "wicked or only desperate" (10:122) in his savage response to Beatrice? and what choices does she have? Beatrice, who lied to protect Giovanni on their first encounter, has the impossible choice between continuing being able to kill other things or letting herself be killed by the antidote (and neither option is of her inventing). Her final attempt to transcend "circumstance" is only a Georgiana-like sacrifice of the woman to save the egocentric male. It is surely no solution, any more than is the narrator's over-simple suggestion that her physical state is merely "an earthly illusion" (10:122).

▼

Thus ends Hawthorne's work at Concord. It had been a period of considerable exploration; it had also identified certain formal requirements for subsequent fiction. However, dismissing the work as "these fitful sketches" (10:34) in his retrospective "The Old Manse," he subsequently decided that "[u]nless I could do better, I have done enough in this kind" (10:34). Nor had there been any "simple perception of what is right, and the single-hearted desire to achieve it" (10:30) (a pretty naive wish anyway), but only complexity without answers. Writing to his publisher, James T. Fields, in 1854 about a reprinting of *Mosses*, he admitted that, "upon my honor, I am not quite sure that I entirely comprehend my own meaning in some of these blasted allegories; but I remember that I always had a meaning, or at least thought I had." The apologetic preface to "Rappaccini's Daughter" acknowledges the "fancy and originality" of his work, but complains about his "inveterate love of allegory" (10:91).

This seems to indicate an uneasiness about the stylistic mode of his fiction, rather than about his subject matter. The image of the poisonous woman, though pushing the dilemmas of desire and circumstance into acute relation, ultimately obstructs the fictional examination of a human relationship. Hawthorne's letters in 1844–1846 also reveal a dissatisfaction with the short-story form: in January 1846 he declares while preparing *Mosses* for publication, "I never mean to write any more stories. . . . It is rather a sad idea— not that I am to write no more in this kind, but that I cannot better justify myself for having written at all. As the first essays and tentatives of a young author, they would be well enough—but it seems to me absurd to look upon them as conveying any claim to a settled literary reputation. I thank God, I have grace enough to be utterly dissatisfied with them" (16:139–40).

Remarks such as these imply a sense of artistic development. On first going to Concord, as Hawthorne recalls in "The Old Manse," he had "resolved at least to achieve a novel, that should evolve some deep lesson and should possess physical substance enough to stand alone" (10:5). From his stay at Concord he emerged with both a clearer, fuller conception of the human subject and, in "Rappaccini's Daughter," the first evidence of the possibility of a fiction that might have sufficient "substance" to express this. Four years later he would begin to write *The Scarlet Letter*, having written in his notebook during the winter of 1844–1845 (the winter of "Rappaccini's Daughter") the germ of its story: "The life of a woman, who, by the old colony law, was condemned always to wear the letter A . . . ." (8:254).

Chapter 7

"Being Serviceable to Mankind

in His Day and Generation"

The Salem Tales

1846–1849

▼ NEARLY ONE AND A HALF YEARS after completing his last substantial work, "Rappaccini's Daughter," Hawthorne entered the Custom House as Surveyor, and the gulf between Concord and Salem became acutely clear. "The Old Manse," postscript to his Concord works, shows the first signs of a shift in perspective, and "The Custom-House" confirms it. The narrator of each piece has entered foreign territory where, if he adopts their language, he knows his former views will look strange: "dreamy," "subtle," "fantastic," "fastidious," "poetic" (1:25) are the adjectives applied in "The Custom-House" to his Concord acquaintanceship, and the attack had been more overt in "The Old Manse."

Both "The Old Manse" and "The Custom-House," two complementary pieces introducing and concluding this new phase of his career, are concerned with understanding the relationship between the Concord-inspired artist and the Salem world to which he has returned—this is the portrait of the artist as Surveyor. At Concord, "Drowne's Wooden Image" and "The Artist of the Beautiful" had brought Hawthorne to a preferred idea of the artist as one who interacts with his community and whose creations have human significance to their audience. In Owen Warland he had seen the perils of an artist separated from social processes, and in the disruptive eroticism of Drowne's statue he also recognized the potentially troubled relationship of an artist to the conservative community he wished to be involved with but in relation to which he had adopted a radically questioning stance.

Now he must live this dilemma, and it is not surprising that we find the "Old Manse" narrator defending himself against an imaginary attack by his readers (10:30). Seen from the coercive perspective of Salem, his previous writings, deeply engaged though they were in the crucial tensions between individual desire and social circumstances, now seem "fitful sketches, with so little of external life about them" (10:34). The "Old Manse" image of the author as a "writer of idle stories" (10:4), so unlike the previous clerical inhabitants, presages that "Custom-House" characterization of the narrator by his imagined Puritan forebears: "A writer of story-books! What kind of a business in life,—what mode of glorifying God, or being serviceable to mankind in his day and generation—may that be?" (1:10). Although the Concord tales had in fact been deeply preoccupied with the position of the human subject within contemporary society, what strikes the narrator of "The Old Manse" is the remoteness of the milieu in which these tales were composed from the Salem world he is now located in, what the sketch variously calls the "material world," the "artificial life," "a morbid activity" (10:3, 25, 29).

Hawthorne now finds himself in the world of "custom" in its several meanings: the world of commerce and money, the state and its citizens' obligations, and notions of ordinary daily living and values that are commonly accepted. He finds the denizens of the Salem Custom House "individuals unlike himself" (1:24). They are also different from the figures peopling *Mosses:* cozily adjusted to a corrupt patronage system (in which Hawthorne failed to retain a place), they have no inner life at all, and as a result resist the efforts of the sympathetic imagination pioneered while at Concord. This is a world, "The Custom-House" reveals, inimical to imaginative writing. "[T]he materiality of this daily life pressing so intrusively upon me" (1:37) made writing very difficult for Hawthorne until he was dismissed from his post in June 1849.

Initially, but only briefly, Hawthorne seems to have half-capitulated to Salem, the embarrassed radical mouthing conservative assumptions, decrying past achievements, resolving to write no more tales, completing "The Old Manse" by writing it "as impersonally as I could" (16:152), and doggedly resolving to learn from the unpromising Custom House company he has landed in. "The Old Manse" is stitched together from a heterogeneous collection of matter culled from his Concord notebooks and half-internalized views of that conservative social order with which he now cohabits. Differing voices compete. It is important to detach the sketch from its customary relationship with *Mosses* to see it for what it is, a work strung out between opposing worlds, the narrator precariously and uncomfortably straddling the two.

But this ambivalence is momentary and strategic; Hawthorne goes on to find his bearings. In the rest of the writing Hawthorne did at Salem, we shall see that Concord was not abandoned. His work does not undergo another huge change of direction, formally or in vision. This is not another swing of the pendulum back to the material and attitudes of the 1830s to take up in a chameleon way the attitudes of the Custom House, nor is he merely patching over a rift opening in his Concord conclusions. What we get here is a shift in emphasis rather than any change in values. The artist investigates the social and artistic consequences of his Concord vision. His artistic radicalism remains intact; all his Salem pieces in some way challenge conventional habits of mind, feeling, or reading.[1]

As a result his final Salem piece, "The Custom-House," shows fewer unresolved tensions than "The Old Manse," though the narrative voice still ducks defensively at times. This was written in 1849–1850 after Hawthorne had composed the four Salem tales, been dismissed from his post as Surveyor, and composed most of *The Scarlet Letter* (the final three chapters being sent to his publisher after the submission of the bulk of the manuscript with its accompanying "Custom-House" sketch). Its tone has the unabashed confidence (unparalleled in Hawthorne's work) of a man who has achieved his prime literary ambition (indeed in the March 1850 "Preface" to the second edition he refuses to alter the sketch in spite of the furor it has evoked [1:1–2]). By late 1849 he feels free largely to reject any self-compromising relationship with Salem.

However, it is not surprising that the return to Salem initially produced very little writing. From October 1845 until May 1848 there are only a handful of pages in his notebooks. Six brief, mostly unexceptional reviews for the *Salem Advertiser* span March 1846 to May 1848.[2] The winter of 1845–1846, from early October until mid-April, was spent fruitlessly trying to write an introductory piece for the projected *Mosses* collection, first mooted in April 1845 (see letter of April 7, 1845 [16:86]) and finally published in June 1846. As he tells his publisher in December 1845, "I write continually—but am conscious, even at the moment, that I am not writing the true thing. . . . Do not think me wilfully idle; for it is not so" (16:136). Two letters of this period, of January 24 and April 15, 1846, state that he has decided to write no more stories (16:139) and that he will "try histories, biographies, and all such stuff" (16:153). But by October he admits that he has still done nothing since taking office (16:188), and his wife reveals in late December of the same year (16:193) and again in mid-September 1847 that he has written nothing: he had, she says, "now lived in the nursery for a year without a chance for one hour's uninterrupted musing, and without his desk being once opened!" (16:213n). The move to a larger house, however, in September 1847 promised change: "I am trying to resume my pen; but the influences of my situation and customary associates are so anti-literary, that I know not whether I shall succeed. Whenever I sit alone, or walk alone, I find myself dreaming about stories, as of old; but these forenoons in the Custom House undo all that the afternoons and evenings have done."[3]

Hawthorne did go on to write four more stories before *The Scarlet Letter*. ("Feathertop," his one last remaining tale, was written shortly before leaving Lenox in 1851.)[4] Hawthorne knew by March 1849 about the campaign to oust him from office and this may have spurred him on to write (see letter of March 5, 1849 [16:263–64]). The precise order in which the four tales were composed is not known, and it is possible that Hawthorne worked on other material that he subsequently destroyed: for example, we do not know what Hawthorne was writing during the winter of 1847–1848 from September onward. We know only that he finished "Ethan Brand" in early December

1848. Hawthorne describes the completion of "Ethan Brand" (which may or may not be the remnant of a failed novel-length fiction) both in terms of a "spell" being "broken" (implying some previous writing block) and as a tremendous struggle: "At last, by main strength, I have wrenched and torn an idea out of my miserable brain" (16:251). We know from a letter, March 8–9, 1849, from Sophia Hawthorne to her mother that her sister Elizabeth Peabody hoped for a piece for her *Aesthetic Papers:* "With regard to the article, my husband began another—rather went on with another, after the first went to New York; & finally it grew so very long that he said it would make a little book. So he had to put that aside & begin another. This has also grown altogether too long for E.'s book, so now he must prepare another from some of his journals" (11:382). We do not know, however, whether "Main-street," given to Elizabeth Peabody for publication in May 1849, was one of those pieces, or what these others were.[5]

The dates of composition for "The Snow-Image" and "The Great Stone Face" have been disputed, but these were in all probability written sometime in 1849 and indeed may be part of that work done in the early months of 1849. Notebook evidence suggests that "The Snow-Image" was definitely composed by September 1849 and could well belong to the spring of 1849, though it probably was not completed then since Elizabeth was given the lengthy "Main-street."[6] Sophia Hawthorne also provides evidence that "The Great Stone Face" was written by early September 1849.[7] Hawthorne lost his post in June 1849, and although his son believes that he began *The Scarlet Letter* the day after his dismissal (1:xix), doubts are cast on this by the editors of the *Centenary Edition,* given Hawthorne's mother's illness and deeply disturbing death at the end of July, his customary inability to write during the summer months, and evidence of plans in early August to write not a novel but a "school book—or, at any rate, a book for the young" (16:293). But the account in "The Custom-House" and the admittedly late evidence of Hawthorne's letter to Samuel Cleveland in January 1863 suggest both that the idea for this novel had been on his mind for "as much as a year before," and that he wrote some shorter pieces before settling to the novel (1:34 and 43).[8] Possibly this writing took the form of revising or completing work begun earlier in the year. Given the impossibility of dating exactly the order in which these tales were composed, this present study treats them as contemporary with one another.

All in all, it was a checkered period of composition; what was achieved prior to *The Scarlet Letter* and "The Custom-House" was written with difficulty and hesitancy. But the work done at Salem is a necessary stage in Hawthorne's development, consolidating his Concord discoveries and exploring their social consequences. It is in this way that Hawthorne sees himself participating more fully in the public realm. When "The Custom-House" speaks of his difficulties of writing *The Scarlet Letter* while employed at Salem, the narrator observes, "The wiser effort would have been, to diffuse thought and imagination through the opaque substance of to-day" (1:37). It has generally been assumed that Hawthorne failed to pursue that option. It appears, however, that the four Salem tales, each carefully located either within his Salem world or a New England village, were indeed his attempt at this project.

▼

The tales written in Salem, unlike the Concord group, do not constitute a concerted enterprise. Although their concerns overlap with one another, each takes on new material in different ways. "Ethan Brand," the first published (though not necessarily the first written) at Salem, is the tale that stands closest to the Concord tales, yet in its important differences it signals a new phase in Hawthorne's development, counterbalancing a too exclusive and dangerously powerful preoccupation with subjectivity as an artistic subject with a brief attempt at a naturalistic portrait of a social community.

Superficially, Brand seems another scientific investigator like Rappaccini or Aylmer, whose desires are projected onto others' lives with terrible effect. The kiln that occupies center stage and the marble heart both suggest that this is another "Allegory of the Heart": "he had thrown his dark thoughts into the intense glow of its furnace, and melted them, as it were, into the one thought that took possession of his life" (II:84). Brand's night meditation "deep within his mind" (II:98) continues the *Mosses* exploration of subjectivity. The notion of "sympathy" is also present here, though the insight it affords into the "chambers or the dungeons of our common nature" (II:99) becomes instead a tool to manipulate other people even more powerfully than had Rappaccini's unsympathetically probing gaze.

Yet "Ethan Brand" does not proceed like a Concord tale. The world of desire is not explored except for Brand's final vigil, nor does the tale recount its protagonist's life story except in brief summary. It is as if Brand's story had already been fully told in the previous detailed accounts of an Aylmer, Owen, or Rappaccini, and this tale is indeed the concluding chapter that it purports to be of a longer romance. The teasing hints of untold incidents do not persuade one that the rest of the novel is necessary to its final understanding of its protagonist. The reason for this is also that his quest is pointless. Whereas Rappaccini converted his external environment into an image of his own mind, Brand's life is one of ultimate introversion, the goal of his search is within himself—diving into the kiln is literally self-absorption. The story thus short-circuits itself: the dog chasing its tail mirrors the structure of Brand's life story.

Brand's fate suggests the need for Hawthorne to move in a fresh direction. Hawthorne cannot be equated with Brand, but some aspects of his artistic project at Concord are clearly paralleled by Brand's activities. By pursuing those to their alarming conclusion, the writer is then pointed toward other different possibilities.9 Brand is an investigator of the psyche, "opening the chambers or the dungeons of our common nature by the key of holy sympathy, which gave him a right to share in all its secrets" (II:99). His initiating impulse was fueled by "love and sympathy for mankind" (II:98). But whereas Hawthorne's explorations lead him to Drowne as representative of the artist's "sympathy," Brand's investigations shift the meaning of "sympathy" away from aspirations toward benevolent action founded on felt understanding and toward an alarming capacity to manipulate others and their will to action.

Hawthorne's Concord work avoided Brand's uncaring intellectual detachment. To use the terms he works out in this present tale, the "heart" was not separate from the "intellect" in *Mosses*—the capacity for a sympathetic response to the individual based on "love" mostly combines with the ability to investigate issues on a more general level. But this tale does evince a certain wariness about possible directions artistically and personally that the exclusive exploration of subjectivity may take.

What was needed as a counterbalance was a fuller representation of public reality, in this case the village community. "External life," as "The Old Manse" had argued, had been missing from *Mosses*. Concord work, in reviewing the clash between individual subjectivity and the subject's positioning within the social order, had focused mainly on the psychological consequences (except where the world of desire attempted to colonize the material world as in "The Birth-mark" and "Rappaccini's Daughter," or more benignly gave form to its dreams in "The Artist of the Beautiful" and "Drowne's Wooden Image"). Arguably, too, "Rappaccini's Daughter" had difficulty in pursuing its complexities partly because its symbolic elements seemed too disengaged from the realm of material fact to deal adequately with the problems presented. Now there seems to be an artistic effort to represent that social world more fully and distinctly, and not only from the introverted protagonist's perspective. Thus the "petty and wearisome incidents, and ordinary characters," the "materiality of this daily life," the "opaque substance of to-day," the "dull and commonplace," which are all identified by "The Custom-House" (1:37), are brought into conjunction with that Concord-imagined world, not to replace it but to complement it. The kiln is now placed in its wider social setting; realism is laid side by side with symbolism.

Much of the tale's setting, inhabitants, and objects (the limekiln; hills; cloudscape; Esther's father; Joe; the soap boiler; the diorama) are in fact drawn directly from the North Adams notebook of 1838 (8:79–151), and hence written during the last period when Hawthorne's writing foregrounded the social world. The sustained and dedicated attention paid in that notebook to his social environment seemed the results of efforts by an acutely miserable Hawthorne (at that time deeply unhappy over his love for Mary Silsbee[10]) to suppress his unvoiced private pain. The material was not used in any of his published works of the time. Released by the Concord years' exploration of frustrated desire, he is now able to return to it. These sympathetic North Adams portraits, created in a place where Hawthorne felt, as at Concord, "independent, and untroubled by the forms and restrictions of society" (8:34), can be now incorporated into his published writing.

The picture of the community is achieved in several ways: by describing its group activities (meeting Brand, viewing the diorama), through certain key images (the stagecoach horn, the church steeples), and through individual characters, some of which are quite carefully particularized rather than typecast (arguably, this applies even to the stage agent, a "specimen of the genus" [II:91] but endowed with individualizing detail). The doctor and the former lawyer both fit well into his Concord vision of the human subject; each is ruined by some disjunction between individual subjectivity and existence within the social order. However, their continued social engagement—an engagement employing those very qualities lacking within established social structures—makes these characters' lives and portraits different from those so lacking a "place" in the *Mosses* sketches. The doctor is "wild, ruined, and desperate," but with "such wonderful skill, such native gifts of healing, beyond any which medical science could impart, that society caught hold of him, and would not let him sink out of its reach" (II:92). This social group is not offered as a simple positive; they are after all the haunters of the barroom, a rough crowd rushing like a mob to see Brand, with limited imaginations and experience and with "vulgar modes of thought and feeling" (II:93). Bartram in particular demonstrates an insensitivity that must qualify the closing scene's impression of peace and harmony.

Nonetheless, "brotherhood" is a word used repeatedly in various forms in this tale (II:90, 98, 99, 100, 101), and it is reinforced by both the new image of a chain ("He had lost his hold of the magnetic chain of humanity" [II:99]) and by more positive versions of the recurrent circle/sphere image (not the self-destructive circles of Brand's obsession): the village "completely shut in by hills" that looks "as if it had rested peacefully in the hollow of the great hand of Providence" (11:101). These are directly opposed to the world of self-imposed loneliness in which Brand, stranger at his own fireside, exists. However, given the brevity of the passages of detailed portraiture and interaction, this notion of the "brotherhood with man" (11:90) remains somewhat formulaic. The short story may be an unsuitable form for exploring it, and at present Hawthorne's interest remains at a general level.

Nonetheless, this tale begins to define some of Hawthorne's more positive social hopes after the more psychologically oriented investigations in the Concord work. Hawthorne begins the moral placing of the psychological studies of *Mosses*. There the word "moral" had elided the idea of an ethical good into the emotional responsiveness of "sympathy," but somehow he had to make sense of the unalleviated vision of indubitable wrong and profound suffering left by "Rappaccini's Daughter." He takes up the idea of the Unpardonable Sin, first noted in his notebooks in the winter and spring of 1844–1845 around the time of the composition of "Rappaccini's Daughter" (8:251). Given that his fundamental vision of desire and circumstance offered a model of humanity not in terms of innate corruption but as a tragedy of misplaced, unexpressed, conflicting needs within an inadequate world, Hawthorne faces the question of how he is to define "evil" out of this welter of competing claims. Brand's is instead an amoral curiosity that has lost its sense of what may be right or wrong.

In spite of fleeting gestures toward a heavenly future, Hawthorne's theology of the Unpardonable Sin remains basically humanistic in its emphasis. Crude superstitions coexist with a basic materialism (Bartram's belief that Brand converses with Satan in the kiln), and these are rejected in favor of a more finely imagined picture of an emotional hell. Brand does not need the devil to explain his actions. Hawthorne's notebook defined the Unpardonable Sin as a "want of love and reverence for the Human Soul" (8:251), an idea that springs directly out of the understanding of the human subject afforded by his Concord work. It is a vital step on Hawthorne's part toward evolving an ethics that is responsive to his increasingly complex sense of the individual's experience within the social order and that is not simply adopted from preexisting moralities. There are also hints that the good needs to be located within the social order, and evil is the product of the suppression or neglect of the "heart" (that is to say, a loving responsiveness).[11] The tale raises the question of what kind of action should follow "sympathy," of how a socially efficacious good can be achieved.

None of this, however, is strongly developed in this tale. Only one small boy demonstrates an innate sensitivity (an "intuition") to Brand, and his "tender spirit" (11:98) is shown to be threatened by the need to grow up into a rougher world. The dawn scene, unparalleled in Hawthorne's previous writing, brings together the human world and Nature in a harmonious relationship that is both greater than its constituent parts and still full of individuality, but the description is somewhat fanciful in the context of the realistic parts of the tale, its anthropomorphism a little obtrusive and its statements heavily qualified. It is also difficult to relate this to Brand's pain and the villagers' wrongs. Not only are the villagers imaginatively insensitive to him but also his sin is unpardonable precisely because it seals him off from everyone else. The tale is important in its reaching toward definitions of both evil and good, but these remain as yet undeveloped. The short story, as Hawthorne is now handling it, is showing clear signs of being formally unsatisfactory for his enlarged artistic project.

▼

"The Old Manse," in reaction to what Hawthorne saw as contemporary social and intellectual restlessness, articulated a need to restore "the simple perception of what is right, and the single-hearted desire to achieve it" (10:30). Brand too much resembles the Concord searchers criticized by that sketch to be deemed able to achieve this, but two other Salem stories, "The Snow-Image" and "The Great Stone Face," explore what happens when the writer attempts to imagine the operation of such "simple" moral insight and benevolent action within ordinary daily life. Unlike *Mosses,* these two works do not focus on individually expressed conflicts between desire and circumstance. Instead, the tales concern themselves with the tension between a personal vision of benevolence and the attempt to act upon this within society. This tension still relates to the common *Mosses* conflicts (*Mosses* contains several examples of the unsuccessful attempts of reformers and such like to act upon their beliefs and perform what they regard as socially useful deeds), but here the focus is on working out the tension in the world of "actual circumstance."

In these tales, Hawthorne imagines the "simple perception of what is right" being actually achieved, and discovers that he can only achieve this through fantasy. Those who succeed are "simple" people—the word recurs several times in relation to the protagonist of "The Great Stone Face," and the children in "The Snow-Image" have a similar undivided subjectivity and apparently unproblematic insight into reality. In both tales the mother encourages the children's faith, listening "with her heart" (II:II). The qualities of Bartram's little Joe are here developed. In the tracing of Ernest's lifelong self-development watching the mountain we are given a story that parallels but also counters Brand's evolution from uneducated laborer to philosopher as he watched his kiln.

But it is not clear how these people have escaped the hitherto inevitable consequences of entering the social order—the splitting of the self, the suppression of desire, and the creation of a troubled unconscious. The closeness to the mother possibly suggests an imagined retention of a supposed pre-oedipal unity of being. These characters fairly successfully oppose the patriarchal authority figures of their family or culture. The qualities that these stories promulgate emanate from what is presented as opposed to the social order: the natural world, and by implication some transcendental power (both tales, but particularly "The Great Stone Face," refer to angels [II:43 and 20]). Both tales take place out of doors, in relation to but still separate from the domestic. The Custom House habitués, shut indoors, achieve nothing in their working life to match Ernest.

Hawthorne has not returned to the moralism of the later 1830s phase that located its source of good in social structures.

Both tales imagine stories that explicitly counteract the darker images or sustain the positive images of recent works. Whereas Concord had left us with Rappaccini's unnatural garden where Beatrice from childhood had only a poisonous plant as her "sister," here the children play with a "snow-sister" (II:II) in a town garden transformed by snow "just fallen from heaven" (II:9). "The Great Stone Face" returns to the landscape of "Ethan Brand" to try to establish positives within a setting where images of hope had previously been considerably qualified. In a literal replay of "Drowne's Wooden Image," the snow image comes alive through love; Ernest responds to the stone face, much as Elliston had to Rosina's.

"Ethan Brand" had contained only passing suggestions of "sympathy" and "brotherhood" in the community. These two tales ask how this might function within the social group. In Ernest, "sympathy" and moral action are, we are told, successfully combined, a success that, however, may merely derive from a plot set up in such a way that Ernest does not have to deal with the kind of pain that the Concord works revealed in others. Little detail is given through plot, and the great array of synonyms for these qualities of sympathy and brotherhood leaves them still curiously vague. Though Ernest, unlike Brand, successfully combines intellect and heart, "thought" here is more like meditation. The emphasis is on emotion, on a range of feeling closely allied to the idea of sympathy already current in Hawthorne's work and apparently exemplifying the emotional reality of "brotherhood."[12] The "heart" and the "expression" of the heart are recurrent focal terms here.

In "The Snow-Image," "sympathy" and practical benevolence are instead separated. The strength of the children's sympathetic imagination, working "knowingly and skilfully" (II:10) to create a visually accurate human representation, brings their statue alive: they endow it with a reality equivalent to their own; they kiss it into life. Their father, whose would-be benevolence destroys, does not simply represent those lacking "sympathy": he is clearly a kindly person (he worries about the frozen child). But his "empty" and "impenetrable" heart (ii:7) indicates his incapacity to imagine lives and needs other than his own, in this case the "stranger" who is not " 'some neighbor's child, I suppose' " (ii:18). He sees her only within the intellectual framework of his own "system" (ii:25). To him she merely "looks like snow," while the more imaginative can grasp that she is "made of snow" (ii:22). Their metaphor insists on another order of reality, while his simile in contrast seems to diminish the difference. His is a comic form of the egotism of a Rappaccini or an Aylmer who create the world in terms of themselves. He is also an example of the notebook entry of between October 1848 and March 1849: "A benevolent person going about the world, and endeavoring to do good to everybody; in pursuance of which object, for instance, he gives a pair of spectacles to a blind man—and does all such ill-suited things" (8:285).

Yet the reader here pauses in some difficulty. The tale is fatally flawed in its conception. Only by taking the tale's fantasy as literally true (and the tale demands this by showing unambiguously that the snow image has indeed moved from the spot on which it was made) can Mr. Lindsey be criticized. However, if the reader tries to take the tale seriously as a practical tale about sympathy and benevolence, translating this moral into ordinary daily reality, the story does indeed collapse into a puddle of water, for in real circumstances the majority of people would behave, not surprisingly, like Mr. Lindsey. Here imaginative insight remains within the realm of miracle. Like the stone face, if one looks too closely, this tale is a "chaotic ruin" (ii:27).

The problem is that although both tales ostensibly deal with "actual circumstance" (i:37), that is, with domestic life based on Hawthorne's extended notebook descriptions of daily life with his children (8:398–436) or the life of an ordinary laborer, we are offered instead a "Childish Miracle" (ii:7) or the legend of the coming of a Christlike hero. Though "The Great Stone Face" depends less on fantasy than does "The Snow-Image," nonetheless it takes on the providential patterns of a moral fable.[13] Both tales seem sentimental compared with the Concord tales in that they deal with an ideal world of goodness while pretending this is how life on earth actually is. It is all made to sound far too easy.

Hawthorne's reported comment on the form (but not the content) of "The Great Stone Face" also pinpoints the problem: "Mr. Hawthorne," wrote his wife in a letter, "says he is rather ashamed of the mechanical structure of the story, the moral being so plain and manifest."[14] The "substance of to-day" is indeed "opaque" ("The Custom-House," 1:37) if the only way the artist can shine light through it is by the use of fantasy or fable. No wonder Hawthorne thought his art at this period a "soap-bubble": it was inherently likely to be "broken by the rude contact of some actual circumstance" (1:37). Some attempt to define the problem can be found in "The Great Stone Face" when the Poet points out the cause of the disparity between what he calls "dreams" and "realities." But Ernest's life, which seeks to resolve that dichotomy, is just another "dream."

"The Snow-Image" and "The Great Stone Face" may seem at face value to be homilies, but they come to recognize and explicitly explore the artistic difficulties in writing works that seek to address practical social issues in a way that may persuade the reader. The narrator of "The Snow-Image" even refuses to give the tale a didactic conclusion because those who need the lesson are least able to appreciate it. The problem is addressed more extensively in "The Great Stone Face." Ernest is a successful moral teacher, but we never hear his words and the crowds are shown to attach themselves to any persuasive figure. The artist's role is split between Ernest and the Poet: on the one hand, the power to turn moral insight to action in daily life and to persuade others similarly; and on the other, sympathetic insight, a concern for ordinary people (II:43), and powerful artistic expression (again no examples given). These two figures come together in conversation, but though the "sympathies of these two men instructed them with a profounder sense than either could have attained alone" (II:45), the tale itself fails to combine these.

▼

The remaining Salem piece, "Main-street," returns to material from American history for the first time for an adult audience in about ten years. In this way Hawthorne is able to show the full, interconnecting range of a particular society from family unit to governor, while also identifying some of the political and moral foundations of his own contemporary society, and understanding better the processes of historical change and the implications of these for social structures. But the persistent attention given to his vehicle, the puppet show, and the interaction between showman and his audience mean that the piece's most important role is to develop the other Salem tales' less extended interest in art, the artist, and his audience. In its concentration on seventeenth-century Salem, the sketch connects more closely to *The Scarlet Letter* than any other of these short pieces (especially in its handling of Puritan punishments and the Quakers); nonetheless, its prime concern seems to be in working out the twin problems of characterization and narrative interpretation. His audience demands realism, so he faces the problem of creating characters to which they can respond. He must also make the narrator an interpreter especially in matters of social and ethical judgment, and this is a special problem since Hawthorne has now taken a dislike to simpler didactic structures. In "Main-street," Hawthorne discovers what is necessary to take his Concord explorations further. He had stayed, he says in "The Custom-House," in his Salem post "long enough to break off old intellectual habits, and make room for new ones" (1:42). It is "Main-street" that identifies these "new" ideas.

"Main-street" gives more attention to two notions already found in other Salem tales, the idea of "sympathy" and the "heart," and the idea of "distance": " 'let me entreat you to take another point of view,' " begs the showman of a vociferous critic, " 'Sit further back, by that young lady, in whose face I have watched the reflection of every changing scene; only oblige me by sitting there; and, take my word for it, the slips of pasteboard shall assume a spiritual life' " (ii:63). Distance does not mean mental detachment. Instead it expresses the spectator's awareness that she or he is responding imaginatively not to actual reality, but to this reality transformed by the artistic imagination and recreated in language. Rather than let them uncritically accept the assumptions built into that model of reality, Hawthorne makes his readers stand at a distance questioning the nature and values of the reality being portrayed. Any demand for realism is resisted, and instead the sketch turns to a strength the artificiality of this pasteboard creation, giving the audience and artist overtly designated roles: "Illusion! What illusion? . . . The only illusion, permit me to say, is in the puppet-showman's tongue' " (II:63).

The most important figure is the showman's "critic," and the puppet show explores the historical origins and consequences of his dangerously limited, loud-mouthed attitude. The sketch will try to offer its audience "experience" (II:72) to countermand attitudes like those of this critic: he urges the audience, "let us watch their faces, as if we made a part of the pale crowd that presses so eagerly about them [the condemned witches]. . . . Listen to what the people say" (II:74).

The critic is a less attractive version of Mr. Lindsey's commonsense man, who says that he makes "it a point to see things precisely as they are" (II:52). The phrase recalls the "Old Manse" conservative criticism of Emerson's visitors—and neither defines this "reality." What this critic "sees" is very little indeed, and his "self-complacent" attitude (II:63) remains undisturbed—like Mr. Lindsey, he believes he knows everything already.

The sketch demonstrates the historical roots of such attitudes by contrasting the "shifting panorama" (II:49) with the inhabitants of each scene. The showman is able to move fluidly both physically and intellectually from one historical period to another, but the inhabitants of these scenes, each of whom at her or his own particular moment of time is incapable of understanding the radically transformative effect of time, think that "their own system of affairs will endure for ever" (II:51). For example, for the latest generation in the late-seventeenth-century colony, their elders' stories cannot make the now obliterated forest "true and real to their conceptions" (II:71), for "[n]othing impresses them, except their own experience" (II:72). Fictional "experience" that will unsettle such fixed ideas is precisely what the sketch tries to offer its contemporary audience.

Puritan rigidity opposes this fluidity and change embodied by history. Although the sketch shows that nothing in morality is fixed absolutely and in perpetuity, the Puritans attempted to achieve such absolutism, stopping inherent historical change by imposing their views on their children, the second generation on American soil, and thereby creating a "system" that was an "iron cage" (II:58) and losing touch with their original inspiration. The showman is trenchant in his condemnation of Puritan moral stasis: "[I]ts rigidity could not fail to cause miserable distortions of the moral nature. Such a life was sinister to the intellect, and sinister to the heart; . . . for these characteristics, as was inevitable, assumed the form both of hypocrisy and exaggeration, by being inherited from the example and precept of other human beings, and not from an original and spiritual source" (II:67–68).

As the narrator points out, this baleful Puritan inheritance is still with the nineteenth century. Arguably the showman's dogmatic critic exemplifies part of these "unfavorable influences which, among many good ones, were bequeathed to us by our Puritan forefathers" (II:68)—so impervious to experience and blind to his own cultural biases. Twenty years previously some of the *Provincial Tales* had taken on the notion of cultural change. Now this idea seems to cause less panic; indeed it is welcomed. It can also be seen that, in line with Concord thinking, this rigidity is antithetical to the sympathetic imagination.

All this means that the genesis of new ideas and challenges to rigidified moral and civil authority become vitally important: the town is depicted as starting with married love (thus echoing "The Old Manse") and not with the desire to establish Puritan principles: "How sweet must it be for those who have an Eden in their hearts, like Roger Conant and his wife [the first Salem inhabitants], to find a new world to project it into, as they have; instead of dwelling among old haunts of men, where so many household fires have been kindled and burnt out" (II:53). Furthermore, the Quakers are now treated less ambivalently and more supportively than in "The Gentle Boy" (compare the narrator's antagonistic presentation of Catharine in that early tale with that of the woman here in sackcloth and ashes preaching at the meetinghouse). In presenting the Quakers as wanderers in the wilderness who bring into the town "the gift of a new idea" (II:69), the narrator creates a parallel with those mental wanderers of Concord—Hawthorne and Channing boating away from the Old Manse to explore intellectual freedom in the woods and returning with a new perspective on the social system. Whereas a journey into the wilderness in some of the *Provincial Tales* caused disruption and crisis of belief, here the Quakers' journey to challenge the state is positive even when sadistically resisted by established authority. Here the Quakers' effect is part of that historical change, "as if a living truth had now, for the first time, forced its way through the crust of habit, reached their hearts, and awakened them to life" (II:70). The mingling of the voice of seventeenth-century repression ("we") with nineteenth-century narrator's historical description ("they" [II:69–70]) brings the differing views sharply into conflict, even at a grammatical level.

As the sketch continues with a comparatively lengthy account of the Salem witches, two things become increasingly clear: a concern for matters of merely institutional truth and civil judgment, and the role of the narrator in relation to this. The narrator emerges more and more from behind his "respectable-looking" (II:49) front with which he introduced himself. The material for "Main-street" after all comes not from the Custom House establishment world but from the neglected attic above it. Although at first the narrator's presentation of key Puritan figures may seem conventionally laudatory in intention, the references to the puppetry (II:61–62) remind us that the historically impossible gathering together here of all these patriotic figures is an ideological construction. Although the showman may say that he proceeds with "the inevitable acquiescence of all public servants" (II:73), this compliance is fairly superficial. He is a showman in two senses: he tries (and revealingly, ultimately fails) to create an entertaining show—a socially acceptable artistic illusion—and he shows (in the sense of reveals), as best he can in this medium, alternative aspects of the situations underneath the publicly accepted images. This may account for the curious uncertainty about voice in the sketch that creates a sense of doubleness: the narrator refers to the showman throughout in the third person as if he were a separate individual, yet it is also implied that the narrator's account of the show and the showman's speech are one.

What the sketch increasingly reveals is the unsafe nature of judicial punishment and majority opinion: the witch trials are presented in terms of the voices of the public with all their contradictions unrelated and unresolved. Yet the showman himself is drawn to interpret the scene (" 'What is all this?' cries the critic. 'A sermon? If so, it is not in the bill' " [II:68]). All through, the reader is made aware that the narrator stands behind the scene ensuring that "the proper light and shadow will transform the spectacle into quite another thing" (II:57). We are reminded that, as "The Great Stone Face" asserted, "Creation was not finished till the poet came to interpret, and so complete it" (II:43). In the late 1830s, although producing largely conformist didactic fictions, Hawthorne had found formal techniques, especially the use of the narrator in the sketch medium, to open narratives to interpretation and social evaluation. "Mainstreet" has developed these; *The Scarlet Letter* will extend this further.

So the narrator's powers of criticism are not suspended in some sympathetic attempt to understand these people. Since the sketch demonstrates, by concentrating on the town, that everyone has "a place in the system of human affairs" whether it is made by them or merely found (II:53), there is no escaping questions of civil right and wrong. Given, too, the town's dangerous judgments of dissidents, it is imperative that the narrator does not stay silent. But he does treat the matter differently from the Puritans, although Colonel Hawthorne, the magistrate responsible for whipping the Quaker woman, is given Nathaniel Hawthorne's own nineteenth-century spelling of the family name, thus suggesting the perils of such judgments as well as a continuing interest in questions of morality.

The sketch also turns out to be as much about certain continuities (the need to consider the moral foundations of a society) as it is about inevitable cultural change. A wire binds the scenes together. This sense of continuity is also embodied in the surviving seventeenth-century houses that the narrator, like his audience, knows from his "daily walks" (II:49). The sketch and its narrator must juggle with these two apparent contraries of continuity and change, recognizing both the conserving and radical forces at work in society.

The sketch ends with a snow scene that gives the illusion of obliterating the town and allowing new possibilities: "the traces of former times and hitherto accomplished deeds being done away, mankind should be at liberty to enter on new paths, and guide themselves by other laws than heretofore" (II:80). Hawthorne may be suggesting something about the possibilities of his art here: the show breaks down and the panorama cannot continue onto pictures of the present day, thus leaving the audience in the snow-covered scene of apparently total possibility. Imagination has made vivid to an audience how the sources of present social structures lie in the past. Although the facts of this past are by their very nature unchangeable (the sketch gives instances where insistence on historical fact gives greater accuracy to these explorations and reconsiderations), nonetheless imagination can, through its powers of illusion, suggest other hypothetical alternatives and other possible ways of looking.

Yet in another sense the sketch has broken down, its medium finally inadequate to the fresh complexities of its material, for all the control exercised over that material in this sketch form. As a work of fiction, it merits the same condemnation that early attempts to write up Hester Prynne's story evoked: "My imagination was a tarnished mirror. It would not reflect, or only with miserable dimness, the figures with which I did my best to people it. The characters of the narrative would not be warmed and rendered malleable, by any heat that I could kindle at my intellectual forge" (I:34). "Rappaccini's Daughter," the most achieved fictional narrative of his Concord phase, proves a better indicator of the formal requirements of his future work.

Nonetheless, the sketch had established roles for both narrator and audience, demanding a complex response weighing up the respective claims of both sympathy and judgment, and thus refusing merely to back an easier establishment view of both past and present social structures. The sketch, as John P. McWilliams has demonstrated, "satirizes the conventions of New England historiography while inverting many of its conclusions."[15] The independence and intellectual fluidity of "Main-street" is paralleled in the movement of "The

Custom-House" from public space to private study, from sitting downstairs with the custom officers to pacing up and down above their heads and disturbing the slumbers of these state employees.

"Main-street" is the work that takes Hawthorne closest to *The Scarlet Letter*, both in the roles assigned to narrator and reader, in its hints of moral complexity in the interaction of individual subjectivity and the social order, and in its revisionary use of history rather than contemporary reality. It was after all not the moonlit domestic sitting room described in "The Custom-House" that was presently to provide the material for his first full-length and most successful fiction—"The Great Stone Face" and "The Snow-Image" clearly show that the imagination had great difficulty in transforming common social reality in a way that created that "neutral territory, somewhere between the real world and fairy-land" (1:36). Instead, the "Custom-House" attic provided the better material and perspectives, and "Main-street" suggested better ways of combining the "Actual" and the "Imaginary" (1:36).

"The Best Harvest of His Mind"

The Scarlet Letter

1849–1850

▼ BY SEPTEMBER 1849 Hawthorne had begun writing *The Scarlet Letter*, his controversial dismissal from the Custom House in June of that year and the trauma of his mother's death in July having been the catalysts. For someone who had been engaged for years in an exploration of subjectivity and the social order, the Custom House experience had given him immediate insights into the institutional workings of a social system, while the death of his mother, recorded with unparalleled intensity in his notebooks, brought psychic disturbances uniquely to the surface:

> ...I found the tears slowly gathering in my eyes. I tried to keep them down; but it would not be—I kept filling up, till, for a few moments, I shook with sobs. For a long time, I knelt there, holding her hand; and surely it is the darkest hour I ever lived. . . . And now, through the crevice of the curtain, I saw my little Una of the golden locks, looking very beautiful; and so full of spirit and life, that she was life itself. And then I looked at my poor dying mother; and seemed to see the whole of human existence at once, standing in the dusty midst of it. (8:429)

Five years later, recalling his overwrought reading to Sophia of the closing pages of this tale of another mother and child, Hawthorne commented: "But I was in a very nervous state, then, having gone through a great diversity and severity of emotion, for many months past. I think I have never overcome my own adamant in any other instance."[1] "The Custom-House," too, describes that time in radically disruptive but potentially transformative terms—"the period of hardly accomplished revolution, and still seething turmoil, in which the story shaped itself" (1:43). It was a "revolution" indeed: he had stayed in Salem, he claimed, "long enough to break off old intellectual habits, and make room for new ones" (1:42).

The Scarlet Letter, however, cannot be seen as a complete break from the slow evolution of his previous twenty-five years' work. Indeed, the prefatory "Custom-House" essay presents Hawthorne's time as a government officer and his escape from this into writing the novel in an ambiguous counterpoint of old and new. He had felt "thrown into a position so little akin to my past habits" (1:25), yet to work in Salem was to return to his own and his family's origins. When, as he expresses it at the turning point of "The Custom-House," he discovered that "the past was not dead" (1:27), its revival involved not only his own presently suppressed creativity but also the recovery of the Puritan world that both underpinned contemporary Salem itself and that had provided the material for his first major works, the Provincial Tales, and for one of his most recent.[2] Hawthorne wrote his novel exceptionally quickly (it was finished by February 3, 1850), but in another sense this long-desired achievement had been many years in the making and was made possible by the many phases of questioning, experimentation, change, and consolidation that his work had undergone in the previous quarter-century.[3]

These continuities and discontinuities influence the way the novel works with tensions between radicalism and conservatism, speculation and orthodoxy, relativism and absolutism, subjectivity and the social order, sympathy and judgment, the "Imaginary" and the "Actual." The first section of this chapter will consider how The Scarlet Letter sets about exploring matters of interrogation, interpretation, value judgments, narrative focalization, and closure—all matters brought to the fore by his most recently written Salem pieces.

The importance of "Main-street" in this is underlined by giving The Scarlet Letter the same (albeit fictional) source, "Surveyor Pue": as in "Main-street," the world of "custom" is better explored through historical material rather than in contemporary scenes. This is because the historical material lends itself particularly well to the creative play of the two elements that "The Custom-House" identifies as central to the artist's project: the "Actual" and the "Imaginary," that is, things as they are or apparently were, and things as they might be or might have been. This is possible, Hawthorne understands, because historical "fact," being itself a fabrication of a specific culture, is always open to question and revision. (Of course, any revisionary enterprise is itself culturally specific, since however much the attempt may have been to produce a historically accurate portrait of seventeenth-century Massachusetts, Hawthorne's preoccupations inevitably have a nineteenth-century perspective). It is specifically the *fictional* use of historical material that allowed for what is historically determined in social existence and what might be open to individual choice to be played creatively against each other. Critical studies have shown that Hawthorne was concerned to reexamine certain historical personages, events, and issues, but it is through wholly imaginary characters and plot that this is achieved.[4] This is why the writer in "The Custom-House" can pose first as "editor, or very little more" of the novel (1:4)—that is, bound by his culture's version of history—and then later as one who allows himself "nearly or altogether as much license as if the facts had been entirely of my own invention" (1:33). And since "invention" is what these "facts" largely are, by implication he has considerable license. Moreover, while the position of mere "editor" provides some cover for the narrator against the attacks of any ultraconservative readership that might take exception to the novel's explorations, the latter position of "license" allows for that desired experimentation.

That innovation was to be a key concern can be seen from Hawthorne's comments on the potential of historical fiction. A review of W. G. Simms, *Views and Reviews in American History*, written just three years previously, suggests that he now held clear artistic principles about such material:

The same themes suggested by him [Simms], viewed as he views them, would produce nothing but historical novels, cast in the same worn out mould that has been in use these thirty years, and which it is time to break up and fling away. . . . [H]e possesses nothing of the magic touch that should cause new intellectual and moral shapes to spring up in the reader's mind, peopling with varied life what had hitherto been a barren waste.[5]

"Main-street" had shown that historical material, even when still somewhat ideologically constrained, could provide a fresh perspective on social processes. Hawthorne's historicist approach is given fullest realization in the meteor scene in *The Scarlet Letter*, where a critical examination of Dimmesdale's seventeenth-century perspective reveals the cultural relativity and subjective influences on the construction of meaning. The illusion of consensus fractures into many facets; both Dimmesdale and the reader discover that the "unaccustomed light" imparts to everything a "singularity of aspect that seemed to give another moral interpretation to the things of this world than they had ever borne before" (1:154).

We have seen how a questioning stance, characteristic of *Mosses*, had been continued in "Main-street" with its championing of the Quakers' "gift of a new idea" (II:69) breaking through the "crust of habit" (II:70). It had been "Main-street" that made clear that there can be no absolute moral authority then or now invested in social institutions; the majority of his historically based tales over the past twenty-five years had also been characteristically seamed with doubts or ironies. *The Scarlet Letter* continues this process of unsettling cultural givens that had begun with the *Provincial Tales* journeys and had been transformed into a more concerted enterprise at Concord.

"The Custom-House" presents contemporary Salem as a stagnant place, utterly resistant to change and in sharp contrast to the self-portrait of the writer's mind: thoughts "so vital and so active . . . revived again" (1:27), and "instinctive curiosity" (1:29) quickened in a man who characterizes himself as one "who felt it to be the best definition of happiness to live throughout the whole range of his faculties and sensibilities!" (1:40) So it was in the attic above his sedentary colleagues' heads that the author bestowed "much thought" (1:34) on Hester Prynne's story. "The Custom-House" positions the writer clearly outside the mainstream—"a citizen of somewhere else" (1:44)—constructing a binary opposition between the imaginative artist and the state employee who is a recipient of "public gold" (1:34). The artist is not conceived of romantically as a free spirit (Hawthorne knew by now he is a creature of a particular culture even when attacking that culture), but the nature of his commitments and associates is deliberately left open here.[6]

All three protagonists are themselves shown to be of a speculative character of mind (though with various degrees of intentionality and willingness to act upon such "free" opinion), living in an age "in which the human intellect, newly emancipated, had taken a more active and a wider range than for many centuries before" (1:164). True, the narrator makes a distinction at this point in the story between purely theoretical speculation (pursued by Chillingworth or Dimmesdale in the privacy of his study) and actual revolutionary challenge or change (the latter exemplified by a brief reference to the English Civil War and by the American and French revolutions and recent European upheavals inevitably present in his readers' minds). But this distinction between theory and practice is quickly dissolved by the subsequent information that the Puritans would have regarded Hester's "freedom of speculation" as a "deadlier crime than that stigmatized by the scarlet letter" (1:164). The phrase "our forefathers," also embedded in that observation, emphasizes the connections between the Puritans and nineteenth-century readers, who might otherwise merely smile dismissively at the former importance assigned to merely mental "speculation." Instead they are made to reflect on the moral priorities and generally conservative social action of their own age, challenged here by some more enquiring elements of an earlier age. *The Scarlet Letter* makes the tensions between speculation and orthodoxy, radicalism and conservatism, central to its debate, and Hawthorne chose a historically pertinent image when he said the novel caused the "greatest uproar that ever happened here [in Salem] since witchtimes" (16:329).

This sense of the historical relativity of social values is essential to a continuing investigation of both human "wrong" and of proposed alleviations of that suffering—the pain that *Mosses* presented as endemic and that had provoked the search for an "open sesame." His present historical perspective does not dissolve this project, nor apparently does it wholly discount at least the possibility of transcendental values, but gives him the necessary detachment to observe the operation of values in any particular society and make generalizations as seem appropriate. The tale "Ethan Brand" had not succeeded any more than its protagonist in understanding the full implications of what "sin" might be (Unpardonable or otherwise) or in evolving an effective response. Its questions still hung fire. "[A] more perplexing amalgamation of good and evil" (the phrase is from "The Intelligence Office," but applies better to the unresolved complexities of "Rappaccini's Daughter") still awaited Hawthorne's attention after the moral simplicities of some of the recent Salem tales. Although at one point Hester despairingly thinks, " 'There is no path to guide us out of this dismal maze!' " (1:173), the novel is nonetheless concerned to explore some way through, if not totally out of, the labyrinth.

Although Hawthorne says he dreamed at Concord of writing a substantial novel that would "evolve some deep lesson" (10:5), "Main-street," "The Snow-Image," and "The Great Stone Face," each in their varying ways, had gone on to warn of the perils of moralizing interpretation and the concomitant problems of the imaginative artist's relationship to his (or her) audience. Work in the 1830s had begun to consider formal techniques of opening up narratives to interpretation, establishing some relationship to social codes. *The Scarlet Letter* had to create fresh ways of approaching such matters. Although thematically concerned with crime and punishment, the novel is less immediately preoccupied with sitting in judgment on the characters themselves than with observing how others judge: for example, the Puritan authorities, whom the narrator assesses are least capable of "sitting in judgment on an erring woman's heart, and disentangling its mesh of good and evil" (1:64); or Chillingworth, who mistakenly "had begun an investigation, as he imagined, with the severe and equal integrity of a judge, desirous only of truth, even as if the question involved no more than the air-drawn lines and figures of a geometrical problem, instead of human passions, and wrongs inflicted on himself" (1:129). There is, however, no reason why Hawthorne's contemporary audience (or indeed any subsequent readership) should prove less blinkered, but as "Main-street" and "The Snow-Image" had demonstrated, what is most to be feared is the obtuse know-it-all unprepared to stay open to the narrative's multiple hypotheses.

The extent to which the novel is able to draw a moral conclusion is in question, and certainly the use of the word "evolve" in "The Old Manse" account of proposing a novel suggests an organic structure. The rose plucked by the narrator and presented to the reader in a gentlemanly gesture in the first chapter may be a covertly satirical protest against the more conventionally minded reader who expects such things from novels,7 and the concluding chapter's attempt to fulfill that promise ("Among many morals which press upon us from the poor minister's miserable experience, we put only this into a sentence" [1:260]) suggests several possibilities: a hesitancy on the narrator's part about his conclusions, or an underlying impatience on the author's part with the whole idea of closing the narrative in this conventional way, or a sense that there are indeed "many" but conflicting insights and none of them final. In presenting himself as the descendant of "persecuting" Puritan judges (1:9), the writer of "The Custom-House" distinguishes himself from their "cruelties" toward witches and Quakers (Hester's historical analogues), and yet, by taking the Puritans' shame upon himself, aligns himself with his forefathers in an attempt to transform what he sees as their seventeenth-century bigotry into the apparently more acceptable nineteenth-century views—a liberalism that itself comes under scrutiny.

A concern with the idea of right action persists in this novel. As we have seen, social engagement—existence within social relations— was a central issue in the Salem phase (there the concern was particularly with the idea of benevolent action), and now this novel takes psychological, social, and spiritual perspectives on it. As we shall presently show, there seems to be a shift away from tradi- tional, usually Christian-based, ethical considerations and toward an exploration of more general cultural and psychological foundations beneath this particular preoccupation with judgment. Thus, for example, to describe Hester as "stained with sin, bowed down with shame, or even burdened with a life-long sorrow" (1:263) is to appeal to three separate, if connected, discourses, those of religion, social propriety, and mental suffering. The novel presents the reader with a complexly imagined world where the Salem moral and emotional simplicities are dissolved, a world where it is possible that hatred and love may be "the same thing at bottom" (1:260), where through some unspecified agency guilty feelings may result in a letter on the flesh of the sinner/sufferer, and where the morally uneasy narrator self-consciously shifts his language so that it is difficult to know whether he is drawing on the Christian discourse of sin or that of mental breakdown, or tracing the connection between these—see, for example, his comment on Dimmesdale as "this sorely tempted, or—shall we not rather say?—this lost and desperate man" (1:219).

The word "moral," which in *Mosses* was used to point to the emotional consequences of social and personal wrong, continues sometimes to straddle the psychological and ethical. The word appears twenty-four times in the novel, but now with a greater emphasis on the impact of civil and religious codes on the processes of subjectivity: "his moral system" (1:222), "his moral force" (1:159), "a softer moral and intellectual fibre" (1:86), "the rays of its moral life" (1:91); and by extension, the "moral solitude" of the letter (1:234), "other moral scenery" (1:124), Hester's "moral agony" (1:70), a "moral wilderness" (1:183—not just a classic Puritan trope but an ethically less specific emotional state).

The Scarlet Letter, Hawthorne's first full-length fiction in maturity, most resembles "Rappaccini's Daughter" in its launching into an uncertain narrative of complex character-interaction and event. Allegedly a short tale in its initial conception, it must always have been lengthy and substantial like the majority of his recent writings, and unlike his earlier tales in structure.[8] "Main-street," in its investigation of fictional representation and audience response, had pointed to the need for this kind of fiction. The primary emphasis on character and event is clear even in the account of the novel's origins. Although "The Custom-House" depicts the letter *A* as the initiating element of the tale, within its folds lay the manuscript summary of Hester's story. Furthermore, donning the letter, the narrator transforms himself momentarily into Hester, and the emotional impact of this experience, with its resistance to rational explanations, is stressed. The deliberately exaggerated account makes the commonsensical reader confront the nonrational power of the sympathetic imagination; the letter's embroidery is a "forgotten art" (1:31) that she or he cannot understand simply by solemnly measuring the piece or picking out the stitches. Moreover, the narrator's account of his first struggles to write the novel focuses entirely on the characters, and Surveyor Pue's manuscript is similarly presented as being concerned with character: "the life and conversation of one Hester Prynne," the "record of other doings and sufferings of this singular woman" (1:32). The cloud of uncertainty that then hangs over these characters, periodically obscuring the reader's full view of them as naturalistically imagined people, has its source in the problems of representing the complex and unstable processes of identity, where what is socially determined is constantly undermined by desire and where desire can be represented only and imperfectly by the semiotic systems of that society. The novel mimics to some extent the varying degrees to which these characters are ever knowable to others.⁹

The narrator's voice is an additional complicating factor in this drama of character, place, and event, and one means of introducing moral analysis into the novel without giving that voice complete authority. The narrator is not identical to the Surveyor/authorial persona in "The Custom-House," let alone to Hawthorne himself.¹⁰ His function is neither simply that of expositor and stage manager, nor that of didacticism's judge and moral spokesman. He is one of the many strands of the novel, out of which is spun a web of confrontations, questions, and doubts. His descriptions always tend to slide into multiple interpretation. Neither does the narrator present himself as the foreknowing oracle of truth, fully in control of his tale. Instead of a story recalled, there is often a sense of unanticipated events jolting him into immediate reaction. Doubt is created in a rush of proffered alternatives (for instance, Hester's motives for staying [1:79–80]), with proliferating conditionals (such as "it might be," "it is probable," "Hester saw or seemed to see," "she felt or fancied"). These clamor impossibly for resolution—impossibly, because of the difficulty of ever knowing any character fully, let alone settling the clash of competing needs and desires.

The narrator, as a liberal democrat trying to transform what he regards as an unsavory seventeenth-century tale of immorality and tyranny into something his nineteenth-century audience can accept without disturbing too much its present notions of gender relations, does not keep a constant position throughout. Challenged by the story, he struggles with his own nineteenth-century social indoctrination. A gap gradually widens between the narrative voice and other possible responses to events, as the tale pushes against the restraining narrative framework and the reader is forced to see the deficiencies of the narrator's responses and the narrator's own failure to see these inadequacies.

The narrator's liberalism initially might appear appealing while it still seems possible to be clear about where post-Puritan sympathies might lie (though, even then, his comments on Hester's exposure on the scaffold, for example, are not an attack on her being condemned but only a criticism of the means by which such condemnation is expressed). However, as early as chapter 5 the narrator has begun to dither, his anxiety being caused by his nineteenth-century preconceptions about woman's nature and place. It is Hester rather than Dimmesdale who disturbs him most and whom he most unambiguously condemns at certain points, not simply because she questions her culture's givens far more radically than the minister, but because it is a woman, conventionally a conserving force in that culture,[11] who is doing this: "The scarlet letter was her passport into regions where other *women* dared not tread. Shame, Despair, Solitude! These had been her teachers,—stern and wild ones,—and they had made her strong, but taught her much amiss" (1:199–200, emphasis added). Cheerfully admitting the lack of evidence of Pearl's fate, he safely envisages her "not only alive, but married, and happy, and mindful of her mother" (1:262).

It is not that the narrator simply becomes conservative. His liberalism sits him uneasily on the fence between condemnation and confirmation, and his language employs both orthodox (indeed Puritan) and also radical rhetorics: see the heavy-handed allegorical formulations of "Remorse" and "Cowardice" (1:148) in the midnight scaffold scene where Dimmesdale's thoughts are elided into the narrator's, as well as the Transcendentalist rhetoric of the "sympathy of Nature" (1:203) in the forest scene.[12] Defining such terms as "conservative" and "radical" is problematic except by being historically specific, and in dealing with social structures and with the desire for change, Hawthorne is indeed specific. This is particularly the case with seventeenth-century Boston's coercive utopianism (radical in that century's English eyes, antilibertarian in nineteenth-century American eyes), but both this and Hester's vision of a better social role for women, which also has its colonial origins, have nineteenth-century parallels to complicate matters further. Increasingly at the end of the novel, the narrator presents events through the townspeople's eyes, partly because the narrator himself seems caught up in the patriotic attractions of the Election Day ceremonies, partly because it lightens the burden he still carries of trying to make up his mind. Like the uncomprehending seventeenth-century Bostonians who "arrange their thoughts" many days after Dimmesdale's death, the narrator is faced both with "more than one account" and with the need to settle on one (1:258). What is disturbing is not his actual inconclusiveness (which is surely understandable) but his continuing desire for neat answers, particularly when this is sought with a sentimental inflection uncharacteristic of the rest of the novel (as in his speculation that, in the afterlife, Dimmesdale and Chillingworth may find their antipathy "transmuted into golden love" [1:261].)[13]

The handling of narrative focalization also ensures that the reader's perspective is in a marked state of constant change and confusion, so that the reader not only experiences the many contradictory viewpoints but also is made aware that the narrator at times obscures our view of a character in the interests of making his own point, or more simply seems not to have the imaginative power to envisage his protagonists' thoughts. There is a conscious deliberation about the way the center of consciousness is moved from character to character, sometimes so that the reader is simultaneously within and outside a character—for example, Dimmesdale on the midnight scaffold, or Hester looking toward her future at the beginning of chapter 5. One device in particular keeps readers on their toes. Occasionally a view of events is presented without introduction so that it appears to be that of the narrator, only to be then followed by a phrase revealing it to be instead one of the characters' possibly idiosyncratic ideas. Tempted by the momentary ambiguity of omniscient narration, the reader then learns that what seemed objectively true or at least validated by the narrator is something only subjectively believed. Indeed, at times it never becomes clear whose thoughts we have been given. Examples of this temporary syntactical ambiguity can be found first in the opening description of Pearl, where two sentences apparently stating the incontrovertible fact of Hester's guilt are followed by, "Yet these thoughts affected Hester Prynne" (1:89); and second in the motives given for Dimmesdale's vigil on the scaffold (1:147–48), where it is not clear until the beginning of the subsequent paragraph that the vivid portrait of his sin is a record of Dimmesdale's thoughts rather than the apparently more authoritative narrator's: "And thus . . . Mr. Dimmesdale was overcome with a great horror of mind" (1:148). This device is a more controlled version of the use of free indirect discourse in some of the *Provincial Tales*.[14]

This device is important because it results in a constant tension between sharing sympathetically and directly with a character or the narrator, and being aware of the limits of such subjective vision and claims. A precarious sense of events is pieced together out of this range of experience, thought, and commentary. Such an unstable narrative mode suggests the attempt both to "sympathize" in a *Mosses* sense and a desire to step back from this to seek a wider pattern of meaning.

Thus, too, the narrator becomes an object of scrutiny himself, and this narrational handling is the apotheosis of a self-consciousness about narrative constructions found in some form or other throughout Hawthorne's earlier work. The more general implications of having an unreliable narrator need also to be considered here. This is something Hawthorne is to use most obviously in two years' time in *The Blithedale Romance,* but it had been foreshadowed most explicitly by the patriotic storyteller of "Legends of the Province-House." It is, however, in the less explicit use of such a conventional voice in the moral fables, also of the 1830s, that we find the closest parallel to using a narrative voice that does not clearly advertise itself as untrustworthy and that depends on the reader's own discovery of its gaps, inconsistencies, and inadequacies. This is possibly all the more powerful and subtle for putting the onus on the reader, although one could argue that, depending as it does on the audience's self-conscious awareness of its own often unexamined attitudes, it potentially weakens the novel's moral analysis. Possibly the inherent ambiguity of the device gives protective cover for charting the many ironies of New England without having to come up with some counteractive positive. It certainly allows Hawthorne to have an unhierarchized and undetermined set of responses, and it might force his audience to hear the hardest thing of all to detect, its own silent assumptions.

▼

So *The Scarlet Letter* represents a new form of writing for Hawthorne. A new stage in his thinking about the human subject is made possible by this combining of the "Actual" and the "Imaginary," the worlds of circumstance and desire, first clearly identified at Concord. While working at the Custom House and oppressed by its hostility to works of the imagination, Hawthorne had visualized creativity in opposition to the world of "custom" and so belonging to a different order of reality from the daily one. As long as the circumstances of his Surveyorship imprisoned Hawthorne in this conceptual opposition, he had indeed been in danger of creating the "snow-images" (1:36) or a "soap-bubble" (1:37), which he talks about in "The Custom-House" sketch. "The Snow-Image" story had consciously explored precisely those dangers, but then in part succumbed to them. The Salem tales, with their use of fantasy in conjunction with the ordinary, were a clear warning that "moonlight," in spite of its usefully defamiliarizing powers, was not necessarily the best way of imagining the medium of fiction. Indeed, it failed to produce *The Scarlet Letter,* and we would be wrong to infer, as critical tradition has usually done, that *The Scarlet Letter* was composed within such a conceptual framework. A careful reading of the "Custom-House" account reveals instead that the novel was written only after he had escaped those circumstances and milieu that had bred that sterile oppositional way of thinking about art.[15]

Now, as a far more complexly realized fictional world supersedes those earlier sentimentalized (if possibly genuinely felt) fantasies of the Salem tales, the full force of contradiction and conflict is unleashed, and *The Scarlet Letter* comes to a full consideration of the interaction of individual subjectivity and the social order. The novel does not resolve the problems of the divided self but rather makes the relationship between self as subject and self as object more complex—or at least as complex as in the most disturbing of *Provincial Tales.* The previous Salem tales had rather neglected or simplified individual subjectivity, while establishing a sense of every person having a "place" within the social order even if she or he sat uncomfortably in it. *The Scarlet Letter* now reintroduces the complexity mostly missing from the Salem tales. This is in part achieved by the simple device of moving his seventeenth-century scene from the Salem of "Main-street," where an idealized happy couple and their children with "an Eden in their hearts" (11:53) are depicted as the founders of the town, to a Boston of the same period, where not only are the first acts of the utopian new colony to make provision for a graveyard and a prison but also the novel's plot is founded on an unsatisfactory marriage, recent adultery, and judicial intervention. The novel's opening scene derives from those North Adams journals (tapped within the past year or two for "Ethan Brand") recording a meeting with a man who had arrived at the village looking for his wife without knowing that she had become a prostitute: "I would have given considerable to witness his meeting with his wife. On the whole there was a moral picturesqueness in the contrasts of this scene" (8:59). "Desire" thus meets "circumstance" head on: the eroticism of "Drowne's Wooden Image" is no longer bundled out of sight of the puritanical elders, or doomed like Beatrice Rappaccini to entirely private enclosure and early death. The narrative issues from the prison door, threshold between private agony and public disgrace (some of the *Provincial Tales* had been located on similar interfaces).

The character of Pearl represents one of the most striking shifts in thinking from the previous Salem tales; she has no precedent in Hawthorne's earlier writing. Ernest, Jo, Peony, Violet, and their mother have a moral simplicity foreign to her. In Pearl, a sharply defined miniature of her parents' situation, we can most usefully begin to trace Hawthorne's newly conceived and complexly imagined interaction of desire and circumstance. His conception of the human subject now reaches maturity.

Inheriting her mother's exclusion from society and unacknowledged by her father, Pearl's nature "lacked reference and adaptation to the world into which she was born" (1:91). Remaining in the pre-oedipal stage of development, she declares to her mother, " 'O, I am your little Pearl!' " (1:97) and " 'I have no Heavenly Father!' " (1:98). She is without the presence of the father—in this case, both her physical male parent and the supreme moral and religious authority expressed in that conventional paternal image of which Pearl has no experience. In consequence, she does not enter the social and symbolic order: she "must perforce be permitted to live her own life, and be a law unto herself" (1:135).[16]

In a conversation between the two absent men of Pearl's life who have therefore little comprehension of her, Chillingworth remarks to Dimmesdale that " 'There is no law, nor reverence for authority, no regard for human ordinances or opinions, right or wrong, mixed up in that child's composition' " (1:134). She does not acknowledge the power structures of the town she inhabits, especially when asked to obey in a matter that focuses on the source of that authority and her submission to it—the refusal to repeat the Shorter Catechism to Mr. Wilson comes at a point when civil and religious authorities seek to intervene most directly in her life and sever her connection with her mother.

Faced with hostile crowds, she even speaks a different language from them ("shrill, incoherent exclamations . . . the sound of a witch's anathemas in some unknown tongue" [1:94]), as if to suggest that in failing to take up a place within this patriarchal society, she has not acquired the language that comes with this, and still speaks a tongue associated with the forbidden, rebellious female. Her experience teaches her only that the world around her is hostile, and this provides her with an interpretative frame. In a paradoxical phrase that encapsulates Pearl's actual subversion of parental authority, we are told that Hester would "permit the child to be swayed by her own impulses" (1:92).

To the normally socialized—that is, everyone else in the novel, adults and children—Pearl's character makes no sense unless they either assume there is no structure to her being, or see her in terms of the Devil (even Hester does this in interpreting Pearl's curses as those of a witch). To Hester, Pearl's facial expression is "inexplicable, so perverse" and "bewildering and baffling" (1:92), yet she realizes that this apparent disorder may consist of elements "with an order peculiar to themselves, amidst which the point of variety and arrangement was difficult or impossible to discover" (1:91). So Pearl does have a "principle of being" (1:134—that is to say, psychological coherence), but it is certainly not discoverable to minds such as Chillingworth's or Dimmesdale's. And "the master-word that should control this new and incomprehensible intelligence" (1:93) cannot be in the possession of the woman whose own actions have provoked the all-too-controlling counteraction of those master/ministers who do claim to own the Word.

This is the world of desire as yet unrepressed by the social order (the "circumstance" of the Concord tales)—although possibly not untouched by that world, given her rages and unpredictable swings of mood. Pearl's scorn of "falsehood" (1:180), however, suggests one whose subjective identity has not yet been divided by completed entry into the social order. On the "stage of her inner world" (1:95) she is still able to create a drama that expresses the emotions that her parents seek to conceal even perhaps from themselves. This is seen most clearly at the climax of the novel when we are told that she "betrayed, by the very dance of her spirits, the emotions that none could detect in the marble passiveness of Hester's brow" (1:228). She is the "living hieroglyphic, in which was revealed the secret they so darkly sought to hide" (1:207), an alien sign system that society cannot read but only interprets within its own symbolic order.

But even in her social marginalization, Pearl cannot remain forever a figure of scarcely modified though embattled desire. Playing with the rock pool and its reflections on the margin between shore and sea (that is, settlement and wilderness), Pearl becomes momentarily split into two persons. The scene shows how Pearl, with no position in the social order other than that of devil child, is ignorant of her own identity except, punningly, her "identity" (1:102) with the scarlet letter. Hence she has no experience of herself as object; she does not recognize herself in the pool. In an earlier incident where she is portrayed as reflected along with her mother in the patriarchal mirror of the Governor's armour, it is only her mother whom she announces she sees. Her mother, having left her side, has created this lack that she feels but does not understand, and this is expressed as another person separate from herself. Here the water image (a nonsocial mirror) represents primarily desire for a companion, someone to reflect her back to herself and create a sense of wholeness again. The rock pool scene comes immediately after the chapter, "Another View of Hester," which charts her mother's increasing separation from her former social world (a mental distance now), and prefaces the moment when Hester begins to break the seven-year deadlock by approaching her former husband to request release from her vow of secrecy about him. The pool shows how things are now beginning to change for Pearl as her mother makes moves toward Dimmesdale, thus severing the exclusive relationship between Pearl and Hester. This mirror is different from the game of the green *A* in which the child appears to mirror her mother through her dress. The water-mirror companion does not draw her into the social order—the pool, " 'a better place!' " is an imaginary place of union, wholeness, and happiness that becomes merely "agitated water" as soon as Pearl seeks to enter it (1:168).

This image of mirror reflections is repeated in the brookside meeting in the forest where Pearl reacts to her mother sitting beside Dimmesdale. A border between two states is again represented, here between the world of the family now completed by the Father and the unsocialized wilderness, the "mother-forest" (1:204). Under that maternal influence, Pearl had been gentler, conflict had been absent (she patted the wolf), and desire untrammeled. The fantastical quality of the scene reflects its discontinuity from social reality and underlines the scene's inherent separation from the categories that normally produce social and psychological meaning. And again, as on the seashore, it is the mother's movement away from the child that precipitates the self-division expressed through a mirroring image.

At first the effect of the stream's reflection is to enhance her lack of a substantial social identity—it is almost as if she has entered the "better place" that the rock pool appeared to offer. But Pearl's response to the entry of her father into her life, and hence separation from her mother, is a fiercely articulated rage at a usurper who is very much not the mirroring companion sought in the rock pool— indeed Dimmesdale's dread that his daughter might resemble him expresses his refusal to connect with her, to mirror her being and hence affirm both her inner and social identity.[17] Even at this point he is quick to liken her instead to the socially condemned, the "witch" (1:210). Pearl, having behaved lovingly to him on only one previous occasion when he had saved her from separation from her mother at the Governor's Hall, finds him a threat that shatters her self into two: "another inmate had been admitted within the circle of the mother's feelings, and so modified the aspect of them all, that Pearl, the returning wanderer, could not find her wonted place, and hardly knew where she was" (1:208). The water reflection gives emphasis to her fury, as does the forest that similarly echoes her shrieks, but this apparent unity of being with the environment is contradicted by the basic splitting of the self in the brook's reflections. Paradoxically, the mirror may symbolize simultaneously both division and the possibility of the wholeness that comes with sympathetic responsiveness from another.

One might be tempted to deduce that Pearl is protesting at the flight of her parents from the social order by insisting on Hester's resuming the "sinful" letter of civil and religious judgment (symbol of her position within that order). But Pearl can have no understanding of adultery and at one level it is merely the "habit" (both in the sense of outer garments and customary behavior) that she insists upon. In that case the letter is revealed as without essential significance. The narrator's later view of Pearl as "a messenger of anguish" (1:256) keeping her mother and eventually her father on the moral straight and narrow is partial and possibly misleading. Pearl has a better understanding of the scene; she sees that the reunification of Hester and Dimmesdale, which superficially seems to be the return of the lover, is actually the return of the Law. This Law is embodied in the Father who will pull her mother and herself back into Boston. Both her mother's conventional words of reproof and authority here ("naughty child" [1:209]) and the novel's final scaffold scene demonstrate the correctness of her view. Pearl can only temporarily reverse power structures by ordering her mother to resume the letter; her reassertion of the dyad (" 'Now thou art my mother indeed! And I am thy little Pearl!' " [1:211]) is contradicted by the triad of father, mother, and child on the scaffold in full public gaze. The ultimate consequence of the forest meeting is Pearl's joining with her parents on the scaffold, and if her destiny is, as the narrator conventionally suggests, "not for ever do battle with the world, but be a woman in it" (1:256), then we should note that this "world" must subordinate all women, since one is clearly not deemed a "woman" if one challenges authority. Not surprisingly, as the final chapter reveals, the world continues to be no secure or necessarily happy place for the many women who come to Hester for help. Pearl cannot be accommodated within American society.

▼

With this image of the mirror, Hawthorne has returned to a motif he had employed at different phases of his career and that has in its different usages indicated how at each stage he was conceptualizing

the self. It is the portrayal of subjectivity in the three adult protagonists that needs now to be explored, starting first with this
image of the mirror. In *The Scarlet Letter,* eyes and water constitute
mirrors of the psyche, and these are different again from the metal
mirror (the armour) of Puritan civil and religious authority. Both
kinds of mirror, social and psychical, are therefore present, and both
embody aspects of the splitting, which existence within the social
order creates in the subject. However, the helmet and breastplate
(mental rigidity and lack of contact with feeling) obliterate any sign
of the individual's subjectivity except insofar as the subject accepts
that letter of condemnation and punishment as a sign of herself. On
the other hand the natural mirrors of eyes, rock-pools, and stream,
together with an individual's private looking glass, do give access to
subjectivity, to that mental space where consciousness can be seen
struggling with the gap between the various positions the subject
is assigned in the social order and those aspects of the self neither
accepted nor represented there.

Another person can constitute such a mirror, as when Hester and
Dimmesdale finally encounter one another in the forest beyond the
physical boundaries of the social system: "the crisis flung back to
them their consciousness, and revealed to each heart its history and
experience, as life never does, except at such breathless epochs. The
soul beheld its features in the mirror of the passing moment" (1:190).
It is notable that these mirrors of subjectivity appear at moments
of crisis and conflict with social institutions and socially created
problems. Hester is on the scaffold when she remembers her beauty
"illuminating all the interior of the dusky mirror in which she had
been wont to gaze at it" (1:58)—a surface that is dark because her
sexuality can find no full acceptable expression in her society. It
is at her bleakest moments when social prescription weighs most
heavily on her that Hester can see in her small daughter only what
the Puritan world would expect her to find: in the "small black
mirror of Pearl's eye" (1:97), she does not see her own image in spite
of this being her customary experience (a mother/daughter dyad
existing outside the symbolic order). Instead she sees the image of

a malevolent Dimmesdale, the hidden half of Pearl's parentage and an image of the anger she feels at his betrayal of her.

The mental lives of Dimmesdale and Chillingworth, again specifically in relationship to the social order, are also described through images of the mirror: the minister's hallucinatory visions in the looking glass of his private study are the creations of constant introspection brought about by socially induced guilt. Chillingworth, in conversation with his former wife, suddenly senses the clash between his former identity within a community (the happy husband) and his present position as the revengeful husband: it is "as if he had beheld some frightful shape, which he could not recognize, usurping the place of his own image in a glass. It was one of those moments—which sometimes occur only at the interval of years—when a man's moral aspect is faithfully revealed to his mind's eye" (1:172).

Considering these moments of internal conflict recorded in mirrors, it would seem that desire can be found in a pure and continuous state only in a Pearl. For Hester, it is something lost in adulthood and then refound—the "mightier touch," the recovery of desire that "awakened all her sensibilities" (1:176), so socially as well as personally disruptive. Moments of undivided and unrepressed desire in others are transitory, brought into being by socially unsanctioned (indeed erotically associated) contact with another person: for example, the "tumultuous rush of new life" (1:153) on the nighttime scaffold when Dimmesdale takes Pearl's hand; or the "exhilarating" rise of his spirits in the forest when Hester volunteers to leave with him (1:201); in the same scene Hester's recovery of her erotic self as she takes off letter and cap, "gushing from the very heart of womanhood" (1:202); and Chillingworth's "wild look of wonder, joy, and horror" and the "ghastly rapture . . . too mighty to be expressed only by the eye and features" (1:138) when he thrusts his hand inside Dimmesdale's clothes in a parody of the sexual act. Also part of this is Dimmesdale's "violence of passion," so forbidden socially that the narrator, backing away in alarm, draws on an unmodified discourse of Puritan orthodoxy to deal with it (it "was, in fact, the portion of him which the Devil claimed" [1:194]).

These rare escapes of feeling from the "dungeon of his [and indeed her] own heart" (1:201) occur in places or at moments that are fully secluded from the gaze of the town when expression can be comparatively less inhibited. As a result of this seclusion and secrecy, such incidents remain marginalized and without clear social reference, except insofar as the fumbling attempts to express such feelings use words and symbols drawn from the social order. This only serves to remind and reintroduce the very social frames of reference that the characters desire to escape. It will presently be considered whether the protagonists do succeed in changing the meaning of that letter and the language of Puritan value to which they paradoxically still have to recourse.

Furthermore, once a character reinserts herself or himself into society, these feelings become distorted and perverse. Desire expressed, for example, on Dimmesdale's return from the forest, takes a corrupted form. When finally in that last, fully public, scaffold scene all characters expose themselves willingly or unwillingly in actions imitating some of those earlier scenes of expressed desire (Dimmesdale holding Pearl's hand and exposing his stigmata beside a demented Chillingworth and Hester pleading desperately again for love), there is only death, disappointment, and diminution. The only other exception to the almost universal repression or social transmutation of that kind of "desire" (and again it is made clear that it has no reference to the Massachusetts social order) are the mariners, dressed in clothes as gorgeous as Hester's letter or Pearl's garments. At the moment of greatest conflict between "desire" and "circumstance" (Dimmesdale in the pulpit awaited by Hester outside), the narrator's attention is lengthily dominated by these sailors, because they "transgressed, without fear or scruple, the rules of behavior that were binding on all others" (1:232)—including, as we are to see, Hester and Dimmesdale. The sea, which the lovers will never reach, is "subject only to the tempestuous wind, with hardly any attempts at regulation by human law" (1:233).

Mostly, the characters experience subjectivity as a regulated and hence confused state. Hawthorne's Concord work expressed a belief that there were innate desires that were not met within the existing social order, and his writings then evolved a model of the human subject that was important for its hypothesis (opposed to the position of nearly all the 1830s works) that individual identity could not be described purely as the creation of any particular society. But such a conception failed to deal with the full complexity of subjectivity as well as leaving "desire" itself as a rather vague concept. Even Hawthorne's most elaborated work of that period, "Rappaccini's Daughter," while unique in his work up to that point for its depiction of intersubjective tensions, could not deal in any detailed way, within that enclosed and fantastical garden, with how each person's desire is given a particular shape by the society of which she or he must be a part. While the men in that tale may suggest the way in which ideas of science and sexuality are culturally constructed, Beatrice, for all her courage, is far too simply presented as a male product with no other connections with life in the Paduan streets.

The Concord tales had also argued that the "Book of Wishes" ("wishes" in the sense of something that preexists the taking up of positions within the social order) was "probably truer, as a representation of the human heart, than is the living drama of action, as it evolves around us" (10:333). This question of what if anything can be said to be essential to the human constitution continues to be important in *The Scarlet Letter*, given its preoccupation both with a social order designed to control its members at all levels and with the possibilities of a child's psychological inheritance and education. Symptomatically, the word "nature" recurs far more frequently with reference to human beings than "nature" in the sense of the nonhuman natural world.[18] The focus, however, is mainly on the qualities that seem to make each person individual, and in consequence unique in her or his circumstances—"the very constitution of his nature" (1:132). Less commonly, the narrator does make generalizations about "human nature" (1:40, 160, 162, 227) and "our common nature" (1:55), and about supposedly essential gender differences (for example, "the very nature of woman" [1:65], the "nature of the opposite sex" [1:165], and motherhood's "sympathies of nature" [1:101]). Such generalizing comments are a product of the narrator's desire for some kind of sympathetic community. Because they slide over those individual traits that make integration into the community so difficult (those to do with sexuality, anger, fear, jealousy), the narrator fails to convince. Sometimes when he does show concerted action based on a "common nature," there is a disturbing moblike quality to this (1:40, 162).

In talking about a particular individual's "nature," however, there is interest in how that personality's basic and distinct disposition operates within the social order and is affected by it; it is not a matter of simply finding the right slot for people. This can be seen in the way the word is used in the discussions of the Custom-House habitués (1:20, 37, 38), of Pearl (1:165, 90, 262), of those who wish to confess and cannot (1:132), of Dimmesdale himself (1:166, 198), and of Hester as nurse (1:161). Particular interest is expressed in apparently innately varied levels of energy in the personality that determines the individual's power to survive and to assert herself or himself to others within a community—that "native energy of character," the "vigour in Pearl's nature," "weakness or force of his original nature," "the ordinary resources of her nature," and Hester's "impulsive and passionate nature," and the "inexhaustible" tenderness in her "nature" (1:84, 184, 38, 78, 57, 161). None of this assumes that one's nature has any inherent moral quality. "Wild," used of a person's nature, may be interpreted positively or negatively (1:79, 244, 262); it merely indicates that something lies outside social forms. Two classic notions of essential human nature are both clearly rejected by the novel: the Romantic conception of presocial innocence, and the Calvinist belief in innate depravity (only mentioned in the novel in the slightly absurd though theologically correct context of a three-year-old child whose character is untamed but hardly vicious).

The Scarlet Letter now suggests that a "truer" representation of the subject will be one that investigates subjectivity within that "living drama of action," which "The Intelligence Office" had discounted. Hester realizes at the novel's outset, as she returns from the prolonged contemplation of memories to her temporarily forgotten situation on the scaffold, that, "Yes!—these were her realities,—all else had vanished!" (1:59). The extensive treatment of the town's religio-political structures as well as a considerable amount of social detail throughout is part of this move to place the subject within an actual social order; indeed, the analysis of the authorities in the Election Day procession show how impressed the narrator is by the substantial nature of the social formation he has to deal with.

The processes of consciousness do not, of course, "vanish" from the tale (as it did when in the 1830s Hawthorne's writing turned its attention to social reality). Nor do they remain an "incommunicable thought" (10:349) as it was in some of the *Provincial Tales* both as far as the protagonist's community was concerned, and also for the baffled reader. Here, despite Dimmesdale's inner isolation, Chillingworth's opting to shed his identity as Roger Prynne, and Hester's constant sense of not belonging to the town, subjectivity is continually placed within and connected to that social order. We have seen how some of the *Provincial Tales* identified the moment when consciousness registered the dividing of the self—the subject's moment of awareness of her or his own subjectivity. Taking its beginning a year after the act of adultery had irrevocably separated self as subject and self as object for Hester and Dimmesdale (and consequently for Chillingworth), *The Scarlet Letter* is more concerned with elaborating the consequences of living thus consciously divided: Dimmesdale's shriek on the midnight scaffold may recall Brown's cry in the forest or Robin's laughter at the procession, but here, unlike those abruptly concluded tales, the novel moves on swiftly to resituate Dimmesdale in his community, firstly within the seventeenth-century mind-set with its interpretative conventions, and then fully in daytime Boston with details and an extended action.

Here, too, adultery has far more repercussions than the climactic events of many of the *Provincial Tales*. Now desire collides publicly with social institutions, rather than secretly and ambivalently inside some young man's head; the fact of Pearl's existence cannot be ignored. The erotic is foregrounded as the central issue that the community has failed to contain within the framework of marriage and institutionalized gender relations.[19] The letter on Hester's dress is the interface between passion and the social order, the point where desire is translated into the terms of Boston's symbolic order. The scaffold functions in a similar way as an interface between different parts of the self, and hence becomes "the one point that gave it [her life] unity" (1:244). The nature of that passion is, however, not wholly assimilated and reduced by that signification. Hester's own meaning, symbolized by her elaborate embroidery of the letter, persists and is given public currency despite her initial conscious rejection of it as self-expression (1:83–84).

The letter, too, indicates how Hester, Dimmesdale, and the cuckolded Chillingworth act out for other people impulses denied, repressed, or negatively framed. It feels for Hester as if "her heart had been flung into the street for them all to spurn and trample upon" (1:55), but for the rest of the community too her function is not merely a celebration of their probity. Even though framed by public condemnation, Hester represents and recalls both the perennial existence of such passions even within the most "righteous" community and the way that society is unable to accommodate them. These New Englanders need Hester to remind them of their own frustrated, repressed, suffering selves: she is the mirror in which they see themselves, even though they tend consciously to deal with that recognition by rejecting that truth and making her a scapegoat. Given the nineteenth-century narrator's ambivalent response to Hester, this observation holds good for Hawthorne's readership too. It was, as he observed in a letter of January 15, 1850, to his publisher J. T. Fields, "rather a delicate subject to write upon," so much so that he had to write in a way that would not offend his readers' sensibilities (16:305).

Because the colony's image is the ideologically sustained one of unity, purpose, commitment, and clear self-definition, Hester cannot at first believe what her experience of wearing the letter tells her: that she is not the only sexual sinner or tempted soul in Massachusetts (surely an otherwise not unreasonable assumption). It is a testimony to the extent to which she is mentally assimilated into Boston that she assumes that her intuitions are false, indeed satanic. At this stage Hester does not know how endemic is her condition as the unloved wife and frustrated lover; only later will her fellow citizens come openly to her for advice on such matters that are not part of the official picture.

She has, it is true, become a safe confidante only by virtue of her self-abnegation: her full feelings may not ever be understood, and indeed she would seem too dangerous to others if those feelings were. In her earlier days when she is a dangerous image, the merest covert or unintentionally expressed hint of shared feelings and experience had for her quickly turned from a sense of relatedness (an alternative community of desire) to her orthodoxly framed belief that her "sin" had merely been repeated (1:86–87). The narrator, who likes the idea of the older Hester as sorrow-stricken counsellor, is characteristically far more disturbed by that community of desire (he clings to a nineteenth-century norm of sexually "pure" femininity). Although he recognizes Hester as "poor victim of her own frailty, and man's hard law" (87)—a phrase that suggests excessive punishment for something she could not wholly prevent—he shies away from the likely (but as yet unverifiable) inference that she is not an exception. The society that buys Hester's gorgeous embroideries (explicitly linked through the *A* and Pearl to the erotic) cannot be one in which desire is wholly suppressed.

So the "labyrinth" (1:166) of Hester's mind is not unique to her, but inevitably reflects the societal labyrinth she inhabits: her inner conflicts (and Dimmesdale's and Chillingworth's) are those of their culture, only more intense and more fully acted out. Boston is not a monolithic structure of fundamentalist oppression, to be seen simply in terms of a depersonalized state opposed by dissenting individuals, nor is it one where a distinction can be sharply drawn between the abstract processes of institutional power and the quite separate actions of private citizens. True, the state can be very dangerous on the few occasions when it totally denies the subjective reality of its members. Language then detaches itself completely from actuality: " 'But, in their great mercy and tenderness of heart, they [the magistrates] have doomed Mistress Prynne to stand only a space of three hours on the platform of the pillory' " (1:63). However, Governor Bellingham does receive Hester at home dressed "in a loose gown and easy cap,—such as elderly gentlemen loved to indue [*sic*] themselves with, in their domestic privacy" (1:108), and Mr. Wilson who is there to assist Bellingham's nonetheless official enquiry into Pearl's upbringing, is at one and the same time the church authority checking on the thoroughness of Pearl's theological education and "a grandfatherly sort of personage, and usually a vast favorite with children" (1:111). The authorities, we are told, are slowest to bend, but eventually even they acknowledge her "good qualities" (1:162). This is not simply hypocrisy, but the inherently mixed nature of existence in social relations.

Hester's treatment at the hands of her fellow citizens is shown to have highly mixed motives: contemptuous condemnation has "its mingled grin and frown" (1:85); praise for her charities comes with mention of her disgraceful past; apparent tolerance may be only the "cool stare of familiarity" (1:86). God's Commonwealth is a complicated place, and all sorts of needs and compulsions are covertly in operation. The chapter, "Another View of Hester," involves us seeing another and more mixed view of Boston from that introductory punitive portrait. It is the narrator, commenting on a tolerance based on self-interest rather than principle, who clings to a liberal hope rather than pursue these harsh contradictions: "As is apt to be the case when a person stands out in any prominence before the community, and, at the same time, interferes neither with public or individual interests and convenience, a species of general regard had ultimately grown up in reference to Hester Prynne. It is to the credit of human nature, that, except where its selfishness is brought into play, it loves more readily than it hates" (1:160).

The utopianism of this society also needs to be incorporated into this picture. The reforming urges of 1840s Concord are here recast and critically scrutinized. This utopianism is central to the tension between desire and actual social conditions, and shows how the structures and ideologies of a society must be related, however retrogressively and with distortion, to the desires of its individual members. This coercive and authoritarian theocracy is the projection of a desire for perfect individuals living in a perfect institution (perfection being of course defined in Calvinist terms), and it has been formed by common choice (that is, at least by those church members with a vote). Dissidents in consequence "would have been sternly repressed, not only by the rigid discipline of law, but by the general sentiment which gives law its vitality" (1:231). Dimmesdale's Election Day sermon, written when we might least expect it, testifies to the vital persistence of such utopianism, and its coexistence and indeed even connection with those other strong desires in his psyche. Hester's vision of better relations between women and men is yet another version of the utopian urge, though one that does not have as its premise the innate depravity of humanity and that does not try to achieve perfection by the use of prisons.

Massachusetts' ideology merely camouflages a paradoxical social reality that includes both injustice and yet a profound longing for absolute justice, and both deep piety as well as disobedience to divine command and the near atheistical fatalism of the scientist honored in their midst. The very attempt to construct such a utopian institution, however, severs that society from other forms of desire: sexuality institutionalized becomes only the legalized (marriage) or the illegitimate (adultery). The inevitable product of such a "civilized society" (1:48) must be suppression and repression.

The conflicts and contradictions, which the protagonists experience internally as well as externally, are therefore representative of inherent divisions within the culture itself. Hester, imagining reform, recognizes how subjectivity is shaped by the particular society in which the individual finds herself or himself: "As a first step, the whole system of society is to be torn down, and built up anew. Then, the very nature of the opposite sex, or its long hereditary habit, which has become like nature, is to be essentially modified" (1:165). The essentialism of the remarks on femininity that then follow this observation testify more to the *narrator's* own conservatism about women than to any belief in innate nature actually established in the text. "The Custom-House" provided further evidence of the social structuring of subjectivity in the fear it expressed that to hold office too long would have been to change one's supposed nature (1:38, 40). So here at last Hawthorne returns to the sense of the social construction of identity, last explored at any length in "Legends of the

Province-House" (again in a historical setting). This time, however, there is the attempt to trace the coexistence of such an identity with a persistent, unsocialized desire, whereas previously he had treated the latter separately though contemporaneously in "Edward Fane's Rosebud" and "The Shaker Bridal," and subsequently in many of the tales written at Concord.

The social construction of identity coexisting with unsocialized desire is clearest in the person of Dimmesdale, possibly because he is most implicated in maintaining this system. His conflict between God and Eros would be merely a cultural commonplace if the intensity of his religious faith, wholly characteristic of New England, had not given those contradictions a revived power and his religious office a central significance, and had not his desperate ambivalence pushed him into extreme, almost absurd positions. The erotic and the religious are so entangled that there is no real surprise in finding him writing his best sermon in praise of God's America on the evening after his decision to resume sexual relations with a woman whose husband he now knows is still alive. His reality is Boston, and his censored feelings can be manifested only in the hidden language of his stigmata. Because his had been "a sin of passion, not of principle, nor even purpose" (1:200), it was all the harder for him subsequently to police such undeliberated impulses. As a result the deed actually hems him in ever more tightly into the belief structures of his society through the need for constant self-surveillance, whereas for Hester the experience pulls down ideological fences. A related paradox of his Christian orthodoxy is that it is an "iron framework" (123) that simultaneously supports and confines, thus indicating in part at least an emotional rather than consciously principled dependence on socially established doctrine. It is a moot point whether Dimmesdale wants Hester sexually when she makes her proposal in the forest. Rather, he wants to be recognized—if not by the town, then by Hester.

Even Hester, the one who comes nearest to being able finally to express undivided desire by the time she meets Dimmesdale seven years later in the forest and has come to see herself as the prophetess of a new social order, evinces a subjectivity structured by this social and symbolic order, whose influence persists even when she appears more liberated. Her feelings about her adulterous act have been mixed. She has infringed the Mosaic/Massachusetts code, and it seems at first that she does at least acknowledge the force of that traditional moral law, at least as one among several kinds of obligation pressing upon her. Yet discussing their marriage with Chillingworth in the prison, Hester does not immediately admit guilt: her remark, "'I have greatly wronged thee'" (1:74), comes as her response to *his* admission of the role played by his own emotional vulnerability in creating this unstable marriage. The comment, "She knew that her deed had been evil" (1:89), is only the prelude (though not one that is dismissed) to a review of the paradoxes and unknowns of having given birth to her daughter. She faces there not only the comfortably familiar paradox of a fortunate fall (the illegitimate, beloved child who may save her soul) but also contradictory but equally culturally derived fears that Pearl is a demonic being, fears that, however, are then recast (though not necessarily more reassuringly) in more materialist and no longer religiously condemnatory terms of genetic inheritance and environmental influence.

It is such mixed sentiments that have to be placed alongside her assertion, "'What we did had a consecration of its own. We felt it so!'" (1:195). She is not simply the Romantic individualist as antinomian, opposing a wholly repressive society. Because of contradictory views within her, the letter is simultaneously both a triumph and a source of shame, even if her sense of guilt is not absolutely identical in its basis to what the public punishment is intended to make her feel. We must not read her apparently assured forest decision (made in the heat of the moment) back into her earlier, more divided responses, even if "consecration" had indeed been felt, as she implies, long ago at the moment of love-making. It takes seven years of social ostracism and the intellectual pursuit of moral understanding (rather than dependence on that authority of feeling) to clarify what is right and wrong for her into a clearly defined personal code of individual responsibility. To express this code she must adapt the language of orthodox morality, and since language in its nature is never immovably fixed, those meanings do shift and express her new sense of things.

Even so, this resistance to social absorption must exist side by side with those forms of social determination.[20] The account given of her reasons for having previously lived out her sentence in Boston indicates not only her confusion but also her earlier attempt to resolve contradiction by a more orthodox censorship of unpermitted feelings and the espousal of punishment—an attempt that must fail because she is in part aware of what she is doing: "What she compelled herself to believe,—what, finally, she reasoned upon, as her motive for continuing a resident of New England,—was half a truth, and half a self-delusion" (1:80). The lengthy analysis of her motives at this point leaves it unclear how much of this we must ascribe respectively to cultural assimilation, or to romantic love, or to less conscious psychological needs to remain in a place that, unlike girlhood in England, has given her an identity. It seems likely that all of these are involved, and none are preeminent at this point.

Hester's rebellion has huge repercussions for her thinking about social structures in general, for she sees that gender relations are central to these. Her thinking moves beyond her own existence to question that of "the whole race of womanhood" (1:165). Superficially, hers might seem an all-too-stereotypical story of a woman faithful unto death to the man she loves: in spite of his dying rejection of her ("'Hush, Hester, hush'" [1:256]), her final words concern "how sacred love should make us happy, by the truest test of a life successful to such an end!" (1:263). (Dimmesdale failed such a test.) For a nineteenth-century audience, this lifelong "sacred love" would only mean marriage and the conventional expectations of woman's role as devoted wife and mother (Hester obediently, if reluctantly, helping Dimmesdale up the scaffold steps).

But Hester's vision resists such assimilation into existing gender norms. The complexities of these four people's unhappy lives suggest that something more than a legalized form of romantic love is needed to reform the social order that so shapes subjectivity. We are not being offered a new version of "The New Adam and Eve," for that utopian "inner sphere which they inhabit together" (10:248) had been reimagined in the disastrous congress of Beatrice and Giovanni. Hester's prophecy of a "life successful to such an end" will not come into being without changes in the way society constructs femininity and masculinity—the Dimmesdales of this world would need to change as do the Hesters. There is, too, an implicit criticism of contemporary nineteenth-century femininity, in particular the loss of energy and sexuality (1:50).

It is the sphere of gender relations specifically to do with intimate relationships—marriage, family, romantic love—that is the critical locus of both connection and conflict between individual passion and social institutions, and consequently the weak point where stresses show and fractures occur. As Hester knows, the meeting with her husband privately in the prison is far more frightening than the previous three hours exposed to the public gaze. However, it is also true that Dimmesdale, Chillingworth, and Hester do each have a public identity and a social role—minister, doctor, nurse—and these must first be taken into account when exploring the ostensibly separate and private world of intimate relations. These social roles are both significant to them and a source of complex ambiguity since the roles are distorted by unexpressed desire, particularly where power over others is involved.

Chillingworth was once a caring man seeking "the advancement of human welfare" (1:172) whose knowledge becomes also the power to torture and control. Dimmesdale, as a minister, has a power that is derived not simply from his official position but also from a private ability that taps the needs and desires of individuals. The connection is established subliminally through the special quality of voice delivering the sermons (1:67), as well as his secret experience of "sin." Disturbingly, "[t]he people knew not the power that moved them thus" (1:142), so that Dimmesdale, meeting the young woman parishioner, consciously recognizes the erotic base of their relation-ship of which she remains unconscious (1:219). The potential for abuse is made clear, though Dimmesdale fights off the temptation: "The virgins of his church grew pale around him, victims of a passion so imbued with religious sentiment that they imagined it to be all religion, and brought it openly, in their white bosoms, as their most acceptable sacrifice before the altar" (1:142). This "deep, almost worshipping respect, which the minister's professional and private claims alike demanded" (1:218), gives him, like Chillingworth the physician, a power that threatens to be corrupting once he mentally steps outside of official controls of the community. Talking to his parishioners on his return, the minister's reluctant power game is stripped of its socially respectable facade. Chillingworth's deliberate abuse, culminating in the surreptitious examination of the sleeping Dimmesdale, similarly arises from his mental separation from the usual social restraints on these powerful desires.

Hester's public work within the community is at once both more incidental (since Dimmesdale and Pearl are her center) and acciden-tal: "She was self-ordained a Sister of Mercy; or, we may rather say, the world's heavy hand has so ordained her, when neither the world nor she looked forward to this result" (1:161). But the sick and suf-fering evoke in her a warmth, pity, and impulse to help that are also part of her response to Dimmesdale. She is quick to drop this role when Dimmesdale needs her, for women in this world are not usually "Able" (1:161)—that is, they do not usually have a public role other than motherhood. Motherhood, however, was society's conventional role for women in both seventeenth- and nineteenth-century New England, and in early Boston it is unusually open to public scrutiny in comparison with other societies. Hester evolves her own style of mothering, negotiating between what the novel presents as the conventional seventeenth-century expectations of her community and the more liberal nineteenth-century readers' sense of a child's needs. We should, however, be cautious about celebrating her too straightforwardly as tender matriarchal rule opposing authoritarian patriarchy, when we see how she still has recourse to Bostonian severity when she feels particularly pressed by the impossible need to meet conflicting demands of child and lover: " 'Do not tease me; else I shall shut thee into the dark closet!' " (1:181). Possibly it is only Dimmesdales's patriarchal presence that drives her thus to threaten her daughter.[21]

It is the personal relationships between the three adult protag-onists ("their mutual world" [1:240]) that both subvert and distort those public, professional subject positions. These personal relationships access desire while at the same time being partly shaped by the characters' social identities. In consequence, another set of subject positions must be taken into account: husband, wife, lover (this last, though not socially recognized, is a relationship defined by Dimmesdale very much within the framework of current nineteenth-century public attitudes). Desire is shaped by socially instituted expectations; both men have conventional expectations of Hester as a woman. "'Wondrous strength and generosity of a woman's heart'" (1:68), mutters Dimmesdale, romanticizing Hester's refusal to name her partner, after having laid on her with consummate ambiguity the burden of confessing for him. In the forest she offers again a similar conventional devotion, albeit—given Chillingworth's existence—in a socially unsanctionable relationship.

For Chillingworth, marriage had been a culturally conceived and idealized compensation for his personality and work: he had hoped "'that the simple bliss, which is scattered far and wide for all mankind to gather up, might yet be mine'" (1:74). Chillingworth, in the conventional language of marital bliss, "needed to bask himself" in her "nuptial smile" (1:176). Ironically, it is Chillingworth's radical restatement of the basis of marriage (during the meeting with Hester in the prison) that Hester adopts and adapts: his experience and intellectual independence allow him to see beyond the simple prohibition of the Mosaic code ("thou shalt not commit adultery"). But this anger and desire are expressed in much more conventionally motivated acts, possibly because that patriarchal world bestows on the frustrated male the power he may lack personally. For all his intellectual distance from the mainstream beliefs of Boston and his acknowledgment of the emotional roots of present difficulties, when it comes to his actions Chillingworth behaves exactly as a cuckolded husband would have been expected to do—if he cannot have Hester, Dimmesdale "'must needs be mine!'" (1:75).

Hester alone tries to distance herself from such conventional forms, responding to her marriage in language that would surely have shocked the novel's original readership: "Such scenes had once appeared not otherwise than happy, but now, as viewed through the dismal medium of her subsequent life, they classed themselves among her ugliest remembrances" (1:176). The form that her love takes complicates matters for everyone: she will not fit Chilling-worth's idea of a wife, nor Dimmesdale's notion of the self-sacrificing woman. She becomes forthright in her condemnation of her husband despite her marriage vows, and clear in her wishes in respect of Dimmesdale (it is she who proposes that they flee Boston together). But she, too, has recourse to ordinary forms: what she intends setting up in Europe is a quite familiar family unit of father, mother, and daughter.

▼

What conclusions then can the novel offer? The final part of this chapter will examine the resolutions sought and outcomes reached, the interweaving of change and limitation. There is neither total freedom nor total determinism. In spite of her subjective involvement in social structures of meaning, Hester still finds it possible to question established moral structures and to try to act upon her ideas—her envisaging a "coming revelation" (1:263) is a gesture toward change. The male protagonists, more securely locked inside its assumptions, destroy themselves or others. In the final scaffold scene, "men of rank and dignity" were "perplexed as to the purport of what they saw,—unable to receive the explanation which most readily presented itself, or to imagine any other,—" (1:253). These men belong to a community that, for all its utopian aspirations, is characterized as "accomplishing so much, precisely because it imagined and hoped so little" (1:64).

Hester, excluded primarily by her sex (rather than solely by her misdemeanor) from participation in political practicalities of this patriarchal state, is instead partially freed to "imagine" and "hope"—attempting creatively to visualize a reformed social order for every-one as well as an alternative life for Dimmesdale and herself. Perhaps it matters less that what she wants is to make a home for Dimmesdale than that she is capable of that initial thrust for wider change. Unlike those Puritans, she has identified the centrality of changing relationships between women and men in any reformation of the community in the interests of justice and happiness. The Puritan attempt to found a better society in New England while maintaining traditional gender relations unaltered had its logical outcome in state punishment for adultery. Hester, in taking a wider view, goes further than the women in "Edward Fane's Rosebud" and "The Shaker Bridal," who challenged male investment in existing status and power only by the fact of their unextinguished love and did not see beyond the personal and particular. It must be noted, however, that Hester the prophetess is quite prepared to suspend her general ambitions for society in order to quit Massachusetts altogether for the arms of Dimmesdale. Her attempt to flee is doomed to failure because it is a personal solution, ignoring her knowledge of the need for wider social change.

The men, more directly implicated in power structures, find it harder to challenge them. Dimmesdale's decision to remove himself from Boston paradoxically inserts him mentally even more securely within it: he is now, in his view, a confirmed sinner and the Massachusetts colony all the more blessed in comparison. His ministerial work has shown him, like Hester, the great extent of guilt and unhappiness, but he has experienced this within an orthodox framework that submits "sinners" to their God. As a result, his glowing image of the Holy Commonwealth and its future remains untarnished by this knowledge. He certainly feels no need for radical social reform, as Hester had felt. The community loves his Election Day sermon, giving as it does such a pleasing, compensatory self-image, and so not surprisingly he thus reaches the pinnacle of his career. The euphoric sense of community caused by this political rhetoric pushes him to try to make himself fully known to it through confession. Hester was accurate in her assessment of his position in the Election Day procession—"he seemed so remote from her own sphere" (1:239)—and the narrator rightly (if in a condescendingly essentialist way) sees her resentment of this as gender based: "And thus much of woman was there in Hester, that she could scarcely forgive him . . . for being able so completely to withdraw himself from their mutual world" (1:240).

Sexual love in this novel leads swiftly to ethical considerations, as Hester tries to evolve for herself ideas of moral right and wrong to replace demonstrably inadequate conventional structures regulating desire. Adultery may be totally prohibited—the narrator never discounts this—but the most that the novel will establish is that seventeenth-century Boston believed it to be so. Yet all three protagonists in different ways have at some point questioned this by asking what marriage means. Hester revises the old language of obligation and condemnation: " 'Yes, I hate him!,' " says Hester of Chillingworth, " 'He betrayed me! He has done me worse wrong than I did him!' " (1:176). Negotiation between promises made to both husband and lover brings a similar shift in the symbolic system of conventional morals, made all the more vivid for Hester having to explain this change to her legal spouse: " 'for, having cast off all duty towards other human beings, there remained a duty towards him [Dimmesdale]; and something whispered me that I was betraying it, in pledging myself to keep your counsel' " (1:170). It is Chillingworth who initially introduces into the discussion of morality and marriage matters of personality, circumstance, and emotion, and Hester has now extended this into what is, for both seventeenth-century and nineteenth-century institutional norms, a profoundly radical rethinking of sexual ethics. Its disruptive power is shown in the narrator's panic, seeing a world "only the darker for this woman's beauty, and the more lost for the infant that she had borne" (1:56).

Hester's skill in adapting the language of that society to articulate her move from traditional codes demonstrates both that change is possible and that there are limits to this. This linguistic flexibility indicates that a more general evolutionary transformation is possible. But flexibility clearly cannot be infinite, and so to some extent the language of New England continues to affect the way she formulates matters even after she has ostensibly rejected that culture. Hester cannot wholly leave behind the thought patterns in which she was raised and has lived, nor indeed will she physically leave Boston in the end. Both linguistically and existentially, change and limitation are inextricably intertwined.

The exploration of moral values goes even further with speculation about what then constitutes the worst sin of all. Indeed, the clearest definition of "evil" in the novel immediately precedes that most celebrated assertion of Hester's new moral good (" 'What we did had a consecration of its own. We felt it so! We said so to each other! Hast thou forgotten it?' " [1:195]). It is Dimmesdale who formulates the new description of sin not simply because he has experienced Chillingworth's influence most, but because he cannot shed the Puritan mentality in which the idea of "sin" plays a central role. Hester, too, in similarly seeing their situation in judgmental terms, testifies to the way her seven-year penal experience (as well as her education) has given her subjectivity a particular shape. This kind of conceptualizing (note the abstract way in which he will refer to himself) can be expected from someone who even after the forest meeting remains a minister, theologically trained to consider such questions: " 'May God forgive us both! We are not, Hester, the worst sinners in the world. There is one worse than even the polluted priest! That old man's revenge has been blacker than my sin. He has violated, in cold blood, the sanctity of a human heart. Thou and I, Hester, never did so!' " (1:195). But here the idea of what constitutes the greatest evil is neither simply the intriguing metaphysical and ethical speculation of "Ethan Brand," nor the ideological reaction of some hypersensitive Puritan. Rather it is a way of investigating the general basis of this moral shift that Hester has begun to express. So arguably the protagonists' patterns of ethical thought are here more a help than a hindrance.

The key notion here seems to be "violation," and it proves useful because it is central to all the characters and their circumstances, and relates directly to the basic conception of human subjectivity underpinning the novel. Evil is not Calvinist Original Sin, that principle of innate corruption operating within human beings. It is seen to lie in those fractures in consciousness, long since identified in Hawthorne's work as productive of suffering and a sense of wrong. Now, however, the focus is not so exclusively on the resulting pains of alienation, but on how others may exploit that gap to their own ends. "Evil" is a perversion of love (violation itself having a sexual as well as a general meaning). Both love and this "evil" involve intimacy, that access to individual subjectivity that "sympathy" makes possible. When this "heart-knowledge" constitutes an unwanted, secret, and undetected access into consciousness, then it gives the interloper power to manipulate, expose, and damage. All three protagonists recognize the potential of such knowledge: Hester had backed off in fear from the intuitions that her letter gave her about her fellow townspeople; Dimmesdale had fought not to abuse the power provided by his intimate knowledge of his parishioners; Chillingworth alone uses this power to hurt. It is a realization that leaves our somewhat conservative liberal narrator in the final chapter both fascinated by the radical implications of this for viewing the customary and far more simply conceived emotional/moral landscape of human interrelationships, and profoundly wary himself of pursuing those disruptive implications any further: "It is a curious subject of observation and inquiry, whether hatred and love be not the same thing at bottom. Each, in its utmost development, supposes a high degree of intimacy and heart-knowledge; each renders one individual dependent for the food of his affections and spiritual life upon another; each leaves the passionate lover, or the no less passionate hater, forlorn and desolate by the withdrawal of his object" (1:260).

At the roots of this notion of "violation" lies the realization that the sympathetic imagination is not the constant and unambiguous instrument for good that most of the Concord works had believed. Such intimacy may be a source of terror rather than the promise of others' loving recognition of that part of the self that remains unexpressed within the social order. Indeed, one reason why it may be unexpressed emerges in this novel—a clearly delineated understanding of the repressive force of a conformist and powerfully controlling social formation, be it seventeenth century or nineteenth century (the "Custom-House" narrator had also been forced to see that). Such a society makes the idea of being "known" generally within the community a dangerously sentimental ideal. Part of the self is therefore extremely vulnerable and in need of protection from the very people by whom it so desires to be recognized and accepted.

The way in which the word "sympathy" is recurrently and variously used throughout the novel further clarifies this matter. The notion of imaginative sympathy, slowly maturing over the years, clearly articulated in his Concord work but made too sweet and easy in the Salem tales, is now explored in all its complexity. The word and its derivatives occur at least forty-one times in *The Scarlet Letter*, and its significance will be distorted unless the full range of meanings is taken on board. It is not a matter of the novel merely charting its ambiguities; instead an attempt is being made to make sense of these, and to explain how it is possible for "sympathy" to lead to either trust or violation.

Basically, "sympathy" here is a morally neutral response, an identity of feeling or physical substance with another person or thing. The word had been used in a similar sense in "Rappaccini's Daughter" when Beatrice, the flowering bush, and Giovanni all came to possess the same physical attribute. Similarly, in that tale it was a question of power that makes such "sympathy" morally suspect and turns it into violation: a power, based on medical knowledge and greater than that of its human subjects, invades the fabric of their being, and obliterates individuality and the ability to make one's own choices. Where "Rappaccini's Daughter" drew on Renaissance scientific terms to provide this meaning of sympathy, *The Scarlet Letter* explores the wider social, moral, and interpersonal implications that the concept came to have later in the eighteenth century. For Adam Smith sympathy was not any particular emotion, but a correspondence or agreement of feeling between people. Sympathy "may give rise to sentiments like pity and benevolence, but it is not itself a sentiment."[22] "Sympathy," as Adam Smith discovered, was central to all social intercourse, and in *The Theory of Moral Sentiments* it becomes the key to thinking about a whole range of issues (all of them also crucial to *The Scarlet Letter*) to do with the nature of virtue and vice, moral judgments, conscience, self-deceit, self-expression, the necessity of living in a society, custom, and education.

In *The Scarlet Letter*, "sympathy" ranges across a spectrum of meaning. There is the simple and not necessarily conscious identification of like with like: the sun around Pearl "attracted thitherward as by a certain sympathy" (1:208) might be a positive Romantic image, but it uncomfortably resembles another connection, this time drawn directly from Renaissance medicine, between Chillingworth and his herbs ("Would not the earth, quickened to an evil purpose by the sympathy of his eye, greet him with poisonous shrubs" [1:175]). This connection can equally be pleasant or painful: the entertainers' "appeals to the very broadest sources of mirthful sympathy" (1:231) are matched by a different sort of connection in which "no human sympathy could reach her [Hester], save it were sinful like herself" (1:89). This may become an unwilled intuition or consciously felt link between two similarly constituted beings: the Surveyor's "mere sensuous sympathy of dust for dust" (1:9) with Salem; Hester, as Pearl's mother, having " 'sympathies which these men lack!' " (1:113); and the letter giving Hester "sympathetic knowledge of the hidden sin in other hearts" (1:86) without any contact with them. Again, chameleonlike, one may take the color of one's surroundings: the townspeople's interest in Hester reviving "by sympathy with what they saw others feel" (1:246), and Pearl's disturbed excitement an example of how "[c]hildren have always a sympathy in the agitations of those connected with them" (1:228).

None of these usages has in essence a moral meaning, even if ethical implications may emerge from it. It is the narrator who leaps to a judgmental and erroneous assumption in commenting that Dimmesdale's encounter with Mistress Hibbins "did but show his sympathy and fellowship with wicked mortals and the world of perverted spirits" (1:222). True, sympathy may seem to be positive: Dimmesdale's connection with Hester makes him a better pastor, because "this very burden it was, that gave him sympathies so intimate with the sinful brotherhood of mankind; so that his heart vibrated in unison with theirs, and received their pain into itself" (1:142). But there is a similar, and indeed similarly expressed, mechanism (though based on hate, not loving pity, and ultimately creating a very different outcome) operating in Chillingworth's perception of Dimmesdale's secret self: " 'There is a sympathy that will make me conscious of him. I shall see him tremble. I shall feel myself shudder, suddenly and unawares' " (1:75).

All this merely establishes the capacity of humans to be receptive to others' emotions. Moral questions arise when consideration is made of which feelings are contacted, how this is achieved, and with what intention and what result. To be "sensitive" (a word used nine times about Dimmesdale)[23] is a two-edged instrument. Only Chillingworth actually cultivates the power of sympathy, but the destruction of the other person's private self as a consequence of an imaginative engagement with him or her was not at all what Hawthorne's writings at Concord had envisaged: "then, at some inevitable moment, will the soul of the sufferer be dissolved, and flow forth in a dark, but transparent stream, bringing all its mysteries into the daylight" (1:124).

Again, it is true that the "sympathies" of the crowd around the scaffold at the novel's conclusion are described by the narrator very positively (at this point in the novel, under pressure of his desire for a resolution for his tale, he makes appeal to a rather vague, fictionally unsubstantiated notion of "the great heart of mankind" [1:243]). But these people's response is both involuntary and at one level based on a misapprehension of the true state of affairs. This response is not properly conscious; neither does it embrace the full otherness of the man: "the people, whose great heart was thoroughly appalled, yet overflowing with tearful sympathy, as knowing that some deep life-matter—which, if full of sin, was full of anguish and repentances likewise—was now to be laid open to them" (1:254). This is certainly not the deliberated, active workings of the sympathetic imagination as conceived in Hawthorne's earlier works. If the crowd had fully understood, it might well have condemned Dimmesdale ("[m]eagre, indeed, and cold, was the sympathy that a transgressor might look for, from such bystanders at the scaffold" [1:50]), though it is possible that the deep emotion evoked by the tone of his voice rather than his words did prove stronger than socially instituted judgments, "beseeching its sympathy or forgiveness,—at every moment,—in each accent,—and never in vain!" (1:243–44). This moment of understanding does not continue beyond his death, so what good it accomplishes unwittingly is profoundly limited. Moreover, it is notable that sympathy works here in this constructive way only when circumstances are rather impersonal (Hester the nurse, and the uncomprehending crowd around Dimmesdale) and when it does not have to deal with more disturbing feelings like hate, sexuality, or the sheer difference between individuals.

For Hester to show "sympathy" for others is instead to provoke in them "terror and horrible repugnance" (1:84). So to take an ethically constructive view of "sympathy" and argue that it is an innate, morally admirable quality whose fully conscious exercise has merely been censored and suppressed by seventeenth-century Boston is to slide over the difficulties and complexities involved in living in any social order. Judicial, religious, and popular judgments will always both coexist and conflict with that loving and forgiving understanding that such a liberal view of "sympathy" aims for, particularly where, as in Massachusetts, social institutions are fundamentally penal in character. While the final scaffold scene shows that this emotionally based understanding does exist, it also demonstrates the fragility of its operation.

Yet without the bonds created by this very "sympathy," the novel suggests, there is only isolation and alienation. As Adam Smith observes, a person who may be aware that others do not understand what he is feeling, "at the same time passionately desires a more complete sympathy. He longs for that relief which nothing can afford him but the entire concord of the affections of the spectators with his own. To see the emotions of their hearts in every respect beat time to his own, in the violent and disagreeable passions, constitutes his sole consolation."[24] It is a passage that brings Dimmesdale swiftly to mind.

Sympathy is presented as a necessary part of a child's development; it will also be shown to be essential to wider social interaction if these relationships are to escape the constricting framework of repressive ideologies. The word is used to explain Pearl's insulation from the social/symbolic order, when her mood of "perverse merriment" as she dances on tombstones removes her "entirely out of the sphere of sympathy or human contact" (1:133). Outside such contact, Pearl could become like Gervayse Hastings of "The Christmas Banquet" (a tale written when Hawthorne first explored the possibilities of the sympathetic imagination), incapable of an active response to others because of a failure to experience emotionally what another may be feeling: "She wanted—what some people want throughout life—a grief that should deeply touch her, and thus humanize and make her capable of sympathy" (1:184). When finally Pearl is fully inserted into the social order, this is achieved not simply through her father's public acknowledgment of her (which is socially misunderstood anyway): "The great scene of grief, in which the wild infant bore a part, had developed all her sympathies" (1:256). "Sympathy" here is simply the capacity to sense what another may be feeling; it does not primarily mean pity, love, or caring, although the knowledge of others that sympathy brings does in this case lead to that.[25]

In Hester's case, "sympathy" does stimulate the kind of benevolent action (Hester's care of the community's suffering) that the Salem tales had found important and that remains important. Such action is dependent on sympathy. Although charity takes second place in Hester's life to Dimmesdale and her daughter and may be construed as the transference of thwarted love, nonetheless "so much power to do, and power to sympathize" (1:161) has considerable importance both in its immediate relief for sufferers, and more significantly in its success in effecting a major shift in the letter's social meaning and hence in Boston's symbolic order. We must grant, however, that the town also has other quite self-regarding reasons for liking Hester in this new but quite conventionally feminine role: "Able; so strong was Hester Prynne, with a woman's strength" (1:161).

Nevertheless, although "sympathy" can then have benevolent effects with some people in certain circumstances, its essentially neutral nature allows it also to be an instrument to abuse others through the knowledge it brings. The sympathetic imagination had earlier in Hawthorne's work meant supportive recognition, revelation, and acceptance of those hidden parts of the subject unrepresented in the social order. *The Scarlet Letter* is deeply preoccupied with images of concealment, detection, exposure, revelation, truth, and being known to others, but it problematizes the notion of revelation and of truth to one's internal sense of being. Paradoxically the need to hide and protect part of oneself in the face of a threatening condemnatory world engenders an increasingly pressing desire within the consequently alienated being to be understood.[26]

The question remains whether "sincerity" (true feeling) has to be sacrificed as the price paid for communal tolerance and affection in Boston, and whether the only chance of being remotely "true" is to "'[s]how freely to the world, if not your worst, yet some trait whereby the worst may be inferred!'" (1:260). Sympathy depends on whether the individual expresses her or his feelings in ways that are generally deemed "proper" by the community. Smith concerns himself with the same notion of "propriety" as he ponders the social problems arising from the idea of imaginative sympathy. The social *presentation* of self turns out not to be the same as the full *representation* of self.[27] Spurning that negotiated sympathy as inauthentic will lead, as Smith himself points out, only to isolation; but to show more than this is to risk ostracization.

This is the tightrope to be walked delicately between assuming a fallacious, hypocritical social mask and meeting the opprobrium consequent on total exposure. Hester's longing thoughts about explaining the letter to Pearl are again couched in terms of "sympathy"—connections and relationship, in this case a loving one ("The thought occurred to Hester, that the child might really be seeking to approach her with childlike confidence, and doing what she could, and as intelligently as she knew how, to establish a meeting-point of sympathy" [1:179]). But dreading her antagonism, Hester lies to Pearl, and this lie ironically creates a greater gap between them: "'If this be the price of the child's sympathy, I cannot pay it!'" (1:181). Dimmesdale is, one presumes, wholly sincere in his final attempt on the scaffold to confess (unlike his earlier two-faced efforts), but chance or hesitations of his rather less than directly expressed confession mean that loving pity is here evoked without the onlookers' having consciously to accommodate the "sinner" within their image of the saintly preacher.

Yet "sympathy" and "truth" are inextricably linked—"a glimpse of human affection and sympathy, a new life, and a true one" (1:200) is how Dimmesdale conceives of it, though in his case the "sympathy" he then seeks is Boston's and the "truth" is Puritanically framed.

This connection between personal integrity and a responsive social relationship is vital given the novel's basic conception of the human subject. Being "true" is dependent on being known, and this must involve mutual, benevolent acknowledgment—sympathy not just in the sense of the faculty that makes for knowledge, but sympathy in a morally positive responsive sense. This Chillingworth realizes, and having discovered Dimmesdale's secret, he deliberately and hence destructively withholds himself until Dimmesdale has a hysterically exaggerated notion of his corruption, concealment having become for the latter an even graver sin: "'Had I one friend,—or were it my worst enemy!—to whom, when sickened with the praises of all other men, I could daily betake myself, and be known as the vilest of all sinners, methinks my soul might keep itself alive thereby. Even thus much of truth would save me!'" (1:192). Chillingworth, however, brings about his own self-destruction by a lack of truth to himself. In addition to hiding his feelings from others from the very first moment he enters Boston marketplace, he fails to acknowledge even to himself the strength of his own anger and frustration as he embarks on the search for his wife's lover, an emotional truth very different from the merely factual "truth" he thinks he is seeking.

The words "truth" and "true" pepper the text, sometimes centrally connected to the theme of revelation and that mirage of unified identity, sometimes merely as the narrator's attempt to establish some fact (for example, "it is true," "it may be true," "It might be true" [1:96, 53, 26]), or as an exclamatory acknowledgment in dialogue ("'True!'" replied he" [1:74]). The overall effect is to jostle the reader repeatedly into an uneasy desire for certainty and the suspicion that this "truth" is not yet forthcoming. Dimmesdale's congregation is "hungry for the truth" of divine revelation (1:191); Chillingworth seeks his wife's lover, "'as I have sought truth in books; as I have sought gold in alchemy'" (1:75); and the reader, seeing both the illusory nature of the doctor's past pursuits and the ambiguities of "the judgment which Providence seemed about to work" (1:253) in the final scene, is wary of trusting either books or God to deliver that "truth." The semantic variety of the word "truth" is itself testimony to the impossibility of unitary meaning.

Both Hester and Dimmesdale seem concerned with the "truth" of their feelings and actions, that is, they are concerned to establish some congruence, if not identity, between these two elements of their being (the mental life and existence in social relations). As we have seen, it is no longer a matter of "desire" opposing "circumstance," but matching consciousness and action within the social arena. "Truth" in this novel is used to cover a range of meanings with reference to a notion of psychic integrity, open relationships with others, and actions based on the adherence to some moral or metaphysical absolute. There is certainly no single truth: while Dimmesdale thinks there is a Christian one, Hester has evolved another based on an individual morality, and the narrator searches fairly unsuccessfully for some common base to both of these.

The primary meaning of "truth" is a psychological rather than an ethical one: the promise of "'Exchange this false life of thine for a true one'" (198) is as much an observation of a psychological need as an assertion by Hester of the greater right of their love over conventional morality. When Dimmesdale meets Hester in the forest, their exchange has fullness, courage, and directness because, although they have different attitudes to their deed, there had been openness between them initially ("'We felt it so! We said so to each other!'" [1:195]), and nothing can now remain concealed between them. This is so even if the social repercussions of this "truth" are nullified, and conventional morality would discern only a different kind of falsity: "Here, seen only by her eyes, Arthur Dimmesdale, false to God and man, might be, for one moment, true!" (1:196). Chillingworth himself evinces a residual desire likewise to be known, exclaiming "'Dost thou know me so little, Hester Prynne?'" (1:73), and later, breaking suddenly but momentarily from his obsession with torturing Dimmesdale to ponder with Hester (for there is no one else to talk to) over his miserable realization of his self-transformation: "'Dost thou remember me, Hester, as I was nine years agone?'" (1:172).

In one respect Dimmesdale is correct in thinking that the letter aids Hester in "truth" in this sense—"'whom the scarlet letter has disciplined to truth, though it be the truth of red-hot iron, entering into the soul'" (1:173). But Dimmesdale's "life of ghastly emptiness" in "this dismal maze" is exacerbated by her need, until this point, to hide her husband from Dimmesdale: "'I must reveal the secret,' answered Hester firmly. 'He must discern thee in thy true character'" (1:173). Hester knows both the difficulty of telling the truth and the multiple repercussions for everyone, including Pearl, of failing to do so. Dimmesdale is also described in terms of a respect for "truth," when the complex psychology of truth-telling both underlies and undermines his far simpler notion about God's truth. By using the word "true" the narrator establishes how Dimmesdale has projected the complete fragmentation of the individual subject in psychological breakdown, emotional confusion, and loss of defined social role into images of divine condemnation, rejection, and annihilation: "that eternal alienation from the Good and True, of which madness is perhaps the earthly type" (1:193). "True" and "truth" are key notions in analyzing the social and mental implications on those radical divisions within him (see "The Interior of the Heart" [1:143–46]). Here we have a model of the human subject where, in a descending spiral of ever-increasing alienation, consciousness experiences a radical separation from social positioning and finally total ontological insecurity:

> To the untrue man, the whole universe is false,—it is impalpable,—it shrinks to nothing within his grasp. And he himself, in so far as he shows himself in a false light, becomes a shadow, or, indeed, ceases to exist. The only truth, that continued to give Mr. Dimmesdale a real existence on this earth, was the anguish in his inmost soul, and the undissembled expression of it in his aspect. Had he once found power to smile, and wear a face of gayety, there would have been no such man! (1:145–46)

Transitory moments where "truth" of a person's being is made clear propel events toward the unraveling of some of the difficulties: Dimmesdale on the midnight scaffold wondering, "'Who is that man?'" [1:156] leads ultimately to the forest scene and then to the final scaffold scene. But the ultimate solution is not as obvious as Pearl thinks it to be: "'Thou wast not bold!—thou wast not true!' answered the child. 'Thou wouldst not promise to take my hand, and mother's hand, to-morrow noontide!'" (1:157). For Dimmesdale, unity of being is sought through public confession, arguably in this novel an act of primarily social and psychological importance for the subject within the social order rather than the religious necessity (which is how it would have been regarded by Puritan Massachusetts). This emphasis is made clear by the problems raised in the extended and highly ironical discussion of confession between Dimmesdale and Chillingworth, with the atheistical, corrupted doctor lecturing the minister on what is good for God's glory and thereby confirming Dimmesdale's most despairing view of himself (and making the reader question it), and Dimmesdale covertly speaking of his dilemma while simultaneously ducking this opportunity to reveal his deed. After such a discussion, it is hard to see confession unambiguously.[28]

Hester has discovered, however, that wearing the letter does not automatically make her wholly known to her townspeople, unsuspecting as they are of her intellectual radicalism and continuing faithfulness to her lover. She recognizes that a unified being within society is impossible for her (or indeed anyone), and although carried away for a time by the possibilities of living within another society (an illusion given Dimmesdale's needs and desires), she settles for the partial truth of life in Boston. To wear the letter for the rest of her life is neither a triumph for the social/symbolic order and a loss of self, nor on the other hand can it be the freedom of Romantic individualism. That Romantic category of independent subjectivity had from the beginning been superseded by another more socially constrained notion of the subject. Nevertheless, to resume the letter "of her own free will" (1:263) is at least partially to transform rather than merely repeat that opening scene where she stepped into the marketplace "as if by her own free-will" (1:52). Resisting still society's dictates, she negotiates some accommodation to social necessity, and so creates a self and a life for herself in Boston—not probably a happy one, but one that matches more her sense of herself, as the affirmation of "so intense a former life" (1:262) testifies.[29]

"Real" is a word similar in its use to "true," and one that resonates throughout the text. "Real," "really," "reality," and "realities" appear more than forty times in the text.[30] Taken together, these words point to the uncertainties of knowing another person, the instabilities of one's own being, and the partially represented nature of these subjectivities. This gives a complex meaning to the remark, "there was a more real life for Hester Prynne, here, in New England" (1:262). Once she had experienced "some mightier touch" than her husband's that had "awakened all her sensibilities" (1:176), she could never mistake anything else for "the warm reality" (1:177). This is not a matter simply of assigning prime importance to sexuality, but is rather the experience (however transitory) of an integrated subjectivity that the erotic may give access to, and it is this that Hester struggles for in her Boston life. It is linked with the Surveyor's "definition of happiness" as living "throughout the whole range of his faculties and sensibilities" (1:40)—which in his case was totally frustrated by Salem. A private realm of feeling is asserted and maintained within that Puritan society (even if it is more faithfulness to a now past reality finally rejected by her partner). It is neither a secret from Boston, nor wholly accepted by it; it does not lead to a wholly unified subjectivity for Hester, but neither is it defeat for her. It seems a better strategy than the dissembling duality of Mistress Hibbins's life, sister to the governor in daytime Boston and a witch in the night forest, who merely espouses Massachusetts' hostile vocabulary of witchcraft to express an opposition that will end in her execution.

Dimmesdale's solution involves the betrayal of Hester and that private realm. He makes himself into an object in the town's eyes, ceasing to be a subject: typically, his confession moves from "I" to "one" and "him" (1:254–55). On his return from the forest he cannot cope with that new and more complex sense of his own nature, and prefers to return to the comparatively simple if painful identity as the "vilest sinner" abjectly seeking society's forgiveness. In the Election Day procession, his mind is separate from his body because at this point his subjectivity is totally absorbed into the ideological destiny of the colony, from which he will seek recognition and acceptance the instant he has delivered his sermon. This human subject is totally unified only at the price of completely denying individual desire. At one level his death is indeed Chillingworth's "completest triumph and consummation" (1:260).[31]

We are left asking whether these different outcomes mean that there may be an element of choice for the protagonists. The American Republic's ideology of progress, happiness, and self-determination, explored in Hawthorne's earlier work, continues to be deeply shadowed in this novel. Chillingworth, helplessly obsessed (1:129) and philosophically a fatalist (1:174), believes there is no choice. He claims, " 'it has all been a dark necessity' " [1:174]), although he did make the initial decision not to reveal himself when "the choice was with himself" (1:118). The narrator, too, is increasingly drawn to a coercive notion of "fate" that would keep his tale morally neat and tidy: "there was a sense of inevitable doom upon her, as she thus received back this deadly symbol from the hand of fate. . . . So it ever is, whether thus typified or no, that an evil deed invests itself with the characters of doom" (1:211). Made uneasy by Hester's mental freedom, he tends to speak of "freedom" rather negatively as the amoral loosening of social and religious ties—"breathing the wild, free atmosphere of an unredeemed, unchristianized, lawless region" (1:201). Hence at the same time as thus condemning Hester, he speaks of Dimmesdale's situation as unalterable: "And be the stern and sad truth spoken, that the breach which guilt has once made into the human soul is never, in this mortal state, repaired" (1:200–201). Dimmesdale is imprisoned mentally (" 'What choice remains to me!' " [1:196]), but rather than an inherent outcome of all breaches of God's law, his acts are shown to be the product both of a particular temperament (an "iron-nerved" criminal would have "choice" [1:148]) and of a particular culture (Hester's kind of individual intellectual freedom not being on the Puritan agenda). The comment that, "[t]empted by a dream of happiness, he had yielded himself with deliberate choice, as he had never done before, to what he knew was deadly sin" (1:222), suggests that it is Dimmesdale himself who sees his alternatives in those starkly opposed moral absolutes, and hence blocks out any other course of action.

Hester demonstrates the existence of some small degree of choice, at least in terms of her continuing sense of moral responsibility toward Dimmesdale. This is something that her husband has lost belief in: " 'Ye that have wronged me are not sinful, save in a kind of typical illusion; neither am I fiend-like, who have snatched a fiend's office from his hands. It is our fate' " (1:174). She grasps this responsibility in the face of the realization that earlier her promise not to reveal her husband was virtually forced. While she accepts that in this she "had made her choice" (1:167), this is also assessed more narrowly as " 'there seemed no choice to me, save to be silent, in accordance with your behest' " (1:170). " 'What choice had you?' " (1:171), comments Chillingworth. It is following this exchange that Hester in the forest seeks to demonstrate the existence of alternatives.

The word "fate" and its derivatives ("fated," "fatality," "fatal," "fateful") are increasingly present in the latter part of the novel from the plot's turning point of "The Minister's Vigil," but this suggests something less doom-laden than the narrator's usage (for example, his exclamation, "O Fiend, whose talisman was that fatal symbol" [1:87]). The word nearly always focuses on the judicial sentence to wear the letter, the act of adultery it represents, and the forest meeting (the "fateful interview" [1:213]) in which the decision is made to repeat the offense ("a colloquy that was to decide their fate" [1:199]).

However, the way "fate" is sometimes used suggests that it steers a middle course between choiceless determinism and freely created destiny. "Fate" becomes the self-created outcome of the interaction of an individual subjectivity with other subjectivities and social structures: "[t]he minister's own will, and Hester's will, and the fate which grew between them" (1:217). The individual appears to be neither wholly self-determining nor completely choiceless, and the "fate and circumstances" (1:190) she or he faces grow multilayered and interdependent with other people and things: "But there is a fatality, a feeling so irresistible and inevitable that it has the force of doom, which almost invariably compels human beings to linger around and haunt, ghost-like, the spot where some great and marked event has given the color to their lifetime" (1:79–80). This may so progress that the possibilities are narrowed to a virtual vanishing point, as when Hester, "as if impelled by inevitable fate, and against her strongest will" (1:252), is pulled out of love for Dimmesdale onto the scaffold, even while her desire for a future together rejects Dimmesdale's solution. In this respect the "heavy footstep of their approaching Fate" (1:240) is, for Hester, that procession of Puritan church and state on the paradoxically named Election Day. But "Providence," in the sense of a divine force active in human lives, appears only as a more ambiguous possible agent, as when Doctor Chillingworth's arrival to keep Dimmesdale alive (121–22) or the birth of Pearl to save her mother's soul (1:89) are ascribed to its agency.

Choice is narrowed, then, partly because the needs and desires of other individuals must be faced, but partly too because this novel does not entertain for long the idea of a life beyond the frontiers of European culture. Subjectivity comes into being within a particular society, and so while Hester might posit that a short journey beyond the settlement will bring Dimmesdale to the place where he is "free" (1:197)—the wilderness being the classic site for the independent Romantic subject in America—in practice existence is here conceived as inherently social, and there can be no such self-standing, let alone unified being beyond the settlement. Another way of looking at this is to say that Hester and Dimmesdale are themselves part of that social formation, and as such they influence its order and course in certain minor but unmistakable ways. Their subjectivity is not wholly contained by it, yet they help to constitute it. Hester may throw away the "fragments of a broken chain" (1:164), but chains simultaneously link as well as bind, and so Pearl is raised on the edge of a community and taught its religious beliefs.[32]

The recurrence of the words "home" and "place" ("home" appearing twenty-six times and "place" well more than twenty times in a variety of meanings) stress the essential importance to the individual subject of a particular social world. Characters in *Mosses* had repeatedly and unsuccessfully sought their "place"; now *The Scarlet Letter* proposes that there is a "place" to be found in one's actual society, though this will not be the ideal one that matches desire, such as those Concord characters had demanded. Although the reflection in the rock pool seems to suggest to Pearl that the looking-glass world of the pool is " 'a better place!' " (1:168), Pearl is to learn that there is no escape from an existence within some already existing society or other. "The Custom-House" established how the "long connection of a family with one spot, as its place of birth and burial, creates a kindred between the human being and the locality" (1:11), and indeed on a physical level, events in *The Scarlet Letter*, beginning with a birth and ending in the graveyard, tend to keep coming back to one very specific "place," the marketplace. "Place" also refers, however, to one's position as ordained by social institutions and custom: the scaffold as the "place appointed for her punishment" (1:54); high and low rank (1:68 and 253); a recognized and accepted role such as Hester finding "her place" (1:161) in times of crisis for the settlement. It also defines a central element in subjectivity, as when Pearl's "wonted place" is temporarily taken by Dimmesdale so that she "hardly knew where she was" (1:208).

Thus the novel comes to show that each person has a consciousness of having a "place" through personal and social relationships, whether or not these are officially sanctioned and generally recognized or not, and that, as the use of the word "home" shows, such positions within the social order may affirm self-definition in some way, however painful. For woman generally in this society, "home" has its traditional meaning of family dwelling and is conventionally her socially sanctioned arena: we can see how the word and image appears in Chillingworth's expectations and dreams of Hester (1:63, 118, 176), as well as in her hopes of a life together with Dimmesdale and their daughter (1:212). Hester, too, creates a home for Pearl in this primary sense, staving off Mistress Hibbins's subversive invitations with " 'I must tarry at home, and keep watch over my litle Pearl' " (1:117). Also conventionally, Dimmesdale can only find a "home" in the "midst of civilization and refinement" (1:215), intending to flee to England, these New Englanders' intellectual and indeed childhood "home" (1:58, 105).

But the word shifts from these simple meanings when Hester decides to remain in Boston, scene of her adultery and shame and her lover's residence. Whereas her childhood home is "foreign" to her, she creates here in New England her "wild and dreary, but life-long home" (1:80)—a phrase that seems paradoxical given the qualities conventionally assigned to "home," but that is subjectively meaningful. The rest of her life is similarly explained: she finally "found a home" (1:263) in Boston, for here was the "home of so intense a former life" (1:262). Mentally, her "home" is in the wilderness (1:199), but unless she accepts the compromises and partialities of life within the colony, she will have "home and comfort nowhere" (1:166). Dimmesdale, ironically shepherded "home" at midnight (1:157) by Chillingworth and again welcomed "home" by him after the forest meeting (1:223), is subjectively homeless until he mounts the scaffold.

Thus situated within the social order, though only partially recognized or subliminally understood, these characters must content themselves with the presentation of "self" rather than full representation of themselves to society. The "Revelation of the Scarlet Letter" is an ironically entitled climax since not only does the town fail to understand but also the narrator refuses to describe the minister's stigmata even to the reader. Likewise, Hester is never fully revealed to the town. Given this perpetuation of ignorance and confusion, it is not surprising that Dimmesdale envisaged the Last Judgment as the chance "to see the dark problem of this life made plain," suggesting that "[a] knowledge of men's hearts will be needful to the completest solution of that problem" (1:132). The obsession with a "talisman," an "open sesame," in Hawthorne's work now fades in the face of nonrevelation and conflicting claims. There are to be no comforting moral permanences here, only a counterpoint of resistance and accommodation, romantic love barely finding a niche there. Christian revelation, a possible transcendent solution to this "dark problem," may attract the narrator, but as far as the plot shows, it can provide only a happy death for Dimmesdale and not a promise to Hester. Divine revelation, if it comes, exists only in the afterlife. Hester's imagined "coming revelation" (1:263)—a humanized and therefore more fragile version of truth-telling—also contains a Catch-22. It will depend on the teaching of a prophetess whose happy life will prove the truth of her vision of a new future society, yet it has already been made clear that present social structures will have to be torn down first before any woman can be happy. Hester remains therefore a prophetess without public power, her message only heard by the reader.

▼

The question remains whether the writing of imaginative fiction (that is, representation), offering as it does a greater "knowledge of men's hearts" than Boston itself has ever had, may instead provide that "truth" through imaginative "sympathy." Clearly it has the ability to represent the human subject far more fully, since she or he dares present only a partial version of herself or himself to fellow members of society. But "The Custom-House" seems to cast doubt on the art of representation, the role of the writer of fiction, and the capacity of the reader to respond to his creations. The problems raised in "Main-street" about both audience and means of representation still remain.

The "Custom-House" narrator begins his introduction by employing some of the key words conveying the subsequent tale's thematic argument: "revelation," "sympathy," "true." He is shown hesitating over "confidential depths of revelation" of his own life, arguing (as the novel will again do through its characters) that these "could fittingly be addressed, only and exclusively, to the one heart and mind of perfect sympathy; as if the printed book, thrown at large on the wide world, were certain to find out the divided segment of the writer's own nature, and complete his circle of existence by bringing him into communion with it"; indeed, "thoughts are frozen and utterance benumbed, unless the speaker stand in some true relation with his audience" (1:3–4). He also describes his struggles with representation and the fictional illusion he must paradoxically create in the interests of truth: "to dream strange things, and make them look like truth" (1:36). Hawthorne has come a long way from his earliest work—dreams that he felt he must reject.

It would seem, then, that fiction reproduces in miniature the problems of existence in social relations. Writing to Horatio Bridge

the day after finishing *The Scarlet Letter,* Hawthorne reviews his
novel, remarking that "my writings do not, nor ever will, appeal
to the broadest class of sympathies," and then expressing the hope
that "The Custom-House" sketch "may be more widely attractive
than the main narrative" (16:311). So it is not surprising that "The
Custom-House" bypasses these problems of audience and convincing fictional representation by pessimistically refusing wholly to trust
the general reader, and proceeding at one level with a factually false
but imaginatively true account of the novel's origins (thus insisting
simultaneously on the illusion of fiction and the reader's capacity
nonetheless to grasp its importance). The sketch finally spends time
describing not the tale itself, but only his failed attempts at writing
fiction. In this way *The Scarlet Letter* is left open in its relationship
to its readers and in its relation to social actuality.

The possibility then remains that the actual novel, which "The
Custom-House" does not describe, but which Hawthorne was will-
ing privately to tell his closest friend was "positively a h-ll-fired
story" (16:312) and in portions "powerfully written" (16:311), does
make dreams "look like truth," and does go some way toward at least
understanding what such ambiguous words like "truth," "revelation,"
and "sympathy" might mean for the socially positioned subject.

The argument seems to be this. Imaginative fiction potentially
allows for the representation of the self that society had otherwise
debarred. In the world of the novel and by extension Hawthorne's
own world, a notion of what is deemed "proper" governs how
the self is presented in actual social interactions. As Adam Smith
realized, sympathy is usually based on a perceived likeness between
the agent and her or his object of observation. The novel revises
this to the extent of conceiving of a crowd able to respond sympathetically on an intuitive level to someone whom, consciously,
these people would reject as different from themselves (arguably,
what they identify with is pain because they have experienced this
too). But Hawthorne seems to expect from his reader a far more
conscious engagement with the characters through the action of
the sympathetic imagination, and a far less sentimental grasp of
the irreducible difference of others: the reader is to maintain an

analytical distance simultaneous with that closeness. Smith, too, had argued that the operation of sympathy involves evaluating our responses by imagining them through the eyes of a fair and impartial judge—what he calls "the impartial spectator." For Smith this "spectator" is not some transcendent figure of absolute values, but an ordinary, responsive but personally uninvolved bystander, who represents the means by which society can achieve some measure of harmony and stability.[33] Failing to find this conscious, well-judged emotional engagement in his fictive Bostonians, Hawthorne seeks "sympathy" in this fullest form from his readers; unlike Smith, he appears to think that only in the medium of imaginative fiction is this relationship possible. This does not, of course, constitute an answer to ills. Hester's "revelation" may be "coming," but it has not yet arrived and might never do so. But after twenty-five years of exploration and experimentation in his writing, an acceptance, at last, of complexity and contradiction makes for the promised newness of this novel.

~ the subject ?

▼ THE WORKS ARE GROUPED according to probable date of composition. Also included after each title is the date of first publication (these are not always identical with year of composition) and, where appropriate, the collection in which the work was subsequently republished. TT = *Twice-told Tales* (1837 and 1842); MOM = *Mosses from an Old Manse* (1846); SI = *The Snow-Image and Other Twice-told Tales* (1852); AMUEK = *The American Magazine of Useful and Entertaining Knowledge.*

CHAPTER 2 (1825–1828)

Fanshawe (published 1828)   *(7) ±2 / novel*
"Alice Doane" (surviving only as part of "Alice Doane's Appeal")
> "The Hollow of the Three Hills" (published 1830) TT

CHAPTER 3 (1828–1831)

Provincial Tales
> "Roger Malvin's Burial" (published 1832) MOM   *12*
"The Gentle Boy" (published 1832) TT
> "My Kinsman, Major Molineux" (published 1832) SI
"The Wives of the Dead" (published 1832) SI
"The Gray Champion" (published 1835) TT
> "Young Goodman Brown" (published 1835) MOM
"The Battle-Omen" (published 1830) uncollected
"An Old Woman's Tale" (published 1830) uncollected
"Mrs. Hutchinson" (published 1830) uncollected
"Sir William Phips" (published 1830) uncollected
"Dr. Bullivant" (published 1831) uncollected
"Sir William Pepperell" (published 1833) uncollected

why this sequence?

CHAPTER 4 (1830–1835)   *+30*

"Sights from a Steeple" (published 1831) TT
"The Haunted Quack" (published 1831) uncollected
"The Seven Vagabonds" (published 1833) TT
"The Canterbury Pilgrims" (published 1833) SI

Material definitely or likely to belong to *The Story Teller:*
"Passages from a Relinquished Work" (published 1834) MOM

"Mr. Higginbotham's Catastrophe" (published 1834) TT
"My Visit to Niagara" (published 1835) uncollected
"Graves and Goblins" (published 1835) uncollected
"A Rill from the Town-Pump" (published 1835) TT
"The Vision of the Fountain" (published 1835) TT
"The Devil in Manuscript" (published 1835) SI
"The White Old Maid" (published 1835) TT
"The Gray Champion" (published 1835) TT
"The Ambitious Guest" (published 1835) TT
"Wakefield" (published 1835) TT
"Sketches from Memory" (published 1835): "The Notch of the White
Mountains," "Our Evening Party among the Mountains," "The Canal Boat"
[all MOM]; "The Inland Port," "Rochester," "A Night Scene" (all uncol-
lected)
"Old Ticonderoga" (published 1836) SI
"The Ontario Steamboat" (published 1836) AMUEK
"The May-Pole of Merry Mount" (published 1836) TT
"The Minister's Black Veil" (published 1836) TT
"The Wedding-Knell" (published 1836) TT
"A Visit to the Clerk of the Weather" (published 1836) uncollected
"The Great Carbuncle" (published 1837) TT
"Fragments from the Journal of a Solitary Man" (published 1837) uncol-
lected
"The Haunted Mind" (published 1835) TT
"Alice Doane's Appeal" (published 1835) uncollected
"The Village Uncle" (published 1835) TT
"Little Annie's Ramble" (published 1835) TT
"Old News" (published 1835) SI

Composition date unknown, but possibly at this time:
"Fancy's Show Box" (published 1837) TT

CHAPTER 5 (1835–1842)

Contributions to the *American Magazine of Useful and Entertaining Knowl-
edge* and *Peter Parley's Universal History*
Earliest extant notebooks (*The Lost Notebook* and parts of *The American
Notebooks*)

Circa autumn 1835
"Monsieur du Miroir" (published 1837) MOM

26 tales +
children's

"Mrs. Bullfrog" (published 1837) MOM
"Dr. Heidegger's Experiment" (published 1837) TT
"The Man of Adamant" (published 1837) SI
"Sunday at Home" (published 1837) TT
"David Swan" (published 1837) TT (composition date unknown, but possibly at this time)

1836
"The Prophetic Pictures" (published 1837) TT

By mid-1837
"A Bell's Biography" (published 1837) SI
"Sylph Etherege" (published 1838) SI
"The Shaker Bridal" (published 1838) TT
"Endicott and the Red Cross" (published 1838) TT
"Peter Goldthwaite's Treasure" (published 1838) TT
"Night Sketches" (published 1838) TT

1837–1838
"Time's Portraiture" (published 1838) uncollected
"The Threefold Destiny" (published 1838) TT
"Edward Fane's Rosebud" (published 1837) TT
"The Toll-Gatherer's Day" (published 1837) TT
"Foot-prints on the Sea-shore" (published 1838) TT
"Snow-flakes" (published 1838) TT
"Chippings with a Chisel" (published 1838) TT
"Legends of the Province-House": "Howe's Masquerade," "Edward Randalph's Portrait," "Lady Eleanor's Mantle," "Old Esther Dudley" (published 1838–1839) TT
"The Sister Years" (published 1839) uncollected
"The Lily's Quest" (published 1839) TT
"Thomas Green Fessenden" (published 1838) uncollected
"Jonathan Cilley" (published 1838) uncollected

1839–1840
"John Inglefield's Thanksgiving" (published 1840) SI

1840–1842
The Whole History of Grandfather's Chair (published December 1840–May 1841)

Biographical Stories for Children (published 1842)

CHAPTER 6 (1842–1845)

Notebooks continue

Winter 1842–Spring/Summer 1843   *2l tales*
"A Virtuoso's Collection" (published 1842) MOM
"The Old Apple-Dealer" (published 1843) MOM
"The Hall of Fantasy" (published 1843) MOM
"The New Adam and Eve" (published 1843) MOM
"The Birth-mark" (published 1843) MOM
"Egotism; or, the Bosom-Serpent" (published 1843) MOM
"The Procession of Life" (published 1843) MOM
"The Celestial Rail-road" (published 1843) MOM
"Buds and Bird-Voices" (published 1843) MOM
"Little Daffydowndilly" (published 1843) MOM

Winter 1843–Spring 1844
"Fire-Worship" (published 1843) MOM
"The Christmas Banquet" (published 1844) MOM   *Sympath. imgin. 1st time*
"The Good Man's Miracle" (published 1844) uncollected
"The Intelligence Office" (published 1844) MOM
"Earth's Holocaust" (published 1844) MOM
"The Artist of the Beautiful" (published 1844) MOM
"Drowne's Wooden Image" (published 1844) MOM
"A Select Party" (published 1844) MOM

Winter 1844–Spring 1845
"A Book of Autographs" (published 1844) uncollected
"Rappaccini's Daughter" (published 1844) MOM
"P.'s Correspondence" (published 1845) MOM

CHAPTER 7 (1846–1849)

Notebooks continue
"The Old Manse" (published 1846) MOM
Reviews to *Salem Advertiser* 1846–48

By December 1848
"Ethan Brand" (published 1850) SI

1847–1849 (probably winter 1848/spring 1849)
"Main-street" (published 1849) SI
"The Great Stone Face" (published 1850) SI
"The Snow-Image" (published 1850) SI

CHAPTER 8 (1849–1850)

The Scarlet Letter, including "The Custom-House" (published 1850)

Notes

Chapter 1   Introduction

1. Henry James, *Hawthorne*, 28.

2. G. D. Josipovici, "Hawthorne's Modernity," 359. This is what Seymour L. Gross, "Hawthorne's Moral Realism," calls "the embarrassing existence of what is perhaps the most artistically uneven canon ever completed by a great artist" (11). Various explanations for Hawthorne's diversity typically mix together works from widely diverse periods of composition: for example, Richard Harter Fogle, *Hawthorne's Fiction: The Light and the Dark;* Roy R. Male Jr., *Hawthorne's Tragic Vision;* Frederick C. Crews, *The Sins of the Fathers: Hawthorne's Psychological Themes,* 10–17; James K. Folsom, *Man's Accidents and God's Purposes: Multiplicity in Hawthorne's Fiction.*

3. For example, Jac Tharpe, *Nathaniel Hawthorne: Identity and Knowledge,* where a thesis of development is based on publication dates, and the use of "a rough chronology based first on the general idea that the more mature followed the less mature" (25). Working by date of publication rather than composition can conceal certain problems: for example, David S. Reynolds, *Beneath the American Renaissance: The Subversive Imagination in the Age of Emerson and Melville,* 114–18, discusses "Young Goodman Brown" (published 1835, but probably written between 1828 and 1831 as part of *Provincial Tales*) with tales like "A Rill from the Town-Pump" (belonging to the *Story Teller* phase and composed between 1832 and 1834). Though useful, Reynolds's diagnosis of Hawthorne's "almost schizophrenic split between the Conventional and the Subversive [literary currents of the time]" needs modification and refining in light of better dating.

4. M. L. Allen, "Hawthorne's Art in His Short Stories," 9.

5. For examples of these three approaches, see Hyatt H. Waggoner, *Hawthorne: A Critical Study,* 64, who indicates a time between 1825 and 1831; Gloria Erlich, *Family Themes and Hawthorne's Fiction: The Tenacious Web,* 1, and Richard H. Brodhead, *Hawthorne, Melville, and the Novel,* 43, who states that Hawthorne's "eventual turn to the novel was not, really, the result of his work's accumulated momentum" (29–30); and Edgar A. Dryden, *Nathaniel Hawthorne: The Poetics of Enchantment,* 11–12.

6. Francis O. Matthiessen, *American Renaissance: Art and Expression in the Age of Emerson and Whitman,* 218. See also Mark Van Doren, *Nathaniel Hawthorne;* and Barton Levi St. Armand, "Hawthorne's 'Haunted Mind': A Subterranean Drama of the Self," 22.

7. Michael J. Colacurcio, *The Province of Piety: Moral History in Hawthorne's Early Tales,* 41. Colacurcio recognizes that his enquiry into Hawthorne's early tales (published between 1830 and 1850) has been "partial and selective" in the sense of privileging historical tales and leaving out "a very great deal of competing (and possibly contradictory) evidence" (484–85), and he raises the problem of what to do with the rest (484–87). Although he offers a brief, wider survey of that Salem career (28–35) and calls for a "fully empirical account" of it (484), he concurs (539n) with Neal Frank Doubleday, *Hawthorne's Early Tales: A Critical Study,* 3, who argues, "The 1825–1838 time span is as clearly defined a 'period' in Hawthorne's work as any we are likely to find in the study of any writer."

8. See Richard P. Adams, "Hawthorne's 'Provincial Tales' " and John J. McDonald, " 'The Old Manse' and its Mosses: The Inception and Development of *Mosses from an Old Manse.*"

9. Nina Baym, *The Shape of Hawthorne's Career,* 7.

10. For studies of Hawthorne's early projects, see Elizabeth Lathrop Chandler, "A Study of the Sources of the Tales and Romances Written by Nathaniel Hawthorne before 1853"; Nelson F. Adkins, "The Early Projected Works of Nathaniel Hawthorne"; and Seymour L. Gross, "Four Possible Additions to Hawthorne's 'Story Teller.' " For information on library borrowings, see Marion L. Kesselring, *Hawthorne's Reading, 1828–1850: A Transcription and Identification of Titles Recorded in the Charge-Books of the Salem Athenaeum.*

11. Baym, *Hawthorne's Career,* blocks these years differently, in part because she chooses not to date some of the shorter works as precisely as this, and therefore groups certain of the tales differently.

12. See David Leverenz, *Manhood and the American Renaissance;* Gillian Brown, *Domestic Individualism: Imagining Self in Nineteenth-Century America;* Lauren Berlant, *The Anatomy of National Fantasy: Hawthorne, Utopia, and Everyday Life;* Joel Pfister, *The Production of Personal Life: Class, Gender, and the Psychological in Hawthorne's Fiction;* Sacvan Bercovitch, *The Office of* The Scarlet Letter; and Richard Brodhead, *Cultures of Letters: Scenes of Reading and Writing in Nineteenth-Century America.*

13. Pfister, *Production of Personal Life,* 1. Pfister traces the emergence of a middle-class psychological discourse to these social changes. See also Brown, *Domestic Individualism:* "nineteenth-century American individualism takes on its peculiarly 'individualistic' properties as domesticity inflects it with values of interiority, privacy, and psychology" (1). Also relevant are

Leverenz, *Manhood and the American Renaissance*; and Berlant, *Anatomy of National Fantasy.*

14. Jeffrey Steele, *The Representation of the Self in the American Renaissance,* particularly 138–39, 151–52, and 172–76, argues that Hawthorne dismantled Emersonian conceptions of a transcendent persona. For an illuminating proposition that Puritan self-reflection was predictive of Romantic problems of subjectivity, see Colacurcio, *Province of Piety,* 370–76.

15. For recent studies focusing on ideological and social shapings of the psyche in Hawthorne's work, see Pfister, *Production of Personal Life;* Brodhead, *Cultures of Letters,* who argues that literary works themselves both subjugated and empowered their readers (42); and Berlant, *Anatomy of National Fantasy,* who notes the attempt to link social regulation to desire through a "National Symbolic" (4–5). See also Sam Girgus, *Desire and the Political Unconscious in American Literature,* especially the opening chapter on the dialogue between the narratives of consensus and desire.

16. John Franzosa, "Locke's Kinsman, William Molyneux: The Philosophical Context of Hawthorne's Early Tales," 5. See also Terence Martin, *The Instructed Vision: Scottish Common Sense Philosophy and the Origins of American Fiction.* Chapters 2 and 3 of this present study explore these matters more fully.

17. Rosalind Coward and John Ellis, *Language and Materialism: Developments in Semiology and the Theory of the Subject,* 76. Their discussion of ideology (67–78) and indeed their whole chapter on "Marxism, Language and Ideology" (61–92) have been very useful in clarifying my sense of what kind of psychological model to work with in Hawthorne's work. I have not found any simpler intrasubjective view of human relations sufficiently complex for Hawthorne's various discourses. Also useful is Elspeth Probyn, *Sexing the Self: Gendered Positions in Cultural Studies,* especially chapter 5, "Technologizing the Self," which, while avoiding any simplified, universal individualism, explores the possibility of self-knowledge and of agency within the material and discursive limits that form the self: "The self can provide a place to speak from by bringing together the practices that we live and the problematizations of those practices" (135).

Chapter 2   *Seven Tales* and *Fanshawe*

1. Moncure D. Conway, *Life of Nathaniel Hawthorne,* 31. Few critics find in *Fanshawe* characteristics of Hawthorne's later work: Robert Eugene Gross, "Hawthorne's First Novel: The Future of a Style"; and Leslie A. Fiedler,

Love and Death in the American Novel, 225–27. *Fanshawe*, "Alice Doane," and "The Hollow of the Three Hills" are seldom discussed together—the exceptions being William Bysshe Stein, *Hawthorne's Faust: A Study of the Devil Archetype*, 52–57; Hyatt Howe Waggoner, *Hawthorne: A Critical Study*, 44–55; and Nina Baym, "Hawthorne's Gothic Discards: *Fanshawe* and 'Alice Doane.'"

2. For discussion of which tales belonged to *Seven Tales*, see Adkins, "Early Projected Works," 121–26; Chandler, "Sources," 8; Alfred Weber, *Die Entwicklung der Rahmenerzählungen Nathaniel Hawthornes: "The Story Teller" und andere frühe Werke*, 42 and 46; and Baym, *Hawthorne's Career*, 24. All agree on "Alice Doane" as part of the project. "The Hollow of the Three Hills" is accepted by Chandler and Adkins; Weber thinks it a possibility, being nearest in theme; Julian Hawthorne, *Hawthorne's Reading*, 103, argues that "The Hollow of the Three Hills" is the other story that survived. Baym also thinks it a probability along with "The Old Woman's Tale," which Chandler, unlike Weber or Adkins, also includes. I have excluded "An Old Woman's Tale" because its material, though resembling the other two tales in its source material, is handled very differently, and because Hawthorne visited the setting of the tale, the Valley of the Connecticut, in 1828 (see Hubert H. Hoeltje, *Inward Sky: The Heart and Mind of Nathaniel Hawthorne*, 94) two years after *Seven Tales* was withdrawn from the Salem publisher. "Alice Doane's Appeal," being fiction, can obviously be used only tentatively as evidence for the survival of two of the *Seven Tales*. However, its references to a "series" of tales and to the publication in the *Token* of "three or four of these tales" (both references being true of Hawthorne's own career) are details that are extraneous to the narrative itself and seem to have been mentioned only because the tale is drawing fully on Hawthorne's own career: "My Kinsman, Major Molineux," "Roger Malvin's Burial," "The Gentle Boy," and "Wives of the Dead" all formed part of *Provincial Tales* and all were printed in the 1832 *Token*. It is therefore possible that the story's immediately succeeding account of the burning of other tales and the survival of two of them—details that are also extraneous to the fictional narrative—can be taken as similarly autobiographical (II: 269).

3. Julian Hawthorne, *Nathaniel Hawthorne and His Wife: A Biography*, 2: 123–24, reports Elizabeth Hawthorne's recollections of this period: "It was in the summer of 1825 that he showed them [the tales] to me"; and "In a letter to me he says that he had 'made good progress on my novel'" (124). See also Horatio Bridge, *Personal Recollections of Nathaniel Hawthorne*,

75–76: "It is well known, that, soon after graduating, he prepared for the press a little volume of tales entitled 'Seven Tales of my Native Land.'" Hoeltje, *Inward Sky*, 82, records the removal of Ferdinand Andrews, the Salem publisher involved with *Seven Tales*.

4. Judith Wilt, *Ghosts of the Gothic: Austin, Eliot, and Lawrence*, 102, and 3, 12–20; and David Punter, *The Literature of Terror: A History of Gothic Fictions from 1765 to the Present Day*, 422–3. See also Paul A. Newlin, "'Vague Shapes of the Borderland': The Place of the Uncanny in Hawthorne's Gothic Vision."

5. See Wilt, *Ghosts of the Gothic*, 110–11. This links with Freud's theories of the Uncanny: see Newlin, "Vague Shapes," 84–85; and Rosemary Jackson, *Fantasy: The Literature of Subversion*, 63–72, especially the discussion of its relation to infantile animism (70–102).

6. See Punter, *Literature of Terror*, 403–11.

7. On "spectres," see Michael J. Colacurcio, "Visible Sanctity and Specter Evidence: The Moral World of Hawthorne's 'Young Goodman Brown,'" 275.

8. This definition of the Gothic appears in Robert D. Hume, "Gothic Versus Romantic: A Revaluation of the Gothic Novel," 289. See also Michael Dunne, "Varieties of Narrative Authority in Hawthorne's *Twice-told Tales* (1937)," though Dunne has no sense of the chronology of these works or of the differing thematic significance of their uses of narrators.

9. See also James L. Williamson, "Young Goodman Brown: Hawthorne's 'Devil in Manuscript.'"

10. Martin, *Instructed Vision*, 107, and 126–48. Useful here is Martin's exploration of this society's mistrust of the novel (57–76) and its attitude to the child's perception of reality (70–71). See too Rita K. Gollin, *Nathaniel Hawthorne and the Truth of Dreams*, on Common Sense philosopher Dugald Stewart's comparison of dreaming to madness (23), on "Alice Doane's Appeal," "The Hollow of the Three Hills," and "The Old Woman's Tale." Donald A. Ringe, *American Gothic: Imagination and Reason in Nineteenth-Century Fiction* is a full survey of this philosophical and literary background. See also Michael Davitt Bell, *The Development of American Romance: The Sacrifice of Relation*, 9–22; and Cathy N. Davidson, *Revolution and the Word: The Rise of the Novel in America*, 38–54, who gives the ideological background to this attack on fiction, especially its perceived "threat to ministerial authority" (42). However, Nina Baym, *Novels, Readers, and Reviewers: Responses to Fiction in Antebellum America*, 26–43, notes the

"deluge" of novels at this period, in spite of sectarian disapproval; reviewers, however, favored the realistic novel because it enforced the social world, and regarded individual fantasy as less serious. Robert Sattelmeyer, "The Aesthetic Background of Hawthorne's *Fanshawe*," finds limited confirmation of certain aspects of Scottish Common Sense philosophy in Hawthorne's novel; he also shows that Hawthorne was reading extensively in works of this philosophical and aesthetic school during March to August 1827. Baym, *Hawthorne's Career*, 8, argues that Hawthorne wrote for twenty-five years under Common Sense attitudes about the imagination and the artist's place in society—a view that this present study will seek to question in later chapters.

11. Martin, *Instructed Vision*, 52.

12. See Reynolds, *Beneath the American Renaissance*, 114; and Jackson, *Fantasy*, 3–7. Jackson also goes on to point out how "nearly all literary fantasies eventually re-cover desire, neutralizing their own impulses towards transgression" (9), a process I would argue is also discernible in Hawthorne's work.

13. See Baym, "Hawthorne's Gothic Discards."

14. Martin, *Instructed Vision*, 69.

15. See the use in Punter, *Literature of Terror*, of Freud's notion of sublimation "whereby unwillingness or incapacity directly to confront experiential contradiction finds expression in an apparently different, but in fact related, system of meanings in which the pain of contradiction is cancelled by the pleasure of fantasy" (85). Unlike a number of critics, for example Weber, *Entwicklung*, 55–57, I do not wish to read *Fanshawe* autobiographically.

16. See Sigmund Freud, "Creative Writers and Day-Dreaming," *The Standard Edition of the Complete Psychological Works of Sigmund Freud*, 9:143–53. For his comments on the connection between narcissism and the young child, see "On Narcissisism: An Introduction," *Complete Works*, 14:75.

17. See Wolfgang Iser, *The Implied Reader: Patterns of Communication in Prose Fiction from Bunyan to Beckett*, 284: escapist texts create the illusion of a consistent pattern, excluding anything that might disturb this. Note also that the novel in an oddly insistent but furtive parenthesis berates those who are attracted to death scenes (3:445), and yet of course *Fanshawe* caters to this desire.

18. This kind of daydreaming needs to be distinguished from what Gollin, *Hawthorne and the Truth of Dreams*, calls "creative reverie" (2).

19. Hume, "Gothic versus Romantic," 282–90. See also Henri Petter, *The Early American Novel*, for a survey of novels of the 1790s and 1810s and 1820s, particularly for characteristics close to *Fanshawe* (368).

20. See Weber, *Entwicklung*, 60; and Baym, *Hawthorne's Career*, 111, who argues for a change sometime between 1828 and 1830.

Chapter 3   The *Provincial Tales* Period

1. Goodrich published "Alice Doane's Appeal" (that is, the revised tale) in the 1835 *Token*, but had expressed reservations about the version he received as part of the *Provincial Tales* collection: "about 'Alice Doane' I should be more doubtful as to the public approbation" (9:489). Since he published the other *Provincial Tales* in the 1832 *Token*, and "Alice Doane's Appeal" then appears so much later in 1835 and in the company of two other pieces written at a later date, it seems likely that it was an earlier and now no longer extant version, "Alice Doane," which was included in *Provincial Tales*. For information on Upham, see note 4 below, and in particular Anne Henry Ehrenpreis, "Elizabeth Gaskell and Nathaniel Hawthorne," 99–105.

2. See Hawthorne's letter to Goodrich, May 6, 1830: "I send you the two pieces for The Token. . . . I have complied with your wishes in regard to brevity" (15:205).

3. See Kesselring, *Hawthorne's Reading*, 21, 27, and 49; and Weber, *Entwicklung*, 100–101. Weber points out that Voltaire is mentioned in "Sir William Pepperell," and his *Zadig*, which is referred to in "The Wives of the Dead," was borrowed from October 5, 1830, until the summer of 1831 (71). Critics who do wish to include "The Wives of the Dead" in *Provincial Tales* have not noted that its length probably excludes it from the original batch sent to Goodrich.

4. See Kesselring, *Hawthorne's Reading*, on borrowing of source material for "The Gray Champion" (17 and 25), and for "Young Goodman Brown" (22). See also Arlin Turner, "Hawthorne's Literary Borrowings," 552. For Hawthorne's visit to the regicide judges' graves, see Randall Stewart, *Nathaniel Hawthorne: A Biography*, 41. Ehrenpreis, "Elizabeth Gaskell," notes that Upham's very popular lectures were delivered in 1831 at the Salem Lyceum while Hawthorne was living in the Manning house (Hawthorne had previously commented on plans to establish the Lyceum); Ehrenpreis comments, "Upham was well known to Hawthorne's family and much admired by aunt Mary Manning" (101). Colacurcio, *Province of Piety*, 554n,

does not explain why, in his opinion, the most likely period of composition of "Young Goodman Brown" is 1833–1834. The Centenary Edition editors argue against the inclusion of "Young Goodman Brown" and "The Gray Champion" in *Provincial Tales* (9:491) on the grounds of their late publication in 1835. However, it is not necessarily "puzzling" that Hawthorne should have waited until 1835 to publish them, if we note that they were published in the company of pieces definitely intended for Hawthorne's projected collection *The Story Teller*. It is a reasonable deduction that after the failure of *Provincial Tales* Hawthorne retained those two tales for *The Story Teller*.

5. The attribution of "The Haunted Quack" is not definite but very probable (see 9:398–99). "An Old Woman's Tale" can be dated as 1830 from Hawthorne's visit "two summers since" (9:241) to the valley of the Connecticut. In considering which of Hawthorne's works belong to his *Provincial Tales* period, I have excluded "The May-Pole of Merrymount" because of its use of Joseph Strutt, *The Sports and Pastimes of the People of England* (cited in the text), which was borrowed in March 1827 but returned the same day, and borrowed again for three weeks in January 1835 (see Kesselring, *Hawthorne's Reading*, 18 and 36). This tale may have been conceived at the time of *Provincial Tales* since its basic debate, as we shall see, resembles those of that collection; nonetheless it is likely to be an extensively revised work because, as chapter 4 will demonstrate, its material, treatment, and conclusions are different from *Provincial Tales* and are closer to work known to have been written at a later period. The extended borrowing of Strutt in 1835, which provided important source material, provides further evidence for this hypothesis. "The Minister's Black Veil," published in the same 1836 *Token*, is also sometimes offered as another candidate for *Provincial Tales*. It is undoubtedly similar to those tales and arguably is a later comment on them (see chapter 4). The tale makes reference to "The Wedding Knell," a tale published in the same *Token*, and further linked in a minor way to its companions, "The Minister's Black Veil" and "The May-Pole of Merrymount," by the contrasting presence of grim realities at a wedding. Since "The Wedding Knell" is not a likely candidate for *Provincial Tales*, this possibly relegates its companion pieces to a later date too. Other critics propose variations on my proposed contents for *Provincial Tales*. Chandler, *Sources*, adds "Dr. Bullivant" and "The May-Pole of Merrymount" to my list (12). Adkins, "Early Projected Works," adds "The May-Pole of Merrymount" and "The Minister's Black Veil"

as possibles and comments, "[i]t is not improbable" that "'The Gray Champion' and 'Young Goodman Brown' were originally part of *Provincial Tales*" (130–31). Adams, "Provincial Tales," rejects "The Wives of the Dead" and "Alice Doane" but adds "The May-Pole of Merrymount" to my list, thus finding a common theme of initiation in the collection (39–40). Weber, *Entwicklung*, adds "The May-Pole of Merrymount," rejects "Young Goodman Brown," arranges the tales chronologically in historical sequence, and focuses on history and the spirit of Puritanism (80, 83, and 95–98). Baym, *Hawthorne's Career*, comments, "my own conservative inclination is to stick with the known group ['Alice Doane,' 'My Kinsman, Major Molineux,' 'Roger Malvin's Burial,' 'The Gentle Boy'], and reject the others because they were all written later than the original four or five" (30n).

6. Colacurcio, *Province of Piety*, states, "I see no need to divide Hawthorne's Salem years into two literary periods, as Nina Baym has done (*Hawthorne's Career*, 15–83): the historical—and even the specifically 'Puritan' interest—is continuous through 1838" (536n). Chapters 3, 4, and 5 of this present study test this view. This period of Hawthorne's work contains more historical tales than any other in his career. He was writing at the peak of the public's interest in historical fiction, which in the 1820s accounted for more than 85 percent of American best-sellers. See Lawrence Buell, *New England Literary Culture: From Revolution through Renaissance*, 195.

7. Punter, *Literature of Terror*, 59. See Punter also for the relationship between the Gothic and the historical novel (58–59).

8. Colacurcio, "Visible Sanctity," 275.

9. See Buell, *New England Literary Culture*, 214–38 and 261–80; Charles W. Upham's *Lectures on Witchcraft* (1831) and his *Salem Witchcraft* (1869) are discussed as examples of this approach (218–24). See also Buell's discussion of "Young Goodman Brown" (76).

10. At this stage in his career Hawthorne is likely to be still influenced by common critical attitudes to female characterization where critics' highest examples approximated a woman to a type rather than individualizing her (see Baym, *Novels, Readers, and Reviewers*, 98–99). I would take issue with Reynolds, *Beneath the American Renaissance*, 339–51, who argues that these types demonstrate a diversity of women's roles in preparation for Hawthorne's later, more complex female characters (368–75).

11. Sattelmeyer, "Aesthetic Background," 205; see also 204–6. Buell, *New England Literary Culture*, 207–10, discusses the nineteenth-century debates on the writing of history.

12. Robert J. Daly, "History and Chivalric Myth in 'Roger Malvin's Burial.' " For Hawthorne's use of his sources in "The Gray Champion," see Michael Davitt Bell, *Hawthorne and the Historical Romance of New England*, 27–33 and 50–53; Doubleday, *Early Tales*, 88–90; and G. Harrison Orians, "The Angel of Hadley in Fiction: A Study of the Sources of Hawthorne's 'The Gray Champion.' "

13. "The Gray Champion" has usually been read as *either* unambiguously patriotic (for example, Baym, *Hawthorne's Career*, 72) *or* an intentional attack on Puritanism (for example, Crews, *Sins of the Fathers*, 39–41), but not as a confusing mix of these. Colacurcio, *The Province of Piety*, 208–20, sees it as an "utterly ironic tale" (216), the narrator of which has been reading too much Cotton Mather (209). I hesitate to see it as coherent and sustained as this. G. R. Thompson, *The Art of Authorial Presence: Hawthorne's Provincial Tales*, published after my study was completed, shares my concern with narrators; Thompson's account of "the Gray Champion" (85–94) focuses on the "ironic mask of a partially obtuse narrator" (94). Stewart, *Hawthorne*, 41, reports that Hawthorne, disappointed by his visit to the regicide judges' grave, was quoted by friends as calling the cave a "humbug."

14. It is important to read the tale in its original version (see 9:613–19 for the deleted passages). Hawthorne's revision for the 1837 collection *Twice-told Tales* is characteristic of his other work in the latter half of the 1830s and tends to simplify the problems that "The Gentle Boy" had posed a decade earlier. Seymour L. Gross, "Hawthorne's Revision of 'The Gentle Boy,' " 196–208, does not attach any significance to Hawthorne's revision of the tale at this stage in his career. Thompson, *Art of Authorial Presence*, 102–119, sees the revision as evidence for an intentional and totally ironic reading that leaves no middle way.

15. "Sir William Phips" shows an analogous configuration: naval adventurer and later stately governor.

16. "The Wives of the Dead" is a critically neglected tale whose importance is clearer when given its *Provincial Tales* context. Only Colacurcio, *Province of Piety*, 100–107; Weber, *Entwicklung*, 79–80; and Baym, *Hawthorne's Career*, 32, discuss the tale in this context, though Colacurcio speculates that it belongs to the "Seven Tales" period but that its historicity links it with other *Provincial Tales* stories. Weber simply links it with "Roger Malvin's Burial" because it is set at the same period. Baym groups it and three other stories in *Provincial Tales* with "The Hollow of the Three Hills"

and "An Old Woman's Tale" as a category of tale where imagination is seen as destructive or alienating. Thompson, *Art of Authorial Presence*, finds "infinite regression" (82), dream within dream, without giving this a wider framework of explanation.

17. See Jackson, *Fantasy*, 19–21 and 26–37.

18. Ibid., 26–27.

19. Allan Gardner Smith, *The Analysis of Motives: Early American Psychology and Fiction*, 97, 119, and 106. See also 77–119 passim. This psychology did not of course have a concept of the unconscious.

20. See John E. Holsberry, "Hawthorne's 'The Haunted Mind,' the Psychology of Dreams, Coleridge, and Keats," 307–21, on these theories of association, sleep, and dreams in Locke, Upham, and Dugald Stewart. For a critique of Romantic constructions of the self, see Catherine Belsey, *Critical Practice*, 67–68 and 122–23; and Belsey, "The Romantic Construction of the Unconscious." David W. Pancost, "Hawthorne's Epistemology and Ontology," 8–13, argues that Hawthorne's metaphysics is a mixture of the Common Sense philosophical tradition and more radical Romanticism.

21. Smith, *Analysis of Motives*, 95–96.

22. Henry Nash Smith, *Democracy and the Novel: Popular Resistance to Classic American Writers*, 23–25, sees the tale as a deliberate challenge to the rationality of the age. See also Jack Kligerman, "A Stylistic Approach to Hawthorne's 'Roger Malvin's Burial,'" 188–94.

23. Analyses of this view of ideology that have been useful for this study are Coward and Ellis, *Language and Materialism*, 67–78; and Steve Burniston and Chris Weedon, "Ideology, Subjectivity and the Artistic Text," 203–33. Thompson, *Art of Authorial Presence*, 94–102, argues that Hawthorne parallels the larger historical cultural pathology with individual psychology.

24. See Roy Harvey Pearce, "Hawthorne and the Sense of the Past, Or the Immortality of Major Molineux," 327–49; Peter Shaw, "Fathers, Sons, and the Ambiguities of Revolution in 'My Kinsman, Major Molineux,'" 559–76; Colacurcio, *Province of Piety*, 130–53; James Duban, "Robins and Robinarchs in 'My Kinsman, Major Molineux,'" 271–88; and Robert Shulman, *Social Criticism and Nineteenth-Century American Fictions*, 114–24. T. Walter Herbert Jr., "Doing Cultural Work: 'My Kinsman Major Molineux' and the Construction of the Self-Made Man," illuminates the text's role in relation to a problematic democratic individualism in the early national period. See also Charles Swann, *Nathaniel Hawthorne: Tradition and Revolution*, 13–15,

on the tale's "repudiation of what [Raymond] Williams calls revolutionary romanticism" (15).

25. Colacurcio, "Visible Sanctity," shows how specter evidence for Hawthorne "became *nothing but* the necessary historical 'figure' for guilty, projective dreams or fantasies" (275).

26. Wilt, *Ghosts of the Gothic,* 19–20.

27. There has been much critical debate on the story's narrative viewpoint: see Harold F. Mosher Jr., "The Sources of Ambiguity in Hawthorne's 'Young Goodman Brown': A Structuralist Approach," for a summary of this and a discussion of the relationship between narrator and narratee. Sheldon W. Liebman, "The Reader in 'Young Goodman Brown,'" delineates various stylistic devices, in particular the way in which "point of view shifts imperceptibly from narrator to character so that the reader sees through the character's eyes even when he thinks he is seeing through the narrator's" (158). David Levin, "Shadows of Doubt: Specter Evidence in Hawthorne's 'Young Goodman Brown,'" resolves the problem historically, but Terence Martin, *Nathaniel Hawthorne,* argues that absolute distinctions between dream and reality founder on this specter evidence. My view is that the pink ribbon deliberately sabotages any detective work on what "really" happened. Stylistic explorations are useful: Taylor Stoehr, "'Young Goodman Brown' and Hawthorne's Theory of Mimesis," 402–3, draws attention to the very many "expressions of *apparent circumstance,*" the "vocabulary of surfaces."

28. Franzosa, "Locke's Kinsman," 6–13, explores how "My Kinsman, Major Molineux," in particular, exploits certain ambivalences in the Common Sense philosophy on matters to do with perception, personal identity, the authority of the mind, and a community of shared meanings.

29. See Holsberry, "Haunted Mind," 319–20, who cites Kames's *Elements of Criticism,* in particular the chapter on "Emotions Caused by Fiction."

30. See Schlomith Rimmon-Kenan, *Narrative Fiction: Contemporary Poetics,* 113, and more generally on free indirect discourse (110–16). See also Brian McHale, "Free Indirect Discourse: A Survey of Recent Accounts"; McHale points out that the "original" direct utterance is not recoverable from FID in fiction (256), and comments on "mutual interpenetration of reported utterance and reporting context" linguistically in uses of FID (263).

31. Rimmon-Kenan, *Narrative Fiction,* 114. McHale, "Free Indirect Discourse," 274, surveys the various resolutions formed by readers' compul-

sions to "motivate" or "naturalize" the following constructions identified by critics: FID as a vehicle of irony, or of empathy, as stream-of-consciousness, or as polyvocality (with its implied "metaphysics of multiple, equipollent authorities" [274]). He comments, "FID may serve as vehicle for lyric fusion with the character or ironic distancing from him, or, most interestingly of all, may be equivocal between the two" (275). Thompson's *Art of Authorial Presence* is the only sustained study of Hawthorne's narrative figure, focusing on the dialogical; the end result is a radical skepticism, a profound indeterminacy, and a stalemate of contesting elements.

32. David Downing, "Beyond Convention: The Dynamics of Imagery and Response in Hawthorne's Early Sense of Evil," argues in relation to "The Hollow of the Three Hills" and "Alice Doane's Appeal" that Hawthorne "begins to imagine a kind of responsiveness, beyond convention, in which one can dialectically move between inside and outside, subjective and objective"; and that "the fullness of subjective responsiveness (unarmoured experience) provides the preconditions for objective knowledge and critical insight" (473). I wish, however, to argue that Hawthorne was not to achieve such a balance.

33. The devil's use of the word "sympathy" suggests a nonethical seventeenth-century usage—a "magic communion between cognate individuals," which is linked to medical theories of correspondences. See Roy R. Male Jr., "Sympathy: A Key Word in American Romanticism," 20. Sympathy (in the customary modern sense) with the villain was something nineteenth-century reviewers worried about; see Baym, *Novels, Readers, and Reviewers,* 177–78.

Chapter 4   *The Story Teller* and Other Tales

1. See Hawthorne's letter to Franklin Pierce, June 1832: "I was making preparations for a northern tour, when this accursed Cholera broke out in Canada. It was my intention to go by way of New-York and Albany to Niagara, from thence to Montreal and Quebec, and home through Vermont and New-Hampshire. I am very desirous of making this journey on account of a book by which I intend to acquire an (undoubtedly) immense literary reputation, but which I cannot commence writing till I have visited Canada" (15:224).

2. Buell, *New England Literary Culture,* 64. See also Thompson, *Art of Authorial Presence,* 202–37, for discussion of the "Oberon" figure, though

Thompson does not distinguish between the *Story Teller* narrator and that of the earlier *Provincial Tales*.

3. See John F. Sears, "Hawthorne's 'The Ambitious Guest' and the Significance of the Willey Disaster," 363.

4. See Colacurcio, *Province of Piety*, 350.

5. Kenneth Dauber, *Rediscovering Hawthorne*, 53, sees this as a questioning of American traditions of intimacy.

6. Stanley Brodwin, "Hawthorne and the Function of History: A Reading of 'Alice Doane's Appeal,'" and Baym, *Hawthorne's Career*, 37–39, both argue for the successful amalgamation of fiction with history or for the superiority of the tale's historical section over the Leonard and Alice Doane section; but neither explore the fictionality of "fact" or the implications of the narrator's emotional bullying of his audience. Swann, *Tradition and Revolution*, 18–43, attacks a simple opposition of fiction to historical fact and sees the tale as attempting to create a historical sense. Baym cites Charles Upham's contemporary Salem witchcraft lectures on the dangers of the "unregulated imagination": "Man is never safe while either his fancy or his feeling is the guiding principle of his nature" (38). If Upham is, as I believe, the "historian" praised by the tale's narrator (II:267), then the narrator ultimately fails to follow this advice.

7. Baym, *Hawthorne's Career*, 39 and 50.

8. Dryden, *Poetics of Enchantment*, 123–28, argues, on the basis of Hawthorne's prefaces, that the Gentle Reader "belongs to a lost world of sympathetic involvement" (128). See also John Franzosa, "A Psychoanalysis of Hawthorne's Style," on Hawthorne's typical relationship with his readers as the illusion of an intimate bond. He sees Hawthorne's career as "a series of negotiations with the shifting expectations of his contemporary readership" (402).

9. See 15:290–637 passim. See, however, the letter of January 20, 1842 (605–6), mocking this self-image. John McWilliams, "The Politics of Isolation," argues that the pose of modesty and marginality was designed to enhance Hawthorne's literary reputation as original and sincere.

10. This approach extends also to popular literary forms; see Seymour L. Gross, "Hawthorne's 'The Vision of the Fountain' as a Parody." "A Rill from the Town-Pump" parodies temperance pamphlets; "Little Annie's Ramble" has self-referential elements. The xenophobic "Ontario Steam-Boat" is a problematic example: surviving only in the *American Magazine of Useful and Entertaining Knowledge*, it has possibly been rewritten to suit

a magazine that Hawthorne despised, rather than intended as a sarcastic critique of these attitudes.

11. Buell, *New England Literary Culture,* 102, and 16.

12. Reynolds, *Beneath the American Renaissance,* 10.

13. Elizabeth Peabody's account appears in Conway, *Life of Nathaniel Hawthorne,* 32.

14. To fit together the surviving pieces into a unified whole we would have to explain the inconsistencies in Oberon's story between "The Devil in Manuscript," "Fragments from the Journal of a Solitary Man," and "Passages from a Relinquished Work." See also problems raised by David W. Pancost, "Evidence of Editorial Additions to Hawthorne's 'Fragments from the Journal of a Solitary Man.'" See Weber, *Entwicklung,* 149, for estimates about the manuscript's submission date.

15. See Adkins, "Early Projected Works," 133. Adkins doubts the unity of the project. Unlike Baym *(Hawthorne's Career,* 41), Weber, in *Entwicklung,* takes seriously the integrity of *The Story Teller,* emphasizes the frame in a novelistic way, and interprets the tales in relation to the protagonist of the frame (indeed at certain points argues for the inclusion of a work on grounds of its possible links with the frame). This study is a work of considerable scholarly imagination, making us speculate about the original collection, but remains for me questionable simply because the collection is not intact and there is suspicion of alterations. Chandler, "Sources," 15–17, does not attempt a reconstruction, and Baym offers a possible order for the tales without working out the canon (47–48). The Centenary Edition of Hawthorne's works (9:492–96) accepts the arguments concerning which tales belonged to *The Story Teller* presented by Adkins, 131–45, and by Seymour L. Gross, " 'Story Teller.' "

16. Adkins, "Early Projected Works," speculates about the early composition of "The Threefold Destiny" (133 and 139), yet effectively cancels this with a further note (139). The Centenary Edition somewhat confusingly remarks that there is a "strong possibility" that some of the *American Monthly* pieces were *Story Teller* material (9:495), and yet later, without explanation, includes "The Threefold Destiny" among those written after *Twice-told Tales* (9:514). "Old Ticonderoga" and "Fragments," both from *The Story Teller,* were published by the *American Monthly* in February 1836 and July 1837 respectively. But if "The Threefold Destiny" (published in the same magazine in March 1838) had also been part of *The Story Teller* rather than a freshly composed piece, it is unlikely that the editor

would have delayed so long in making use of it, having already published far less substantial and sustained pieces from that collection. Kesselring, *Hawthorne's Reading*, 45, provides evidence for "Old News."

17. For full details, see chapter 3, note 5. See also Gross, " 'Story Teller.' " The evidence on this matter is typically hard to pin down. Adkins, "Early Projected Works," 143–45, speculates about the dismembering of the collection, quoting Elizabeth Peabody as evidence that Goodrich was the villain. George E. Woodberry, *Nathaniel Hawthorne*, 70, however, quotes Hawthorne to Elizabeth Peabody in 1857: "I perceive that your recollections are rather inaccurate. For instance, it was Park Benjamin, not Goodrich, who cut up the 'Storyteller.' " Lillian B. Gilkes, "Hawthorne, Park Benjamin, and S. G. Goodrich: A Three-Cornered Imbroglio," argues that, since Benjamin and Goodrich were not on speaking terms, it was probably Hawthorne himself who decided which tales went where. Colacurcio, *Province of Piety*, 656n, suggests that the case for including "The Minister's Black Veil" in *The Story Teller* is "very strong indeed" because of the connection between Abbott and Hooper.

18. Weber, *Entwicklung*, 161, concurs that at least five of these 1837 *Token* pieces are new, and although the Centenary Edition (9:495–96) only notes that some could have been written earlier, it does not attempt to distinguish which particular tales it has in mind, thus leaving this suggestion highly speculative. Hawthorne's own footnote to "The Prophetic Pictures" notes that its source is William Dunlap, *A History of the Rise and Progress of the Arts of Design in the United States*, which Kesselring, *Hawthorne's Reading*, shows was borrowed under Hawthorne's name from Salem Library in March and May 1836 (38). During this time Hawthorne was in Boston editing a magazine, and as Arlin Turner notes in *Hawthorne as Editor: Selections from His Writings in the* American Magazine of Useful and Entertaining Knowledge, 266, Dunlap is drawn on or mentioned four times in the magazine by Hawthorne and was one of those books doubtless borrowed by Elizabeth Hawthorne (in answer to Hawthorne's frantic calls for material), but used only to supply direct quotation. For Hawthorne's use of *Ductor Dubitantium* in "Fancy's Show Box," see Doubleday, *Early Tales*, 155–59. Kesselring (36) gives details of library borrowing.

19. Both Chandler, "Sources," 16, and Adkins, "Early Projected Works," 142, think "The Great Carbuncle" is an early tale, and cite "Our Evening Party." The problems of trying to date any tale simply from internal evidence are exemplified in the case of this story: it is very likely to have been

part of *The Story Teller* because of its material, but its handling of didactic elements is more characteristic of the work of the later 1830s. For "The Ontario Steamboat," see Adkins, 140n. Weber, *Entwicklung*, speculates that Hawthorne kept a first copy of the piece when he sent out the manuscript (158–59). The sketch's concluding paragraph on "foreign vice" and native virtue seems a later coda.

20. Weber, *Entwicklung*, 136–37, suggests that "The Seven Vagabonds" and "The Canterbury Pilgrims" were possibly written at the time of Hawthorne's journey (summer 1832).

21. On "The Village Uncle," see Chandler, "Sources," 17, and Adkins, "Early Projected Works," 126. Adkins speculates that it might be part of *Seven Tales*, but cites Elizabeth Hawthorne's story in a footnote. Holsberry, "Haunted Mind," 322–28, argues for interesting parallels between this sketch and the poems of Coleridge and Keats (borrowed from the library in 1833) in addition to Hawthorne's late 1820s and early 1830s reading of Common Sense psychology, and from this I deduce that the sketch could well have been written around 1833, although presumably Hawthorne's knowledge of the poets was not confined to library reading. On the putative frame, see Weber, *Entwicklung*, 259, 261, and 274–75. "Alice Doane's Appeal" is treated by Weber as a parody of the framed narrative (259), and "Little Annie's Ramble" (157–58) is tentatively included as a return to Oberon's reverie (261).

22. Woodberry, *Nathaniel Hawthorne*, 48. I would also argue that since Hawthorne was on bad terms with Goodrich at this point, it seems rather unlikely that he would be reserving more tales for him. For commentators who assume that Hawthorne stopped writing and disposed of all manuscripts, see Gross, " 'Story Teller,' " 93 and 95, and Chandler, "Sources," 17—an assertion made without evidence.

23. The Centenary Edition (9:500) says this was in late 1835, but gives no evidence for this assertion. A letter from Bridge (who, unknown to Hawthorne, had been helping financially to back the collection's publication) talks in September 1836 as if the plans were well in hand (9:501).

24. See Chandler, "Sources": "the year 1836 closed a distinct phase of Hawthorne's life [the Lonely Chamber]" (21). Chandler, having grouped together what I would take to be three different phases into one (1825–1837), then sees the publication of *Twice-told Tales* initiating a new phase early in 1837. Baym, *Hawthorne's Career*, 15–83, divides the period differently into "Beginnings, 1825–1834," which explores *Provincial Tales* and

the *Story Teller* pieces (though only Oberon, the framing narratives, and some of the stories), and the *"Twice-told Tales* Period, 1834–1839," containing moralized fiction and the sketch. In this latter group she includes tales and sketches generally considered to have been composed for *The Story Teller* ("The Wedding-Knell," "The Minister's Black Veil," "The May-Pole of Merry Mount," and "The Great Carbuncle"; and "Little Annie's Ramble," "Sights from a Steeple," and "The Village Uncle"). Also included in this later phase are two other works contemporary with *The Story Teller*, "Fancy's Show Box" and "The Haunted Mind," which she considers to be "quite different from the bulk of material Hawthorne produced in these years" (57). I would argue that one reason that these last two sketches are different is that they were written at an earlier and different stage in Hawthorne's development from the late 1830s moralized writing. No other critic has commented on a break between the work in the early and late 1830s, and none divides the decade in the way I have done. Colacurcio, *Province of Piety*, 28–35, divides Hawthorne's career into four stages: studies of Puritanism up to 1838; taking on Romanticism up to 1849; mastering the formal problems of full-scale romance, 1849–1852; and his last phase. Terence Martin, "The Method of Hawthorne's Tales," *Hawthorne Centenary Essays*, ed. Roy Harvey Pearce, sees the whole period up to 1850 as one of artistic experiment. Van Doren, *Nathaniel Hawthorne*, 84–91, notes the bulk of mystical and moral tales and daylight sketches of the 1830s and a failure to unite the moralist with the haunted mind. Stein, *Hawthorne's Faust*, 66–84, believes Hawthorne spent the 1830s making moral investigations of conduct mostly in contemporary life.

25. See Colacurcio, *Province of Piety*, 370–76, on the discovery of self: Hooper's problem "seems more deeply that of ineluctable selfhood than necessary sin" (370).

26. See William Charvat, *Literary Publishing in America, 1790–1850*, 67–71: poets were on the defensive in the 1830s.

27. See Buell, *New England Literary Culture*, 269. This attitude to history is presented by these works' narrators—a view not necessarily shared by Hawthorne, who continues to use history to define and explore. See, for example, James Duban, "The Skeptical Context of Hawthorne's 'Mr. Higginbotham's Catastrophe,'" and Colacurcio, *Province of Piety*, on "Wakefield" (490–92), "The Minister's Black Veil" (314–85), and "The May-Pole of Merry Mount" (253–77).

28. Herbert Schneider, quoted by Martin, *Instructed Vision*, 15. Martin, 3–13, demonstrates how this philosophy intellectually sanctioned the basic conservatism of Revolutionary and post-Revolutionary America.

29. Baym, *Novels, Readers, and Reviewers*, 270–72, shows the prime importance of plot in the critical reception of contemporary fiction. See also C. S. B. Swann, "The Practice and Theory of Storytelling: Nathaniel Hawthorne and Walter Benjamin."

30. On the use of stereotypes, see Baym, *Hawthorne's Career*, 65–66, who sees their use to control private reality; Claudia D. Johnson, "Hawthorne and Nineteenth-Century Perfectionism," traces these views to Thomas Upham's doctrine of Christian perfectionism; Colacurcio, *Province of Piety*, 487–89, argues that "The Haunted Mind" deals with views of the mind, not with the mind itself.

31. See, for example, "manuscripts in which I gave that dark idea a sort of material existence" (II:171); "I plunged into my imagination for a blacker horror" (II:279); "dipping her image into my mind and coloring it of a thousand fantastic hues" (II:312); Annie giving "life" to her doll (II:125); "my fancy" making historical Ticonderoga seem an actuality (II:189); the Show Box making the hypothetical seem actual; Hooper's acting out of "so dark a fantasy" (II:47).

32. See later chapters for an exploration of the relationship between notions of "sympathy" in Hawthorne's work and the ideas of Adam Smith, Hume, and Burke. For the reception of Adam Smith in America, see John Stafford, "Sympathy Comes to America": Smith was "an essential element in America's exposure to sympathy" (29), his theories taken into account in almost every work of moral philosophy after 1760 in America, even as late as 1823. Smith was part of Hawthorne's college curriculum, and Hawthorne borrowed *The Theory of Moral Sentiments* from the Salem Athenaeum in 1827 (see Kesselring, *Hawthorne's Reading*, 18). Gordon Hutner, *Secrets and Sympathy: Forms of Disclosure in Hawthorne's Novels*, notes that sympathy became a "cultural by-word" (12), but sees it having Romantic origins for Hawthorne, interpreting the term in his works predominantly as a "special intuition" (8) with social and moral meaning; he does not attempt to distinguish Hawthorne's different uses of the term at various phases of his career. Pancost, "Hawthorne's Epistemology and Ontology," which also traces "sympathy" back to the Cambridge Platonists, argues for a mixture of Common Sense philosophy and Romanticism in Hawthorne's work, this time linking sympathy with Romanticism, "the mind's imaginative

identification with the object of its contemplation" (11), progressing to "love" (12). I doubt if Hawthorne's work had yet achieved "sympathy" thus defined. Dryden, *Poetics of Enchantment,* also discusses "sympathy," arguing that it is not purely personal and has a certain detachment to it (25–30).

33. Baym, *Novels, Readers, and Reviewers,* 141, and 141–45. See also Martin, *Instructed Vision,* 112–15 on "right judgement," on the development of the moral sense and the discouragement of undue speculation (4–5), and on the problems early American fiction had in fulfilling the professed desire to make fiction didactic (126–36).

34. Reynolds, *Beneath the American Renaissance,* 182. See also his discussion of Hawthorne's use of popular secularized religious allegories of the 1830s (38–39). Daniel Walker Howe, "Victorian Culture in America," *Victorian America,* 22–26, comments on the moral seriousness and the profound didacticism of this culture, and on the home as the "most important locus for cultural transmission" (25). Baym, *Novels, Readers, and Reviewers,* 190–94, commenting on reviewers' moral preoccupations, notes the preaching of necessity, resignation, cheerfulness, neighborliness, "domestic virtues," duty, and the subordination of the individual to the institution in the interests of stability.

35. Jonathan Arac, *Commissioned Spirits: The Shaping of Social Motion in Dickens, Carlyle, Melville, and Hawthorne,* 188. Brodhead, *Hawthorne, Melville, and the Novel,* explores Hawthorne's dual interest in both conceptual schemes and experience (the latter taking the form of a story) (10–25).

36. Baym, *Hawthorne's Career,* 52, finds the greatly expanded authorial presence beginning earlier in "The Canterbury Pilgrims" and "Sights from a Steeple," but sees this as a "reinforcer of social values" rather than as a more flexible and varied interpretative presence.

Chapter 5   The Work of the Later 1830s

1. Although Turner, *Hawthorne as Editor,* 10, suggests that "there remained some opportunity for him to follow his own inclinations," Hawthorne's letters show him casting around unashamedly for any copy (15:234–35), extracting from books (as Turner reveals [8]), and admitting to reviewing fulsomely a book he has not read: "My way is to take some old magazine and make an abstract—you can't think how easy it is" (15:235).

2. See, for example, LN [11]–[13]. These characteristics continue up to the first half of 1837. James R. Miller, *Hawthorne in His Times,* describes Bridge's

response to Hawthorne's letters: Bridge complains of their "desperate cool-
ness," and writes, "I fear that you are too good a subject for suicide, and that
some day you will end your mortal woes on your own responsibility" (74–
75). Publishing was a precarious business until the late 1840s, as described
by Charvat, *Literary Publishing*, 38–60, so Hawthorne's "neglect" was wholly
typical. However, the disabling self-image of the artist as patrician writer,
independent of money and democratic patronage, survived anachronisti-
cally until 1850 and later; see William Charvat, *The Profession of Authorship
in America, 1800–1870: The Papers of William Charvat*, 292. Buell, *New
England Literary Culture*, 375–97, makes a quantitive analysis of authorship
as a profession in New England, which provides evidence that Hawthorne
was typical in class, education, politics, and religion, but where he differed,
apart from not preferring poetry as a genre, was in seldom having another
paying profession.

3. The entry was written between October 26, 1835, and August 31, 1836.
These notebooks are outstandingly impersonal, but this may be a rare
reference to his own life. For evidence of Hawthorne having not stopped
writing at this time, see chapter 4.

4. Buell, *New England Literary Culture*, 8. Buell, commenting on Hawthorne's output in general, argues that his individuality lies not in a theoretical resistance to overt moralism or in his use of moral frameworks, but
rather "in his awareness of the difficulty of refining the moral sensibility so
that it can enhance an aesthetic design through subtlety of interpenetration
rather than distort it through a too abrupt closure" (68).

5. See Smith, *Democracy and the Novel*, 13, on the "powerful element of
naive nationalism" and the conviction that "religion was necessary to keep
institutions in place, maintain public order, and preserve the sanctity of
private property"; introspection was discouraged. Howe, "Victorian Culture
in America," 11–12, comments on the propagation of these values as an
attempt to humanize the industrial-capitalist order, with an emphasis on
social responsibility and strict personal morality. Charvat, *Literary Publishing*, 27–29, finds some writers oppressed by the particularly provincial
tastes of Boston readers, and quotes Longfellow: "The tyranny of public
opinion there surpasses all belief." Baym, *Novels, Readers, and Reviewers*,
215, comments on reviewers' unease over any novels advocating social
change; public peace was a paramount issue.

6. For the notebook entry, see 8:61–63, dated July 28, 1837. Where the
biographical sketch speaks of Cilley's "power of sympathy" (TS 608) and

says he was "as true a representative of the people as ever theory could portray" (TS 612), the notebook sees insinuation and calculation, and doubts that he will take a prominent part in Congress. Hawthorne's distress at Cilley's death must also have affected the sketch.

7. See chapter 4, note 18.

8. For "A Bell's Biography" and "Chippings with a Chisel," see AMUEK 185 and 117–18; "The Sister Years" and "Time's Portraiture" are *Salem Gazette* New Year Addresses; Joseph Barlow Felt's *Annals of Salem,* borrowed from the library in September 1833 and December 1834 (see Kesselring, *Hawthorne's Reading,* 35 and 36), is a source for "Endicott and the Red Cross"; there is notebook evidence for "Peter Goldthwaite's Treasure" (LN [19]), "Edward Fane's Rosebud" (LN [12]), "The Threefold Destiny" (LN [40]), "Foot-prints on the Sea-shore" (LN [41] and [52–55]), "The Lily's Quest" (LN [36]), "Legends of the Province-House" (LN [37], [41], [56], [62], and [64–65]); "John Inglefield's Thanksgiving" (LN [17]). This leaves only "Night Sketches," "Sylph Etherege," "Snow-flakes," and "The Toll-Gatherer's Day" for which there is no evidence of these kinds. For assistance in dating of all the above (though they are not placed in the same groups or phases as this present study), see Chandler, "Sources," 19–20, and Baym, *Hawthorne's Career,* 55–62.

9. Chandler, "Sources," 15, is typical. Seymour L. Gross, "Hawthorne and the Shakers," argues that the tale is based on Thomas Brown, *An Account of the People Called Shakers,* borrowed from the library on August 27, 1831, and "almost certainly written soon after" the 1831 trip to Canterbury. No commentator, however, has explained why such a well-written tale should then be held from publication for so long.

10. Hawthorne regarded his journalism and writing for children as distinct from his imaginative work: "I see little prospect but that I must scribble for a living. But this troubles me less than you would suppose. I can turn my pen to all sorts of drudgery, such as children's books &c" (letter to Longfellow, June 1837 [15:252]). His copy for the compendium *Peter Parley's Universal History,* later in 1836, follows his historical sources or the preceding volumes' moral judgments so closely that very little of his personal stamp can be found: "it should be read out of the Hawthorne canon," argues B. Bernard Cohen, "Hawthorne and *Parley's Universal History,*" 90. Colacurcio, *Province of Piety,* 497, suggests that after the dismantling of *The Story Teller,* a dispirited Hawthorne sought to accommodate audience and publishers by producing tales that "often read like parodies of the earlier

work." <u>Baym</u>, *Hawthorne's Career*, 85–98, associates Hawthorne's work for children, *Grandfather's Chair* and its sequels including *Biographical Stories*, with the succeeding work done at Concord ("The Manse Decade"), but I hope to show that they are closer to what I take to be the characteristics of the late 1830s.

11. Though there is a faint hint that the Painter's pictures may have given Walter the idea of attacking Elinor, this is both questionable and not foregrounded. No critic interprets the tale in relation to the compositional date and contemporary works.

12. Wayne Allen Jones, "Hawthorne's First Published Review," 498. Jones's view, which argues that this review relates to a change from a theory of imagination as earthbound (supposedly shown in the early works) to more ethereal productions in the 1830s and then in *Mosses* (500), ignores the contexts in which this review appears.

13. See Buell, *New England Literary Culture*, 304–18, on the cult of the New England village and its literary depictions as a "codification of a repertoire of motifs" (305).

14. The chameleon, Keats's image of the ideal poetical character, was probably suggested by Hazlitt, who "inherited the eighteenth-century tradition of sympathy in both its moral and its critical aspects" (see James Engell, *The Creative Imagination: Enlightenment to Romanticism*, 146–47). Stafford, "Sympathy," notes the popularity of Hazlitt's "sympathetic imagination" in American literary criticism at the time (35).

15. See Evan Carton, *The Rhetoric of American Romance: Dialectic and Identity in Emerson, Dickinson, Poe, and Hawthorne*, 170–90, for a finely detailed argument that "history is art's construct as well as its subject, and art not only makes history but is made by it" (170); "the narrator himself has become more and more entangled in the forms and values of an un-ideal past" (185). Colacurcio, *Province of Piety*, 389–482, finds in these tales "an ironic commentary on the pattern of emerging American historiography" (392).

16. Buell, *New England Literary Culture*, 15, and 68–69.

17. See J. Donald Crowley, ed., *Hawthorne: The Critical Heritage*, 15–16, 53–67, and 79–101; quotations are from a typical review of *Twice-told Tales* in the *Salem Gazette*, March 1837, reprinted in *Critical Heritage*, 53. See also Gross, "Hawthorne's Revision of 'The Gentle Boy.'" It is worth noting that short stories did not pay, and collections of them were commercially almost valueless; see Charvat, *Literary Publishing*, 56.

Charvat, *The Profession of Authorship*, 294, also comments that a writer was less vulnerable to publishers' ideas of public taste if he could invest capital in the venture—something that Hawthorne did not believe he could not do. For further comment on predominant contemporary taste, see Ralph Thompson, *American Literary Annuals and Gift Books, 1825–1865;* and Frank Luther Mott, *A History of American Magazines, 1741–1850,* 1:419–20 and 501–2. Baym, *Hawthorne's Career,* 83, speculates that Hawthorne's selection to comply with an imagined public opinion may mask anger or a lack of confidence.

18. This is to take issue with Waggoner, *Hawthorne,* who argues, "Where Hawthorne's beliefs are surest, he writes most traditionally" (261). Interestingly, at this unsettled point in his life Hawthorne deliberately sought the friendship of the conservative poet, Fessenden, whom he praised in the 1838 sketch for his "simple faith in his fellow-man" (TS 582) and for having "caught the rare art of sketching familiar manners" (TS 572).

19. Martin, *Instructed Vision,* 126–36, discusses early American fiction's difficulties in discovering a novelistic form in the principles of social-moral organization, which expected a didactic literature along Common Sense lines.

20. Baym, *Hawthorne's Career,* takes a different view on this matter, arguing that during the *Twice-told Tales* period (dated 1834–1839), Hawthorne desired to write in compliance with what he assumed to be society's values and norms in order to secure a public (54), and did not declare independence from these until writing "The Custom-House" in 1849 (81). I shall argue that *Mosses* is a clear departure after this period of playing ambivalently with moralistic conventions.

21. For Hawthorne's comments, see letter to Sophia, September 1841: "I recollect that the Man of Adamant seemed a fine idea to me, when I looked at it prophetically; but I failed in giving shape and substance to the vision which I saw. I don't think it can be very good" (15:572–73).

22. John P. McWilliams Jr., *Hawthorne, Melville, and the American Character: A Looking-Glass Business,* discusses commemorative versions of the past that were current in the nineteenth century, especially in oratory, and shows that *Grandfather's Chair* departs only slightly from this tradition (36–39). See also his discussion of "Endicott and the Red Cross": Endicott was apparently usually treated as the heroic masculine, but not by Hawthorne, who uses paradox to expose the simplicity of contemporary accounts (46–48). Sacvan Bercovitch, "Endicott's Breastplate: Symbolism and Typology

in 'Endicott and the Red Cross,' " shows through scriptural parallels that, as well as a heroic image, there is protest here against Puritanism. Hawthorne's historical work for children at this period fits closely with the huge quantities of such work in the early nineteenth century; see John C. Crandall, "Patriotism and Humanitarian Reform in Children's Literature, 1825–1860." Crandall describes an "impressive campaign of informal indoctrination of young Americans by their solicitous elders" (3), as part of an adult culture characterized by a self-conscious and self-assured nationalism, intent on preserving a glorious tradition and celebrating a society "unique, superior and nearly perfect" (5).

23. McWilliams, *Hawthorne, Melville, and the American Character*, discusses Hawthorne's contemporaries' attitudes to the Revolution; Hawthorne subtly challenges these (72–85).

Chapter 6   The Concord Period

1. "Monsieur du Miroir" was one of very few pre-Concord tales reprinted in *Mosses*, possibly included because its mirror image was in line with his current thinking on divided selfhood.

2. This chapter offers a very different view from the few other critics who consider this period of Hawthorne's work. McDonald, "*Mosses*," argues for only a subtle change of direction, writing more immediately of contemporary social reality (79–80). Again, in "The Old Manse Period Canon," McDonald finds formal experimentation to deal with contemporary reality. The only other critic to focus at length on this period of Hawthorne's work, Baym, *Hawthorne's Career*, 98–116, takes a very different view, finding instead Hawthorne playing the role of the assured, successful man of letters negotiating a way between reform and materialism (102). She argues that he produced mostly works of little significance (101), and that "[w]e should not try to force his writings from this period into a meaningful statement about the relationship between imagination and life" (103). David M. Van Leer, "Aylmer's Library," 211 and 219n, sees this as the second phase of Hawthorne's career, briefly suggesting a "subtle difference" from earlier Puritan writing. Two other biographical studies have also dismissed Hawthorne's work at this time. Turner, *Hawthorne: A Biography*, believes that most Concord works were "more concoctions than creations; some are experimental in method and hence of special interest" (156). Erlich, *Family Themes*, finds Hawthorne in midlife crisis and takes his strictures on his Concord work at face value (16–19). Other

critics attacking *Mosses* for failure in thought, imagination, artistry, and lack of progress include Robert Cantwell, *Nathaniel Hawthorne: The American Years*, 386–87; Richard P. Adams, "Hawthorne: The Old Manse Period," 151; Van Doren, *Nathaniel Hawthorne*, 129; and Neal Frank Doubleday, "Hawthorne's Satirical Allegory."

3. Hawthorne's relationship with his Transcendentalist neighbors remains highly debatable. He seems attracted to Transcendentalist radicalism, its denial of economic materialism and questioning of social conventions: see Arlin Turner, *Nathaniel Hawthorne: An Introduction and Interpretation*, 85–89. I find persuasive Buell's argument, *New England Literary Culture*, 74–77, that there is a certain kinship between Hawthorne and Emerson in spite of classic differences: they "belong together, as masters of the controlled irony that stems from questioning orthodoxies of their own making or invoking" (74). As Steele, *Representation of the Self*, remarks generally of the age: "deconstruction and construction, rhetorics of regeneration and demystification are intertwined in an endless dance" (185); see also his view of Hawthorne's materializing of the psyche in contrast to Emerson's (1–10, and 151–59). Colacurcio, *Province of Piety*, 29–31, suggests *Mosses* may be viewed as a series of explorations and critiques of Transcendentalism. Also of interest is John S. Martin, "The Other Side of Concord: A Critique of Emerson in Hawthorne's 'The Old Manse.'"

4. This present study uses the authoritative chronology of all Hawthorne's Concord work provided by McDonald, "Canon." Commentary on the entire corpus of work at this period as a distinct whole is mostly partial or sketchy. Only Adams, "The Old Manse Period," McDonald, *"Mosses,"* and Baym, *Hawthorne's Career*, 98–112, cover the range. Adams looks at Hawthorne's maturing attitudes to the individual's and the artist's place in society. Baym does not wish to distinguish between the children's stories written just before his marriage, the work composed at Concord, and the four tales written at Salem after quitting the Old Manse (she speaks of the "Manse Decade" of 1840–1849), stating that "it is difficult to find consistency of matter or manner" in the only six works she identifies as fictions (105). McDonald, too, does not wish to overstress the unity of Hawthorne's work at this time. Changes in terms of satire, not individual psychology, are noted by Doubleday, "Satirical Allegory"; Van Doren, *Nathaniel Hawthorne*, 127–29; Turner, *Hawthorne: An Introduction*, 42–44; and Harold P. Miller, "Hawthorne Surveys His Contemporaries."

5. Dryden, *Poetics of Enchantment*, 25, argues for a similar dynamic: "But just as Roderick's self-contemplation begets otherness so concentration on the other leads back to self."

6. Smith, *Theory of Moral Sentiments*, 18.

7. See Alfred S. Reid, "Hawthorne's Humanism: 'The Birth-mark' and Sir Kenelm Digby." Male, "Sympathy," 20–21, contrasts this with eighteenth-century theories of sympathy of Hume's *Treatise of Human Nature* and Adam Smith. See also Van Leer, "Aylmer's Library," who emphasizes the seventeenth-century context.

8. Allan Gardner Lloyd Smith, *Eve Tempted: Writing and Sexuality in Hawthorne's Fiction*, 35–42, explores the "whole issue of essence versus exteriority" (35) and the irreducible concept of the heart in some of the later *Mosses* stories, pointing out, for example, "the whole vocabulary of inner and outer; surface and depth; material and spiritual; artificial and natural" in "Rappaccini's Daughter" (38).

9. Stephen Adams, "Unifying Structures in *Mosses from an Old Manse*," similarly interprets the Concord myth of Eden in terms of "acts of sympathetic imaginative perception which free man from the burden of the past and reconcile him to complex earthly life" (147).

10. Engell, *Creative Imagination*, 149 and 144. Engell's entire chapter, "The Psyche Reaches Out: Sympathy" (143–60), is very useful here. I disagree with Male, "Concept of Sympathy," 148–49, who argues that Hawthorne rejected the idea that imaginative sympathy had a moral value.

11. Smith, *Theory of Moral Sentiments*, 4.

12. For instance, for prototypes of Priscilla and Zenobia, see 10:303; and posssibly 10:302 for Holgrave.

13. The conjunction of these three tales at this point of Hawthorne's development has gone almost unnoticed; see Baym, *Hawthorne's Career*, 110–12, who notes the conjunction of the first two. Leland S. Person Jr., *Aesthetic Headaches: Women and a Masculine Poetics in Poe, Melville, and Hawthorne*, discusses Hawthorne's "progressive effort to liberate a powerful female figure, clearly identified with his own creative power" (96). These two tales are also examined together, though not in the context of his development, by Stein, *Hawthorne's Faust*, 93–97; Bewley, *The Eccentric Design: Form in the Classic American Novel*, 135–38, who like Baym also finds Hawthorne's positive in Drowne; and Millicent Bell, *Hawthorne's View of the Artist*, 94–111 and 127–34, who finds in these two artists an unresolved duality

present throughout Hawthorne's career. Person, 114, finds Drowne realizing Hawthorne's ideal, a reciprocal relationship between the male artist and his female subject.

14. Engell, *Creative Imagination*, 155. See also Engell, 151–53. Male, "Concept of Sympathy," 141–42, links Drowne's life-giving touch with an organic theory of art based on sympathy, a concept defined by him, however, in terms of an essential homogeneity of all life. Carl F. Strauch, "Emerson and the Doctrine of Sympathy," 152n, wishes to distinguish Emersonian metaphysical sympathy from the eighteenth-century ethical social principles that this study sees underlying Hawthorne's use of the term.

15. The tale does not, in the view of this present study, move beyond the original notebook suggestions (8:158, 165, 185), which contrast Owen's artifact with Nature and call it a trifle. Smith, *Analysis of Motives*, 101, links Owen with Combe's psychological account of monomania in his *Observations on Mental Derangement* (1834). Combe's *Physiology* is mentioned in Hawthorne's notebooks (8:235–36) with reference to "The Birth-mark."

16. It is necessary to distinguish between Hawthorne's different artist figures, and to see this tale in the context of his previous years' work in defining desire and circumstance. Commentators' failure to do this and the customary one-to-one identification of Owen with Hawthorne's artistic role have tended to provoke divisive readings and much tangential debate about the relative importance of the ideal and the material world. For example, Dauber, *Rediscovering Hawthorne*, 81–86; Bell, *View of the Artist*, 94–111; Martin, *Hawthorne*, 74–75; Adams, "Old Manse," 134–37; Sheldon W. Liebman, "Hawthorne's Romanticism: 'The Artist of the Beautiful.'" Buell, *New England Literary Culture*, 71–72, places the tale in the context of contemporary responses to Romanticism, finding that the image of Owen as the "creator of life" is "inseparable from the image of Owen as hapless misfit." June Howard, "The Watchmaker, the Artist, and the Iron Accents of History: Notes on Hawthorne's 'Artist of the Beautiful,' " usefully locates the story in the historical moment of industrialization and alienated labor.

17. Una was born March 3, 1844, "Drowne's Wooden Image" was sent off March 11, and it is conjectured that "The Artist of the Beautiful" was finished by mid-May (McDonald, "Canon," 30).

18. Julian Hawthorne, *Hawthorne*, I:360. Given Una's birth, the argument for an autumn 1844 composition date (see McDonald, "Canon," 32) seems more convincing than the Centenary Edition's spring date.

19. The majority of critics, especially those finding Christian or Neoplatonic symbolism, see the tale as a consistent allegory or moral parable: for example, Thomas F. Walsh Jr., "Rappaccini's Literary Gardens." However, Don Parry Norford, "Rappaccini's Garden of Allegory," explores the tale as the story of the artist's problems as allegorist. Michael T. Gilmore, *American Romanticism and the Marketplace*, 53–70, sees the tale as a "fictionalized version of Hawthorne's circumstances in 1844" (53). Carol Marie Bensick, *La Nouvelle Beatrice: Renaissance and Romance in "Rappaccini's Daughter*," argues against allegorical interpretations and reconstructs in detail the sixteenth-century philosophical, scientific, and medical context. John Downton Hazlett, "Re-Reading 'Rappaccini's Daughter': Giovanni and the Seduction of the Transcendental Reader," explores the destructive power of allegorizing.

20. Beatrice's poison is a notorious crux, nearly always discussed in a vacuum that ignores the context of Hawthorne's explorations at Concord, with the result that the tale is usually interpreted in either religious, scientific, or sexual terms. For example: Waggoner, *Hawthorne*, 111–25; Crews, *Sins of the Fathers*, 117–35, and Charles E. Boewe, "Rappaccini's Garden." A more useful approach for my reading is to focus on problems of perception and interpretation; for example, John Franzosa, "The Language of Inflation in 'Rappaccini's Daughter'"; and Michael J. Colacurcio, "A Better Mode of Evidence: The Transcendental Problem of Faith and Spirit." Richard Brenzo, "Beatrice Rappaccini: A Victim of Male Love and Horror," is closest to my study's reading. Bensick, *La Nouvelle Beatrice*, 99–112, argues the poison is syphilis. Pfister, *Production of Personal Life*, 59–79, exploring cultural anxieties about creative women, sees montrosity as a patriarchal allegory of women.

21. See Dryden, *Poetics of Enchantment*, 60–68, for a discussion of Hawthorne's concept of the "sphere," embodying "the basic intersubjective tension which torments Hawthorne's characters" (67).

Chapter 7   The Salem Tales

1. There is no discussion of all four tales together as a distinctive group or in relation to *Mosses* and to *The Scarlet Letter*, although there has been general or retrospective discussion of individual themes. See Baym, *Hawthorne's Career*, 117–19, who finds a "throwback" (118) to views held a decade earlier. Tom Quirk, "Hawthorne's Last Tales and 'The Custom-House,'" discusses together "The Snow-Image," "The Great Stone Face,"

"Main-street," and "Feathertop" (erroneously dated) as concerned with problems of artistic creation. See also Swann, *Tradition and Revolution*, 44–74, who explores "Ethan Brand" and "Main-street" together as preparation for *The Scarlet Letter* and the "matter of history."

2. These reviews, reprinted in Randall Stewart, "Hawthorne's Contributions to *The Salem Advertiser*," give only small clues to Hawthorne's literary tastes, since mostly they voice very general, conventional sentiments, if possibly ones genuinely held.

3. Letter, November 11, 1847 (16:215). Sophia Hawthorne confirms this in a letter of November 23, 1847: "My husband began returning to his study on the first of November and writes every afternoon" (16:216n).

4. See letter of December 4, 1851: "I happened to have a little time, just before leaving Lenox, which I could not fill up better than by writing this story; otherwise I should not now have had it on hand" (16:513). The unsupported assertion (see Seymour L. Gross and Alfred J. Levy, "Some Remarks on the Extant Manuscripts of Hawthorne's Short Stories") that the tale was written years before and merely revised, seems impossible in view of this statement.

5. See 9:381–82 for details. The Centenary Edition does not try to explain why it believes "Main-street" is both the tale that was too long for Elizabeth Peabody and yet was finally accepted by her. While I agree it is indeed "highly improbable that Hawthorne completed lengthy tales during the period, without publishing them" (11:382), it seems not unlikely he could have started a number, even indeed *The Scarlet Letter* (see note 9).

6. "The Snow-Image" was printed in November 1850, the only definite date for it. Adkins, "Early Projected Works," suggests 1850 for its composition (148–49). However, while the notebooks entry for February 1, 1849 (8:418–22) provides the tale's foundations, an entry in another notebook dated between March 1849 and September 1849 (8:287) notes, "The same children who make the little snow-girl shall plant dry sticks &c." Since this notebook had made no previous mention of this "snow-girl," it must refer to a drafted or completed story. What is not clear is whether this entry was made in the first half of 1849 so that the entry beginning "Monday, September 17th, 1849" (287) indicates by its dating (as it seems to do elsewhere in the notebooks) that Hawthorne is resuming this notebook after some lapse of time, and that the "dry stick" note that immediately precedes this noted date in September 1849 was therefore actually written long before. We know that he kept a journal

of his family doings around this period (March 19, 1849 to September 1849 [8:398–436]), and given the length of those journal entries on his children, wife, and mother, it is likely that Hawthorne was writing little or even nothing else during that period. The temporary cessation of this family journal on September 9, 1849, dovetails into the possible resumption of the other notebook recording ideas for fiction, and may confirm that the second story planned around these children was indeed noted before March 1849. However, it is also possible, given plans in early August to write a "school book—or, at any rate, a book for the young" (letter to Horace Mann [16:293]), that "The Snow-Image" and possibly "The Great Stone Face" were already written (or at least started) and could be used as suitable works for children. It is not unlikely (this is the most one can speculate) that Hawthorne during those first weeks after losing office revised and completed stories already begun, as Sophia had described, in the first months of that year. Julian Hawthorne, *Hawthorne and His Wife*, 1:312 and 330, avers that "The Snow-Image" was a product of those Salem years.

7. See Sophia Hawthorne's letter of September 2, 1849, on her husband's reaction to the tale, quoted by Julian Hawthorne, *Hawthorne and his Wife*, 1:354.

8. See letter to Samuel Cleveland, January 8, 1863: "It [*The Scarlet Letter*] had occasionally occupied my thoughts for, as much as a year before; but I had no time to write it till after being turned out of the Custom House in Salem, when, after recovering the practice of the pen by writing two or three shorter tales, I sat down seriously to it" ("Hawthorne to Samuel M. Cleveland," 1).

9. Several critics wish to see Brand as the artist, discounting the fact that his quest is to do with "truth," rather than expression: see Male, *Hawthorne's Tragic Vision*, 85–89; and Bewley, *Eccentric Design*, 117–23. Baym, *Hawthorne's Career*, 118, identifies the imagination here with solipsism and insanity, whereas I would argue for the additional presence of another, more vivifying kind of imagination.

10. Turner, *Hawthorne: A Biography*, 113.

11. When it is not placed within the pattern of Hawthorne's development, the Unpardonable Sin has perplexed the critics as much as it did Brand: see, for example, Stein, *Hawthorne's Faust*, 97–100. See, however, Swann, *Tradition and Revolution*, 44–62, on the tale as an ironical treatment of an attenuated Puritan tradition.

12. Later Emersonian extensions of the eighteenth-century idea of sympathy have been added here; see Male, "Concept of Sympathy," 140–42, though I disagree that this organicism can be found across Hawthorne's career.

13. See James J. Lynch, "Structure and Allegory in 'The Great Stone Face.'" In "The Snow-Image," I would trace to this problematic choice of vehicle the critical debate about the value and status of the imagination in this tale. For example, see Baym, *Hawthorne's Career*, 118; and Dennis Berthold, "Anti-Idealism in Hawthorne's 'The Snow-Image.'" Shannon Burns, "Hawthorne's Literary Theory in the Tales," 266–70, and Darrel Abel, "'A Vast Deal of Human Sympathy': Idea and Device in Hawthorne's 'The Snow-Image,'" both seek a theory applicable to the entire corpus of Hawthorne's work.

14. Julian Hawthorne, *Hawthorne and His Wife*, 1:354.

15. McWilliams, *Hawthorne, Melville, and the American Character*, 63. See also Swann, *Tradition and Revolution*, 62–74, on the tale's treatment of history as a cultural construct, and its relating of past and present fictions.

Chapter 8   *The Scarlet Letter*

1. Entry for September 14, 1855, *The English Notebooks*, 225. In "The Custom-House," while struggling to write this tale of mother and child, the author imagines in his sitting room a figure who might well be his mother: "a form, beloved, but gone hence, now sitting quietly in a streak of this magic moonshine" (1:36).

2. Carton, *Rhetoric of American Romance*, 154–56, also links Hawthorne's literary future with this return to the past, identifying a subtle dialectical engagement with those Salem sources and models: "self-differentiation and ancestral representation are interdependent."

3. Surprisingly few accounts of *The Scarlet Letter* consider it within the context of his earlier work: Stein, *Hawthorne's Faust*, 104–22 (Faust theme); Van Doren, *Nathaniel Hawthorne*, 145–46 (Hawthorne's last tale); Allen, "Hawthorne's Art," 41 (structural experimentation); and Martin, "Method of Hawthorne's Tales," 28 (the "master product of the methods of Hawthorne's tales," especially the use of a central symbol). However, Baym, *Hawthorne's Career*, 142, argues, "Clearly, *The Scarlet Letter* is quite different from all of Hawthorne's earlier work" (142).

4. Historicist readings argue that Hawthorne's "story really does presuppose a pre-fictive, 'historical' world": see Michael J. Colacurcio, "'The

Woman's Own Choice': Sex, Metaphor, and the Puritan 'Sources' of *The Scarlet Letter*," 104. While this essay and its precursor by the same hand ("Footsteps of Ann Hutchinson: The Context of *The Scarlet Letter*") demonstrate how important—not to say essential—it is to understand what Colacurcio identifies as "Hawthorne's studied historicism" ("Woman's Own Choice," 116), I wish to speculate what it was about his contemporary scene that initiated that interest and in what ways those nineteenth-century preoccupations inflected that rewriting of history. The antinomian controversy that Colacurcio demonstrates as one of the historical centers of the text does relate to a version of that divided self that this present study has been exploring: "At one primal level, the whole antinomian controversy is about the inner and the outer, the private and the public person: what do our outward works, positive and negative, really reveal about our salvation status, or, in naturalized form, about our selves?" ("Footsteps," 484). For other comments on why Hawthorne chose a historical setting, see Zelda Bronstein, "The Parabolic Ploys of *The Scarlet Letter*," who finds the text's resort to the past a critique of contemporary democratic politics; Swann, *Tradition and Revolution*, who sees the novel as a "complex narrative meditation on signs and meanings in history" (80); and Quentin Anderson, *The Imperial Self: An Essay in American Literary and Cultural History*, 61–64: "He had to build his own Boston," to create a sense of "society as a reciprocal affair" (61).

5. *Salem Advertiser*, May 2, 1846, reprinted in Stewart, "Contributions to *Salem Advertiser*," 331–32.

6. Baym, *Hawthorne's Career*, 145–46, noting the novel's genesis in this attic, interprets this, however, as a Romantic escape to freedom through fantasy (143). Note, too, the argument (Henry Nash Smith, *Democracy and the Novel*, 18–22) that Hawthorne's fiction was implicitly subversive of the established value system of the day (urbane rationalism and developing capitalism); and Swann, *Tradition and Revolution*, on "history as comprised of the conflicting claims of tradition and revolution, history as continuity and attempted rupture, history as a struggle for new beginnings or as a series of returns of that which it had too optimistically been hoped had been escaped from or transcended" (3). This is to take issue with commentators who read *The Scarlet Letter* in various ways more conservatively: Bercovitch, *Office*, sees the novel ("thick propaganda" [89]) as an exploration, in the context of European revolutions and sectional conflict in America, of processes leading to a liberal pluralism, that is, consensus, compromise,

and the law. See also Larry Reynolds, "*The Scarlet Letter* and Revolutions Abroad."

7. See Baym, *Novels, Readers, and Reviewers*, 174 and 216.

8. The "Introduction," Centenary Edition of *The Scarlet Letter* (1: xxii) expresses doubts as to whether the novel could ever have been a short story. For a discussion of how the general decay of the often allegorical and moralistic popular tale as a form in the 1850s fostered the development of the more realistic, dramatic short story, see Robert F. Marler, "From Tale to Short Story: The Emergence of a New Genre in the 1850s."

9. From Henry James onward, critics have tended to respond to the indeterminate nature of Hawthorne's characterization by opting to argue for one extreme or the other—they are fully created characters, or unrealistic, symbolic figures. A few recent critics have attempted to grapple with this instability of characterization: David Van Leer, "Hester's Labyrinth: Transcendental Rhetoric in Puritan Boston," especially 69–75; and Carton, *Rhetoric of American Romance*, 99–202. See also the emphasis on a character's life in the original notebook entry: "The life of a woman, who, by the old colony law, was condemned always to wear the letter *A*, sewed on her garment, in token of her having committed adultery" (8:254). This entry, written between October 1844 and March 1845, around the time of the composition of his last substantial dramatic fiction at Concord, "Rappaccini's Daughter" (finished mid-November 1844), is the only idea noted that winter that has the promise of extended development into plot and character.

10. See the way the narrative voice both returns to the "Custom-House" scenario at the end of the novel, while simultaneously and ironically withdrawing from this line of informants stretching back to gossip: "In fine, the gossips of that day believed,—and Mr. Surveyor Pue, who made investigations a century later, believed,—and one of his recent successors in office, moreover, faithfully believes,—that Pearl was not only alive, but married, and happy, and mindful of her mother" (1:262).

11. See Colacurcio, "Footsteps of Ann Hutchinson," 472, who identifies these conventional expectations of femininity, and the novel's "clear recognition of the antisocial meaning of self-conscious female sexuality." See also Darrel Abel, "Hawthorne on the Strong Division-Lines of Nature"; and Nina Baym, "Thwarted Nature: Hawthorne as Feminist." David Leverenz, "Mrs. Hawthorne's Headache: Reading *The Scarlet Letter*," notes "unresolved conflicts about anger, authority, and female autonomy" (555).

12. For an exploration of the confusions of Puritan and Transcendentalist vocabularies, though in relation to epistemological issues, see Van Leer, "Hester's Labyrinth." See also Buell, *New England Literary Culture*, 274–75.

13. In recent years—much to my agreement—there has been a small but growing number of critical voices urging us not to trust the *Scarlet Letter* narrator, or at least not to read him simply as "Hawthorne" to whose views we have direct and unequivocal access. Only two studies deal with the problem fully and at length. For an evasive narrator who believes the only correct response to Puritan law is artistic withdrawal rather than rebellion, see Daniel Cottom, "Hawthorne versus Hester: The Ghostly Dialectic of Romance in *The Scarlet Letter*." Leverenz's account, "Mrs. Hawthorne's Headache," I find the most illuminating, giving full attention to the implications behind an ambivalent narrator "[p]erpetually oscillating between subjectivity and authority" (567), and "[a]t once rebel and inquisitor" (557), proposing a false transcendence of the novel's difficulties. I would, however, argue that the mixture of sympathy and judgment is not "evasive" (566) throughout, but a necessary negotiation between competing realities. See also Van Leer, "Hester's Labyrinth"; Colacurcio, "Woman's Own Choice," 120 and 123–24; and Schulman, *Social Criticism*, 185–88. See also Berlant, *Anatomy of National Fantasy*, 97–159, who explores the narrator's desire to represent and reinstate in his citizen/reader a proper attitude toward the "law," and his increasing tendency to undermine Hester's self-knowledge and archaic, private identities.

14. Other examples of this syntactical ambiguity in *The Scarlet Letter* are as follows: 1:79–80—the beginning of the second paragraph ("another feeling") establishes that the preceding paragraph may also be her thoughts; 1:87—there seems a possible but far from clear slippage from Hester to narrator near the end of the paragraph; 1:176–77—it is not clear whether the final paragraph on the page is Hester's or the narrator's view on her marriage, because the point of view oscillates; 1:201—a doubtful example, when Dimmesdale is fighting against flight, that I am inclined to read as the narrator's recoil from a new turn of events but that seamlessly evolves from an account on the previous page of Dimmesdale's feelings; and 1:222—it is not clear here whether the judgment on Dimmesdale's encounter with Mistress Hibbins is the narrator's, since its terms are very much those of the Puritan minister's moral world. There is no precise, critical comment on this device, although point of view, ambiguity, multiple choice, doubt, and the narrator's problematic presence have, of course, been much discussed.

15. The considerable difficulties that commentators have met when trying to match *The Scarlet Letter* to the "Custom-House" passage on romance seem not to have alerted them to the fact that the passage is not actually talking about this novel. Only three recent commentators share my view that *The Scarlet Letter* and the sketch's discussion of the workings of the imagination are separate and distinct from each other in some way or other. Carton, *Rhetoric of American Romance*, 157–59, links this passage with "a precious or fetishized notion of imagination that better suits 'The Artist of the Beautiful' than the artist of *The Scarlet Letter*" (158). Van Leer, "Hester's Labyrinth," 67–69, argues that *The Scarlet Letter* itself undermines this passage. Michael Bell, "Arts of Deception: Hawthorne, 'Romance,' and *The Scarlet Letter*," sees the passage as a deliberate attempt to divert attention from Hawthorne's subversive commitment to the artist's creative imagination. None of these commentators explains the passage by relating it to Hawthorne's immediately preceding compositions at Salem, in particular "The Snow-Image" and "The Great Stone Face."

16. See Michael Ragussis, "Family Discourse and Fiction in *The Scarlet Letter*," on the pervasive silencing and displacement of the father. Girgus, *Desire and the Political Unconscious*, 49–78, discusses Hawthorne generally in the historical context of a search for unity of self and culture in an increasingly fragmented world, but sees Hester and Pearl occupying the domain of the imaginary. Brodhead, *Cultures of Letters*, 13–47, discusses new nineteenth-century, middle-class theories of socialization—discipline through love rather than corporal punishment. See also T. Walter Herbert Jr., "Nathaniel Hawthorne, Una Hawthorne, and *The Scarlet Letter*: Interactive Selfhoods and the Cultural Construction of Gender."

17. The object relations psychoanalytic model is useful here, and in particular the use made of the mirror as an image of interrelationship, especially between mother and infant: see D. W. Winnicott, "Mirror-Role of Mother and Family," *Playing and Reality*, 111–18.

18. On a rough count (because some usages are not clear), "nature" refers to humans forty-five times, compared to about fifteen examples of the nonhuman natural world. The word is used to refer also to characteristics of objects; to Pearl (on about eleven occasions); and to genetic inheritance (1:10, 94, 130, 116). See also Seymour Katz, "'Character,' 'Nature,' and 'Allegory' in *The Scarlet Letter*": "Nature is morally neutral. It is undirected impulse or potential energy which the individual will expend and express in various ways in the course of his life" (4).

19. See Colacurcio, "Woman's Own Choice," 101–35, who uncovers the novel's historicist subtext of Puritan controversies around sexuality and state institutions. Brown, *Domestic Individualism*, 112–16, takes a more optimistic view than this present study, and argues that the novel eventually erases adultery, rewriting the past as a way of imagining "the cancellation of moral debts and resolution of social conflict" (112).

20. For commentaries that question the romantic individualism and essentialism of the forest scene, suggesting that its liberation from history, culture, and language is only apparent, see Carton, *Rhetoric of American Romance*, 210–12; Smith, *Eve Tempted*, 19–23; Van Leer, "Hester's Labyrinth," 81–83; and John Carlos Rowe, "The Internal Conflict of Romantic Narrative: Hegel's *Phenomenology* and Hawthorne's *The Scarlet Letter*." See also Louise K. Barnett, "Speech and Society in *The Scarlet Letter*."

21. There seems to be conflicting influences at work in the novel's presentation of Hester as mother. The novel's picture of authoritarian parenting by all the other Puritans seems a product of nineteenth-century assumptions rather than historically based (for all Hawthorne's historicism elsewhere): for a revisionary history of Puritan child-rearing with an accent on tenderness and instruction, see David Leverenz, *The Language of Puritan Feeling: An Exploration in Literature, Psychology, and Social History.* Hawthorne's experience of his own daughter (a child described in his notebooks in terms very different from Victorian stereotypes) is an important ingredient in his portrait of Hester's mothering. For other useful views of Hester's maternal role, see Leverenz, "Reading *The Scarlet Letter*"; and Baym, "Thwarted Nature," 73–74.

22. T. D. Campbell, *Adam Smith's Science of Morals*, 94. For further discussion of this point, see 94–96.

23. See 1:133, 134, 139, 148, 171, 193, 200, 208, 239. The only other times the word seems to be used in the novel are to describe Hester's response to wearing the letter (1:86) and to an imagined observer of the opening scaffold scene (1:53).

24. Smith, *Theory of Moral Sentiments*, 23.

25. For a suggestive exploration and comparison of Rousseau's views on the teaching of sociability in the child with those of Adam Smith (who regarded sympathy as natural), see Peter France, "Rousseau, Adam Smith and the Education of the Self." Both Rousseau and Smith seek to ground social living on sympathy. I see the portrayal of Pearl (who fits neither of these views completely) as an exploration of this issue.

26. See my earlier chapters for the historical background of these uses of "sympathy" and for Hawthorne's earlier use of the word. Given the complex operations of sympathy here, I take a different view from Lester H. Hunt, "*The Scarlet Letter:* Hawthorne's Theory of Moral Sentiments," who sees the novel as a criticism of Smith's ideas and an illustration of how the social regulation of conduct ruptures relationships of sympathy. Some critical studies of "sympathy" focusing on *The Scarlet Letter* opt to read it *either* entirely positively *or* entirely negatively: see Kent Bales, "Hawthorne's Prefaces and Romantic Perspectivism"; and William Manierre, "The Role of Sympathy in *The Scarlet Letter.*" For studies that take a more negative view, see Leverenz, "Mrs. Hawthorne's Headache" (an evasion of real intimacy and a fascination and participation in violation); and Van Leer, "Hester's Labyrinth" (seen as a more inherently confused and implicitly materialist term than in this present study). Where these find muddle, I see a more controlled investigation into the problematic and multiform nature of "sympathy," of which the narrator's pity and Chillingworth's inquisitorial violation are only two of several possibilities.

27. See Peter France, "The Commerce of the Self"; and France, "Rousseau, Adam Smith."

28. Public confession was common in Puritan New England for church and civil reasons. See Ernest W. Baughman, "Public Confession and *The Scarlet Letter.*" Baughman points out, "On a purely social level, it was the means by which an individual can remain part of society" (540). See also Thomas L. Hilgers, "The Psychology of Conflict Resolution in *The Scarlet Letter:* A Non-Freudian Perspective" (cognitive dissonance). Orestes Brownson's sternly Christian attack (in Crowley, ed., *Critical Heritage,* 175–79) on the protagonists' desire to preserve "integrity of their character" and failure to realize their offense against God, places all this in its nineteenth-century context.

29. For the idea that sympathy is a "process of negotiation between individuals," see France, "Rousseau, Adam Smith," 37.

30. Quite a sizable number of these citations relate clearly to the individual's sense that what she or he is doing, or is perceived to be doing, is congruent with a particular subjective sense of self (a sense of identity that may of course be an internalized version from external social expectations). See, for example, 1:23, 44, 59, 78, 83, 93, 100, 133, 139, 146, 161, 164, 177, 191, 216, 224, 240, 262. These words are used both of consciousness and of life within the world of social interaction, often contrasting the one with the

other; see, for example, 1:23, 57, 59, 78, 145, 164. In spite of their significance in asserting ontological certainty, these words are often used in contexts that paradoxically inculcate doubt (1:82, 100, 120, 175, 178, 179, 214, 219), especially when syntactically this doubt is reinforced by the use of conditionals and questions or the hypothetical (see 1:83, 100, 120, 133, 175, 214, 219, 240), or when the sense asserts the truth of something that is patently not true (1:16, 241). This extends into the realm of imaginative fiction and questions of the fantastical constrasted with realism: for example, 1:36, 37, 43, 44, 204, 208, 222, 251.

31. For critiques of Dimmesdale's sermon, see Bell, *Hawthorne and Romance,* 141–44 ("a ranting political oration" [142]); and McWilliams, *Hawthorne, Melville, and the American Character,* 67–68. Leverenz, "Reading *The Scarlet Letter,*" 570, attacks Dimmesdale's "spiritualized male narcissicism as the way to complete one's divided self" (570).

32. In relation to this, see Arac's argument, "Politics of *The Scarlet Letter,*" 258–59, that the political impasse of the 1850s affected Hawthorne's ability fully to actualize the revolutionary Hester as a character.

33. For the "impartial spectator," see Smith, *Theory of Moral Sentiments,* 97 (I: 2: 2), though he uses many synonyms throughout. I am following up Campbell's interpretation of this figure (134–45). See also Campbell's comment that "Smith's concept of the impartial spectator . . . represents the means whereby the social consensus necessary for the harmony and therefore the stability of society is achieved" (138–39). That a sufficiently sensitive and complex spectatordom is achievable only through a reader's sympathetic imagination is my conjecture.

Bibliography

Abel, Darrel. "Hawthorne on the Strong Division-Lines of Nature." *American Transcendental Quarterly* 14 (1972): 23–31.

———. " 'A Vast Deal of Human Sympathy': Idea and Device in Hawthorne's 'The Snow-Image.' " *Criticism* 12 (1970): 316–32.

Adams, Richard P. "Hawthorne: the Old Manse Period." *Tulane Studies in English* 8 (1958): 115–51.

———. "Hawthorne's 'Provincial Tales.' " *New England Quarterly* 30 (1957): 39–57.

Adams, Stephen. "Unifying Structures in *Mosses from an Old Manse*." *Studies in American Fiction* 8 (1980): 147–63.

Adkins, Nelson F. "The Early Projected Works of Nathaniel Hawthorne." *Papers of the Bibliographical Society of America* 39 (1945): 119–55.

Allen, M. L. "Hawthorne's Art in His Short Stories." *Studi Americani* 7 (1961): 9–42.

Anderson, Quentin. *The Imperial Self: An Essay in American Literary History.* New York: Knopf, 1971.

Arac, Jonathan. *Commissioned Spirits: The Shaping of Social Motion in Dickens, Carlyle, Melville, and Hawthorne.* New Brunswick, N.J.: Rutgers University Press, 1979.

———. "The Politics of *The Scarlet Letter*." In *Ideology and Classic American Literature*, Sacvan Bercovitch and Myra Jehlen, eds., 247–66. Cambridge: Cambridge University Press, 1986.

Bales, Kent. "Hawthorne's Prefaces and Romantic Perspectivism." *ESQ* 23 (1977): 69–88.

Barnett, Louise K. "Speech and Society in *The Scarlet Letter*." *ESQ* 29 (1983): 16–24.

Baughman, Ernest W. "Public Confession and *The Scarlet Letter*." *New England Quarterly* 40 (1967): 532–50.

Baym, Nina. "Hawthorne's Gothic Discards: *Fanshawe* and 'Alice Doane.' " *Nathaniel Hawthorne Journal* 4 (1974): 105–15.

———. *Novels, Readers, and Reviewers: Responses to Fiction in Antebellum America.* Ithaca: Cornell University Press, 1984.

———. *The Shape of Hawthorne's Career.* Ithaca: Cornell University Press, 1976.

———. "Thwarted Nature: Hawthorne as Feminist." In *American Novelists Revisited: Essays in Feminist Criticism*, Fritz Fleischmann, ed., 58–77. Boston: Hall, 1982.

Bell, Michael Davitt. "Arts of Deception: Hawthorne, 'Romance,' and *The Scarlet Letter.*" In *New Essays on* The Scarlet Letter, Michael J. Colacurcio, ed., 29–56. Cambridge: Cambridge University Press, 1985.

———. *The Development of American Romance: The Sacrifice of Relation.* Chicago: University of Chicago Press, 1980.

———. *Hawthorne and the Historical Romance of New England.* Princeton: Princeton University Press, 1971.

Bell, Millicent. *Hawthorne's View of the Artist.* New York: New York State University Press, 1962.

Belsey, Catherine. *Critical Practice.* London: Methuen, 1980.

> ———. "The Romantic Construction of the Unconscious." In *Literature, Politics and Theory,* Francis Barker et al., eds., 57–76. London: Methuen, 1986.

Bensick, Carol Marie. *La Nouvelle Beatrice: Renaissance and Romance in 'Rappaccini's Daughter.'* New Brunswick, N.J.: Rutgers University Press, 1985.

Bercovitch, Sacvan. "Endicott's Breastplate: Symbolism and Typology in 'Endicott and the Red Cross.'" *Studies in Shorter Fiction* 4 (1967): 289–99.

———. *The Office of* The Scarlet Letter. Baltimore: Johns Hopkins University Press, 1991.

Berlant, Lauren. *The Anatomy of National Fantasy: Hawthorne, Utopia, and Everyday Life.* Chicago: University of Chicago Press, 1991.

Berthold, Dennis. "Anti-Idealism in Hawthorne's 'The Snow-Image.'" *Arizona Quarterly* 38 (1982): 119–32.

Bewley, Marius. *The Eccentric Design: Form in the Classic American Novel.* London: Chatto, 1959.

Boewe, Charles. E. "Rappaccini's Garden." *American Literature* 30 (1958): 37–49.

Brenzo, Richard. "Beatrice Rappaccini: A Victim of Male Love and Horror." *American Literature* 48 (1976): 152–64.

Bridge, Horatio. *Personal Recollections of Nathaniel Hawthorne.* London: Osgood, 1893.

Brodhead, Richard H. *Cultures of Letters: Scenes of Reading and Writing in Nineteenth-Century America.* Chicago: University of Chicago Press, 1993.

———. *Hawthorne, Melville, and the Novel.* Chicago: University of Chicago Press, 1976.

Brodwin, Stanley. "Hawthorne and the Function of History: A Reading of 'Alice Doane's Appeal.'" *Nathaniel Hawthorne Journal* 3 (1973): 116–28.

Bronstein, Zelda. "The Parabolic Ploys of *The Scarlet Letter*." *American Quarterly* 39 (1987): 193–210.

Brown, Gillian. *Domestic Individualism: Imagining Self in Nineteenth-Century America*. Berkeley: University of California Press, 1990.

Buell, Lawrence. *New England Literary Culture: From Revolution through Renaissance*. Cambridge: Cambridge University Press, 1986.

Burniston, Steve, and Chris Weedon. "Ideology, Subjectivity and the Artistic Text." *Working Papers in Cultural Studies* 10 (1977): 203–33.   ⌃

Burns, Shannon. "Hawthorne's Literary Theory in the Tales." *Nathaniel Hawthorne Journal* 7 (1977): 261–77.

Campbell, T. D. *Adam Smith's Science of Morals*. London: Allen and Unwin, 1971.

Cantwell, Robert. *Nathaniel Hawthorne: The American Years*. New York: Rinehart, 1948.

Carton, Evan. *The Rhetoric of American Romance: Dialectic and Identity in Emerson, Dickinson, Poe, and Hawthorne*. Baltimore: Johns Hopkins University Press, 1985.

Chandler, Elizabeth Lathrop. "A Study of the Sources of the Tales and Romances Written by Nathaniel Hawthorne before 1853." *Smith Studies in Modern Languages* 7 (1926): 1–64.

Charvat, William. *Literary Publishing in America, 1790–1850*. Philadelphia: University of Pennsylvania Press, 1959.

———. *The Profession of Authorship in America, 1800–1870: The Papers of William Charvat*. Ed. Matthew J. Bruccoli. Columbus: Ohio State University Press, 1968.

Chase, Richard. *The American Novel and Its Tradition*. Garden City, N.Y.: Doubleday, 1957.

Cohen, B. Bernard. "Hawthorne and *Parley's Universal History*." *Papers of the Bibliographical Society of America* 48 (1954): 77–90.

Colacurcio, Michael J. "A Better Mode of Evidence: The Transcendental Problem of Faith and Spirit." *ESQ* 54 (1969): 12–22.

———. "Footsteps of Ann Hutchinson: The Context of *The Scarlet Letter*." *ELH* 39 (1972): 459–94.

———. *The Province of Piety: Moral History in Hawthorne's Early Tales*. Cambridge, Mass.: Harvard University Press, 1984.

———. "Visible Sanctity and Specter Evidence: The Moral World of Hawthorne's 'Young Goodman Brown.'" *Essex Institute Historical Collection* 110 (1974): 259–99.

———. "'The Woman's Own Choice': Sex, Metaphor, and the Puritan

'Sources' of *The Scarlet Letter.*" In *New Essays on* The Scarlet Letter, Michael J. Colacurcio, ed., 101–35. Cambridge: Cambridge University Press, 1985.

Conway, Moncure D. *Life of Nathaniel Hawthorne.* London: Walter Scott, 1891.

Cottom, Daniel. "Hawthorne versus Hester: The Ghostly Dialectic of Romance in *The Scarlet Letter.*" *Texas Studies in Literature and Language* 24 (1982): 47–67.

Coward, Rosalind, and John Ellis. *Language and Materialism: Developments in Semiology and the Theory of the Subject.* London: Routledge, 1977.

Crandall, John C. "Patriotism and Humanitarian Reform in Children's Literature, 1825–1860." *American Quarterly* 31 (1969): 3–22.

Crews, Frederick C. *The Sins of the Fathers: Hawthorne's Psychological Themes.* New York: Oxford University Press, 1966.

Crowley, J. Donald, ed. *Hawthorne: The Critical Heritage.* London: Routledge, 1970.

———. "The Unity of Hawthorne's *Twice-told Tales.*" *Studies in American Fiction* 1 (1973): 35–61.

Daly, Robert J. "History and Chivalric Myth in 'Roger Malvin's Burial.'" *Essex Institute Historical Collection* 109 (1973): 99–115.

Dauber, Kenneth. *Rediscovering Hawthorne.* Princeton: Princeton University Press, 1977.

Davidson, Cathy N. *Revolution and the Word: The Rise of the Novel in America.* New York: Oxford University Press, 1986.

Doubleday, Neal Frank. *Hawthorne's Early Tales: A Critical Study.* Durham: Duke University Press, 1972.

———. "Hawthorne's Satirical Allegory." *College English* 3 (1942): 325–37.

Downing, David. "Beyond Convention: The Dynamics of Imagery and Response in Hawthorne's Early Sense of Evil." *American Literature* 51 (1980): 463–76.

———. "The Swelling Waves: Visuality, Metaphor, and Bodily Reality in *The Scarlet Letter.*" *Studies in American Fiction* 12 (1984): 13–28.

Dryden, Edgar A. *Nathaniel Hawthorne: The Poetics of Enchantment.* Ithaca: Cornell University Press, 1977.

Duban, James. "Robins and Robinarchs in 'My Kinsman, Major Molineux.'" *Nineteenth Century Fiction* 38 (1983): 271–88.

———. "The Skeptical Context of Hawthorne's 'Mr. Higginbotham's Catastrophe.'" *American Literature* 48 (1976): 292–301.

Dunne, Michael. "Varieties of Narrative Authority in Hawthorne's *Twice-told Tales* (1937)." *South Atlantic Review* 54 (1989): 33–49.

Ehrenpreis, Anne Henry. "Elizabeth Gaskell and Nathaniel Hawthorne." *Nathaniel Hawthorne Journal* 3 (1973): 89–119.

Engell, James. *The Creative Imagination: Enlightenment to Romanticism.* Cambridge, Mass.: Harvard University Press, 1981.

Erlich, Gloria. *Family Themes and Hawthorne's Fiction: The Tenacious Web.* New Brunswick, N.J.: Rutgers University Press, 1984.

Fiedler, Leslie A. *Love and Death in the American Novel.* Rev. ed. London: Cape, 1967.

Fields, James T. *Yesterdays with Authors.* Boston: Osgood, 1872.

Fogle, Richard Harter. *Hawthorne's Fiction: The Light and the Dark.* Norman: Oklahoma University Press, 1964.

Folsom, James K. *Man's Accidents and God's Purposes: Multiplicity in Hawthorne's Fiction.* New Haven: College and University Press, 1963.

France, Peter. "The Commerce of the Self." *Comparative Criticism* 12 (1990): 39–56.

———. "Rousseau, Adam Smith and the Education of the Self." In *Moy Qui Me Voi: The Writer and the Self from Montaigne to Leiris,* 28–51. Eds. George Craig and Margaret McGowan. Oxford: Oxford University Press, 1989.

Franzosa, John. "The Language of Inflation in 'Rappaccini's Daughter.'" *Texas Studies in Literature and Language* 24 (1982): 1–22.

———. "Locke's Kinsman, William Molyneux: The Philosophical Context of Hawthorne's Early Tales." *ESQ* 29 (1983): 1–15.

———. "A Psychoanalysis of Hawthorne's Style." *Genre* 14 (1981): 383–409.

Freud, Sigmund. *The Standard Edition of the Complete Psychological Works of Sigmund Freud.* Ed. James Strachey. 24 vols. London: Hogarth, 1953–1974.

Gilkes, Lilian B. "Hawthorne, Park Benjamin, and S. G. Goodrich: A Three-Cornered Imbroglio." *Nathaniel Hawthorne Journal* 1 (1971): 83–112.

Gilmore, Michael T. *American Romanticism and the Marketplace.* Chicago: University of Chicago Press, 1985.

Girgus, Sam. *Desire and the Political Unconscious in American Literature.* Basingstoke: Macmillan, 1990.

Gollin, Rita K. *Nathaniel Hawthorne and the Truth of Dreams.* Baton Rouge: Louisiana State University Press, 1979.

Gross, Robert Eugene. "Hawthorne's First Novel: The Future of a Style." *PMLA* 78 (1963): 60–68.

Gross, Seymour L. "Four Possible Additions to Hawthorne's 'Story Teller.'" *Papers of the Bibliographical Society of America* 51 (1957): 90–95.

———. "Hawthorne's Revision of 'The Gentle Boy.'" *American Literature* 26 (1954): 196–208.

———. "Hawthorne's Moral Realism." In "Symposium on Hawthorne." Eds. Carl F. Strauch et al. *New England Quarterly* 25 (1961): 11–13.

———. "Hawthorne and the Shakers." *American Literature* 29 (1958): 457–63.

———. "Hawthorne's 'The Vision of the Fountain' as a Parody." *American Literature* 27 (1955): 101–5.

Gross, Seymour L., and Alfred J. Levy. "Some Remarks on the Extant Manuscripts of Hawthorne's Short Stories." *Studies in Bibliography* 14 (1961): 254–57.

Hansen, Elaine Tuttle. "Ambiguity and the Narrator in *The Scarlet Letter*." *Journal of Narrative Technique* 5 (1975): 147–61.

Hawthorne, Julian. *Hawthorne and His Circle*. New York: Harper, 1903.

———. *Hawthorne's Reading*. Cleveland: Rowfant Club, 1902.

———. *Nathaniel Hawthorne and His Wife: A Biography*. 2 vols. Boston: Osgood, 1885.

Hawthorne, Nathaniel. *The Centenary Edition of the Works of Nathaniel Hawthorne*. Eds. William Charvat et al. 20 vols. to date. Columbus: Ohio State University Press, 1962– .

———. *The English Notebooks*. Ed. Randall Stewart. New York: Modern Language Association of America, 1941. Rpt., New York: Russell, 1962.

———. *Hawthorne as Editor: Selections from His Writings in the* American Magazine of Useful and Entertaining Knowledge. Ed. Arlin Turner. Baton Rouge: Louisiana State University Press, 1941.

———. *Hawthorne's Lost Notebook 1835–1841*. Transcript and preface by Barbara S. Mouffe. University Park: Pennsylvania State University Press, 1978.

———. "Hawthorne to Samuel M. Cleveland: An Autobiographical Letter." *Nathaniel Hawthorne Journal* 2 (1972): 1–5.

———. *Tales and Sketches*. Library of America edition. New York: Viking Press, 1982.

Hazlett, John Downton. "Re-Reading 'Rappaccini's Daughter': Giovanni and the Seduction of the Transcendental Reader." *ESQ* 35 (1989): 43–68.

Herbert, T. Walter, Jr. "Doing Cultural Work: 'My Kinsman Major Molineux' and the Construction of the Self-Made Man." *Studies in the Novel* 23 (1991): 20–27.

———. "Nathaniel Hawthorne, Una Hawthorne, and *The Scarlet Letter:* Interactive Selfhoods and the Cultural Construction of Gender." *PMLA* 103 (1988): 285–97.

Hilgers, Thomas L. "The Psychology of Conflict Resolution in *The Scarlet Letter:* A Non-Freudian Perspective." *American Transcendental Quarterly* 43 (1979): 212–24.

Hoeltje, Hubert H. *Inward Sky: The Heart and Mind of Nathaniel Hawthorne.* Durham: Duke University Press, 1962.

Holsberry, John E. "Hawthorne's 'The Haunted Mind,' the Psychology of Dreams, Coleridge, and Keats." *Texas Studies in Literature and Language* 21 (1979): 307–21.

Howard, June. "The Watchmaker, the Artist, and the Iron Accents of History: Notes on Hawthorne's 'Artist of the Beautiful.'" *ESQ* 28 (1982): 1–10.

Howe, Daniel Walker. "Victorian Culture in America." In *Victorian America,* 3–28. Ed. Daniel Walker Howe. Philadelphia: University of Pennsylvania Press, 1976.

Hume, Robert D. "Gothic versus Romantic: A Revaluation of the Gothic Novel." *PMLA* 84 (1969): 282–90.

Hunt, Lester H. "*The Scarlet Letter:* Hawthorne's Theory of Moral Sentiments." *Philosophy and Literature* 8 (1984): 75–88.

Hutner, Gordon. *Secrets and Sympathy: Forms of Disclosure in Hawthorne's Novels.* Athens: University of Georgia Press, 1988.

Iser, Wolfgang. *The Implied Reader: Patterns of Communication in Prose Fiction from Bunyan to Beckett.* Baltimore: Johns Hopkins University Press, 1974.

Jackson, Rosemary. *Fantasy: The Literature of Subversion.* London: Methuen, 1981.

James, Henry. *Hawthorne.* London: Macmillan, 1883.

Jehlen, Myra. *American Incarnation: The Individual, the Nation, and the Continent.* Cambridge, Mass.: Harvard University Press, 1986.

Johnson, Claudia D. "Hawthorne and Nineteenth-Century Perfectionism." *American Literature* 44 (1973): 585–95.

Johnston, Mark Evan. "The Receding Narrator: The *Spectator,* the *Rambler* and Hawthorne's Shorter Fiction." *Essays in Arts and Sciences* 6 (1977): 20–46.

Jones, Wayne Allen. "Hawthorne's First Published Review." *American Literature* 48 (1977): 492–500.

Josipovici, G. D. "Hawthorne's Modernity." *Critical Quarterly* 8 (1966): 351–60.

Katz, Seymour. "'Character,' 'Nature,' and 'Allegory' in *The Scarlet Letter*." *Nineteenth Century Fiction* 23 (1968): 3–17.

Kesselring, Marion L. *Hawthorne's Reading, 1828–1850: A Transcription and Identification of Titles Recorded in the Charge-Books of the Salem Athenaeum.* New York: The New York Public Library, 1949.

Kligerman, Jack. "A Stylistic Approach to Hawthorne's 'Roger Malvin's Burial.'" *Language and Style* 4 (1971): 188–94.

Leverenz, David. *The Language of Puritan Feeling: An Exploration in Literature, Psychology, and Social History.* New Brunswick: Rutgers University Press, 1980.

———. *Manhood and the American Renaissance.* Cornell: Cornell University Press, 1989.

———. "Mrs. Hawthorne's Headache: Reading *The Scarlet Letter*." *Nineteenth Century Fiction* 37 (1983): 552–75.

Levin, David. "Shadows of Doubt: Specter Evidence in Hawthorne's 'Young Goodman Brown.'" *American Literature* 34 (1962): 344–52.

Liebman, Sheldon W. "Hawthorne's Romanticism: 'The Artist of the Beautiful.'" *ESQ* 22 (1976): 85–95.

———. "The Reader in 'Young Goodman Brown.'" *Nathaniel Hawthorne Journal* 5 (1975): 156–67.

Lynch, James J. "Structure and Allegory in 'The Great Stone Face.'" *Nineteenth Century Fiction* 15 (1960): 137–46.

Male, Roy R., Jr. "Hawthorne and the Concept of Sympathy." *PMLA* 68 (1953): 138–49.

———. *Hawthorne's Tragic Vision.* Austin: University of Texas Press, 1957.

———. "Sympathy: A Key Word in American Romanticism." *ESQ* 35 (1964): 19–23.

Manierre, William. "The Role of Sympathy in *The Scarlet Letter*." *Texas Studies in Literature and Language* 13 (1972): 497–507.

Marler, Robert F. "From Tale to Short Story: The Emergence of a New Genre in the 1850s." *American Literature* 46 (1974): 153–69.

Martin, John S. "The Other Side of Concord: A Critique of Emerson in Hawthorne's 'The Old Manse.'" *New England Quarterly* 8 (1985): 453–58.

Martin, Terence. *The Instructed Vision: Scottish Common Sense Philosophy and the Origins of American Fiction.* Bloomington: Indiana University Press, 1961.

———. "The Method of Hawthorne's Tales." In *Hawthorne Centenary Essays,* Roy Harvey Pearce, ed., 7–30. Columbus: Ohio State University Press, 1964.

———. *Nathaniel Hawthorne.* Rev. ed. Boston: Twayne, 1983.

Matthiessen, Francis O. *American Renaissance: Art and Expression in the Age of Emerson and Whitman.* New York: Oxford University Press, 1941.

McDonald, John J. "'The Old Manse' and Its Mosses: The Inception and Development of *Mosses from an Old Manse.*" *Texas Studies in Literature and Language* 16 (1974): 77–108.

———. "The Old Manse Period Canon." *Nathaniel Hawthorne Journal* 2 (1972): 13–39.

McHale, Brian. "Free Indirect Discourse: A Survey of Recent Accounts." *Poetics and the Theory of Literature* 3 (1978): 249–87.

McWilliams, John. "The Politics of Isolation." *Nathaniel Hawthorne Review* 15 (1989): 2–7.

McWilliams, John P., Jr. *Hawthorne, Melville, and the American Character: A Looking-Glass Business.* Cambridge: Cambridge University Press, 1984.

Miller, Harold P. "Hawthorne Surveys His Contemporaries." *American Literature* 12 (1940): 228–35.

Miller, James R. *Hawthorne in His Times.* Boston: Houghton Mifflin, 1980.

Mosher, Harold F., Jr. "The Sources of Ambiguity in Hawthorne's 'Young Goodman Brown': A Structuralist Approach." *ESQ* 26 (1980): 16–25.

Mott, Frank Luther. *A History of American Magazines, 1741–1850.* Cambridge Mass.: Belknap Press of Harvard University Press, 1939–1957. 5 vols.

Newlin, Paul A. "'Vague Shapes of the Borderland': The Place of the Uncanny in Hawthorne's Gothic Vision." *ESQ* 18 (1971): 83–96.

Norford, Don Parry. "Rappaccini's Garden of Allegory." *American Literature* 50 (1978): 167–86.

Orians, G. Harrison. "The Angel of Hadley in Fiction: A Study of the Sources of Hawthorne's 'The Grey Champion.'" *American Literature* 4 (1932): 257–69.

Pancost, David W. "Evidence of Editorial Additions to Hawthorne's 'Fragments from the Journal of Solitary Man.'" *Nathaniel Hawthorne Journal* 5 (1975): 210–26.

———. "Hawthorne's Epistemology and Ontology." *ESQ* (1973): 8–13.

Pauly, Thomas H. "The Literary Sketch in Nineteenth-Century America." *Texas Studies in Literature and Language* 17 (1975): 489–503.

Pearce, Roy Harvey. "Hawthorne and the Sense of the Past, or The Immortality of Major Molineux." *ELH* (1954): 327–49.

———. "Hawthorne and the Twilight of Romance." *Yale Review* 37 (1948): 487–506.

Person, Leland S., Jr. *Aesthetic Headaches: Women and a Masculine Poetics in Poe, Melville, and Hawthorne.* University of Georgia Press: Athens, 1988.

Petter, Henri. *The Early American Novel.* Columbus: Ohio State University Press, 1971.

Pfister, Joel. *The Production of Personal Life: Class, Gender, and the Psychological in Hawthorne's Fiction.* Stanford: Stanford University Press, 1991.

Probyn, Elspeth. *Sexing the Self: Gendered Positions in Cultural Studies.* London: Routledge, 1993.

Punter, David. *The Literature of Terror: A History of Gothic Fictions from 1765 to the Present Day.* London: Longman, 1980.

Quirk, Tom. "Hawthorne's Last Tales and 'The Custom-House.'" *ESQ* (1984): 220–31.

Ragussis, Michael. "Family Discourse and Fiction in *The Scarlet Letter.*" *ELH* (1982): 863–88.

Reid, Alfred S. "Hawthorne's Humanism: 'The Birth-mark' and Sir Kenelm Digby." *American Literature* 38 (1966): 337–51.

Reynolds, David S. *Beneath the American Renaissance: The Subversive Imagination in the Age of Emerson and Melville.* Cambridge, Mass.: Harvard University Press, 1989.

Reynolds, Larry. "*The Scarlet Letter* and Revolutions Abroad." *American Literature* 57 (1985): 44–67.

Rimmon-Kenan, Schlomith. *Narrative Fiction: Contemporary Poetics.* London: Methuen, 1983.

Ringe, Donald A. *American Gothic: Imagination and Reason in Nineteeth-Century Fiction.* Lexington: University of Kentucky Press, 1982.

Rowe, John Carlos. "The Internal Conflict of Romantic Narrative: Hegel's *Phenomenology* and Hawthorne's *The Scarlet Letter.*" *MLN* (1980): 1203–31.

Sattelmeyer, Robert. "The Aesthetic Background of Hawthorne's *Fanshawe.*" *Nathaniel Hawthorne Journal* 5 (1975): 200–209.

Sears, John F. "Hawthorne's 'The Ambitious Guest' and the Significance of the Willey Disaster." *American Literature* 54 (1982): 354–67.

Shaw, Peter. "Fathers, Sons, and the Ambiguities of Revolution in 'My Kinsman, Major Molineux.'" *New England Quarterly* 49 (1976): 559–76.

Shulman, Robert. *Social Criticism and Nineteeth-Century American Fictions.* Columbia: University of Missouri Press, 1987.

Smith, Adam. *The Theory of Moral Sentiments.* Reprints of Economic Classics. New York: Augustus M. Kelley, 1966.

Smith, Allan Gardner. *The Analysis of Motives: Early American Psychology and Fiction.* Costerus New Series 27. Amsterdam: Rodophi, 1980.

Smith, Allan Gardner Lloyd. *Eve Tempted: Writing and Sexuality in Hawthorne's Fiction.* London: Croon Helm, 1984.

Smith, Henry Nash. *Democracy and the Novel: Popular Resistance to Classic American Writers.* New York: Oxford University Press, 1978.

St. Armand, Barton Levi. "Hawthorne's 'Haunted Mind': A Subterranean Drama of Self." *Criticism* 13 (1971): 1–25.

Stafford, John. "Sympathy Comes to America." In *Themes and Directions in American Literature: Essays in Honor of Leon Howard,* Ray B. Browne and Donald Pizer, eds., 24–37. Lafayette, Ind.: Purdue University Studies, 1969.

Steele, Jeffrey. *The Representation of the Self in the American Renaissance.* Chapel Hill: University of North Carolina Press, 1981.

Stein, William Bysshe. *Hawthorne's Faust: A Study of the Devil Archetype.* Gainesville: University of Florida Press, 1953.

Stewart, Randall. "Hawthorne's Contributions to *The Salem Advertiser.*" *American Literature* 5 (1934): 327–41.

———. *Nathaniel Hawthorne: A Biography.* New Haven: Yale University Press, 1948.

———. "Recollections of Hawthorne by His Sister Elizabeth." *American Literature* 16 (1945): 316–31.

Stoehr, Taylor. "'Young Goodman Brown' and Hawthorne's Theory of Mimesis." *Nineteenth Century Fiction* 23 (1969): 393–412.

Strauch, Carl F. "Emerson and the Doctrine of Sympathy." *Studies in Romanticism* 6 (1967): 152–74.

Swann, C. S. B. "The Practice and Theory of Storytelling: Nathaniel Hawthorne and Walter Benjamin." *Journal of American Studies* 12 (1978): 185–202.

Swann, Charles. *Nathaniel Hawthorne: Tradition and Revolution.* Cambridge: Cambridge University Press, 1991.

Tharpe, Jac. *Nathaniel Hawthorne: Identity and Knowledge.* Carbondale: Southern Illinois University Press, 1967.

Thompson, G. R. *The Art of Authorial Presence: Hawthorne's Provincial Tales.* Durham: Duke University Press, 1993.

Thompson, Ralph. *American Literary Annuals and Gift Books, 1825–1865.* New York: H. W. Wilson, 1936.

Turner, Arlin. *Hawthorne as Editor: Selections from the Writings in The American Magazine of Useful and Entertaining Knowledge.* Baton Rouge: Louisiana State University Press, 1941. Rpt., Port Washington, N.Y.: Kennikat Press, 1972.

———. "Hawthorne's Literary Borrowings." *PMLA* (1936): 543–62.

———. *Nathaniel Hawthorne: A Biography.* New York: Oxford University Press, 1980.

———. *Nathaniel Hawthorne: An Introduction and Interpretation.* New York: Barnes and Noble, 1961.

Van Doren, Mark. *Nathaniel Hawthorne.* London: Methuen, 1949.

Van Leer, David M. "Aylmer's Library." *ESQ* (1976): 211–20.

———. "Hester's Labyrinth: Transcendental Rhetoric in Puritan Boston." In *New Essays on* The Scarlet Letter, Michael J. Colacurcio, ed., 57–100. Cambridge: Cambridge University Press, 1985.

Waggoner, Hyatt H. *Hawthorne: A Critical Study.* Rev. ed., Cambridge, Mass.: Harvard University Press, 1963.

Walsh, Thomas F. "Rappaccini's Literary Gardens." *ESQ* (1960): 9–13.

———. " 'Wakefield' and Hawthorne's Illustrated Ideas: A Study in Form." *ESQ* (1961): 29–35.

Weber, Alfred. *Die Entwicklung der Rahmenerzählungen Nathaniel Hawthornes: "The Story Teller" und andere frühe Werke.* Berlin: Erich Schmidt, 1973.

Williamson, James L. "Young Goodman Brown: Hawthorne's 'Devil in Manuscript.'" *Studies in Shorter Fiction* 18 (1981): 155–62.

Wilt, Judith. *Ghosts of the Gothic: Austin, Eliot, and Lawrence.* Princeton: Princeton University Press, 1980.

Winnicott, D. W. *Playing and Reality.* London: Tavistock, 1971.

Woodberry, George E. *Nathaniel Hawthorne.* Boston: Houghton Mifflin, 1902.

Index

Adkins, Nelson F., 3
Adultery, 16–17, 26, 213–14, 225, 226, 241
Alienation, 7–10 passim, 14, 94, 139
Allegory form, 146, 155, 166
American Magazine of Useful and Entertaining Knowledge, The, 79, 80, 98, 100, 102, 108, 110
American Monthly, 77, 79–80
Artist/Art, theme of: in *Seven Tales* and *Fanshawe,* 16, 17–18, 25; in early 1830s, 65–75, 83, 93; in later 1830s, 99, 108–14; in Concord period, 136–42, 155–61, 167–68; in Salem Period, 167–68, 181, 182; in "The Custom-House," 192–93
Audience, internal: in early 1830s, 62, 64, 69, 70, 72; in later 1830s, 100; in "Main-street," 182–83, 186, 187

Baym, Nina, 3, 26, 94; *The Shape of Hawthorne's Career,* 3
Benjamin, Park, 77, 78, 79
Bridge, Horatio, 13, 79, 98, 245; *Journal of an African Cruiser,* 135
"Brotherhood," 175–76, 179
Buell, Lawrence, 33, 66, 74, 99, 115

Centenary Edition, 3, 171
Chandler, Elizabeth, 3
Channing, Ellery, 133, 145, 185
Choice, questions of: in *Fanshawe,* 20, 23, 24; in later 1830s, 99, 120, 124; in *The Scarlet Letter,* 240–42
Christianity: in *Provincial Tales,* 51, 52, 55; in early 1830s, 68, 95; in late 1830s, 99, 101, 118–19; in Concord period, 133; in *The Scarlet Letter,* 195–96, 218, 236, 244
Chronology. *See* Dating of Hawthorne's works
Cilley, Jonathan, 101
"Circumstance": opposed to "desire," ix, x, 7; in Concord period, 135, 139, 142–44, 148–50, 154, 156, 161, 165; "actual," in Salem tales, 178, 180, 181

Class, 6, 148, 162
Cleveland, Samuel, 28, 171
Colacurcio, Michael J., 3

Dating of Hawthorne's works: importance of, x, 2–4; and publishing history, 3, 253*n*3; by library borrowings, 4; *Seven Tales* and *Fanshawe,* 12–13, 256–57*n*2–3; *Provincial Tales,* 29–32, 259–61*n*1–5; works of early 1830s (including *The Story Teller*), 76–80, 267–69*n*16–23; of later 1830s works, 101–3, 268*n*18, 274*n*8–9; Concord period, 135–36; Salem tales, 169–72, 282–83*n*5–6
Desire: as opposed to "circumstance," ix, x, 135, 144, 149–54, 161–62; in *Fanshawe,* 20, 23, 24; in *Provincial Tales,* 41, 46, 55; in Concord period, 135, 139–40, 142–44, 149–54, 161–62; representation of, 139–40, 197, 213–15; and its realization, 142–44, 157, 158–59, 162; in *The Scarlet Letter,* 197, 202–3, 204–5, 210, 213–14, 216–17, 218, 221–24, 236, 240
Development: importance of, ix-x, 1–6, 62. *See also* Hawthorne, Nathaniel—Compositional phases; *The Scarlet Letter* in relation to previous, 190, 247
Didacticism: in early 1830s, 66, 69, 95; in late 1830s, 100, 107–8, 109, 114–15, 120–21; rejected in Concord period and Salem tales, 137, 181, 182. *See also* Moralizing
Domesticity: domestic life, 6, 180; in *Provincial Tales,* 52–53, in early 1830s, 72, 75, 83, 86–90, 95; in later 1830s, 117–18; marginalized in Concord period, 131–33; Salem tales, 180
Douglass, William, *British Settlements in North-America,* 30
Dreaming: in *Seven Tales* and *Fanshawe,* 11, 15, 19, 20, 22–25; daydreaming,